# WHY MY

# WHY MY CHILD?

## *Supporting the families of victims of child sexual abuse*

Freda Briggs

ALLEN & UNWIN

First published in 1993
Allen & Unwin Pty Ltd
9 Atchison Street, St Leonards, NSW 2065 Australia

National Library of Australia
Cataloguing-in-Publication entry:

Briggs, Freda.
Why my child?

Bibliography.
Includes index.
ISBN 1 86373 345 0.

1. Child abuse. 2. Parents of sexually abused children – Counseling of. 3. Parents of sexually abused children – Services for. 4. Group counseling I. Title.

362.7686

Set by Graphicraft Typesetters Ltd., Hong Kong
Printed by SRM Production Services Sdn Bhd, Malaysia

10 9 8 7 6 5 4 3 2 1

# Contents

# Tables and figures

## Tables



## Figures

# Exercises

# Acknowledgements

This book represents the efforts and experiences of many people. It was written at the request of two specific groups: first, the parents who care for child victims of sexual abuse and, second, the community workers who provide support for these families.

Over a period of three years, the author listened to parents and support workers working in Australia, New Zealand, England and Canada. The first manuscripts were distributed to the founders of parent groups in England, Australia and New Zealand. Special thanks are due to Sue Clark and Maxine Hodgson of Parentline, Hamilton, New Zealand, Robyn Rummings of Parent Help, Auckland, senior social workers in the Department for Social Welfare in Auckland and Hamilton and New Zealand Police. Considerable assistance was received from NCH Touchline (Leeds), Jill Trueman, founder/coordinator of SAMS (Southend and Basildon) and Angela Rivera of ISO-SAC (London).

In Australia, manuscripts were shared with the group leaders of PACE (Melbourne), PACSA-WA (Perth), PACT (Brisbane), PACA (Sydney), FACT and PACSA (Adelaide).

Social worker Marie Hume, then working with groups in Chatham, Ontario, Canada, provided samples of therapeutic programmes used in parent and survivor groups. Psychologist Professor Marie O'Neill, then at the University of Newfoundland read the manuscripts and submitted suggestions for the chapters on the management of children's behaviours. Parents and support workers of FACT read and discussed each section and presented their ideas. The sections on volunteering were written with the assistance of Margaret Curtis, Joy Noble and the Volunteer Centre of South Australia, Inc. The sections on the training of volunteers were completed with the help of Cathy Sillard of SPARK, FACT and PACSA, all in South Australia.

Thanks are due to all the contributors, but extra special thanks must go to parent support workers Kathleen Lewis (Adelaide) and Barbara Horgan (Perth) who saw the need for this book and were involved, page by page, in its construction.

# Introduction

Throughout the 1980s, Western countries experienced a dramatic increase in the number of reported cases of child sexual abuse. Where statistics were published, reports doubled in each successive year. No-one knows whether this represented an increase in the number of offences committed against children or whether the publicity given to the problem heightened public awareness and gave people the confidence to report suspicions of abuse. Unfortunately, the increase in the provision of services for child victims and their families failed to keep pace with the increase in cases.

Child protection is now a complex, multiprofessional concern. When a case is reported, the (non-offending) parents have to traverse a professional maze.

Some children are subjected to several interviews by child protection workers, police, child psychologists or psychiatrists, hospital social workers, paediatricians, therapists and court counsellors, as well as lawyers and judges. Each interviewer has a different and very narrow focus. Police, for example, are only interested in whether or not an offence has been committed, who the perpetrator is and whether there is sufficient evidence to prosecute, while social workers concentrate on the safety of the child. Parents are passed from professional to professional, often becoming confused by their different priorities, apparent detachment and use of incomprehensible jargon. Dazed parents are left unsupported with a hundred and one unanswered questions.

Families endure the deficiencies of the 'protection' process because they believe that, in the end, there will be justice for their children. When separation, divorce and access orders are involved, or when offenders are prosecuted and plead 'not guilty' (as most do), cases may continue for up to two years. The outcome may be that abusers remain free and unimpeded in their capacity to harm others because of some legal technicality which has no obvious relevance to the violation of children. Parents become angry. Their confidence in themselves and society is shattered. Their powerful emotions are often immobilising and prevent them from giving their children the support and stability that is vital to their well-being.

To whom can parents turn for help? Social workers are overloaded and lack the time to provide the patient, slow-handed care that parents need. They do not have the facility to support mothers who suddenly find their partners accused of using their children for sexual gratification. Furthermore, few case-workers or family counsellors have the knowledge or specialist skills required to help parents whose painful memories of their own abuse are revived by their children's disclosures. The inadequacy of support services to meet the needs of (non-offending) parents has resulted in many different kinds of initiatives. As with other successful support groups such as Compassionate Friends (for bereaved parents), Rape Crisis Centres (for victims of sexual assault) and Parents Anonymous (which supports parents at risk of hurting their children), the people who are best qualified for the supportive role are often those who have suffered the same experience, worked through it and who are willing to help others.

Increasingly, out of sheer necessity, parents and child survivors of sexual abuse are turning to community, family and neighbourhood centres for help. Where inappropriate family services exist, they form their own informal groups in a desperate attempt to restore some semblance of order to their shattered lives. A range of workers and volunteers now cater, formally and informally, for the wider needs of (non-offending) parents of child victims of sexual abuse. The major task shared by all groups is the support of families during times of need. Without that support, and also education about child protection, parents are unlikely to know how to respond to the disclosure of sexual abuse in psychologically helpful ways. Parents need help so that they, in turn, can help their children to cope with the traumas associated with abuse.

It is clearly in the interests of child protection and community health that professionals refer (non-offending) parents to support services immediately after the disclosure of sexual abuse. Ideally, the professional should make the first contact on behalf of, and with the consent of, the parent. Parents resist making that first approach because of the embarrassment of telephoning strangers about their problem. If no parent group exists, it is in the interests of health and community services to take steps to remedy the deficiency.

This book is for parent counsellors and all professionals, paraprofessionals and volunteers whose work brings them into contact with families. The first four chapters provide information on the problem of child sexual abuse, handling disclosures, offenders and what happens to children and protective parents in the justice system. Chapter 5 contains hints for parents and caregivers on the management of children's difficult, emotionally disturbed behaviours associated with sexual abuse. Chapters 6 to 9 explain why parent support groups are necessary and help readers to establish and manage such groups. In the last three chapters, the grief process is looked at and therapeutic programmes for parents are discussed.

This book was written in consultation with, and at the request of, workers in parent support services in Australia, Canada, New Zealand and the United Kingdom. They pointed to the fact that while there are books available for social workers, health workers and even teachers on the subject of child sexual abuse, little has been written about the needs of parents who are left to pick up the pieces after abuse has been reported. They argued, rightly, that, unless parents receive appropriate and well-timed help, they are unlikely to be able to provide the necessary support for child victims.

# 1 How children become trapped in sexual abuse

When parents first hear that their children have been sexually abused by known and trusted adults, their first reaction is usually one of disbelief. 'If that was happening, I would have known about it. My child would have told me', is the common response. When abuse is confirmed, parents are often angry because their children did not tell them about the sexual misbehaviour when it began. They are also hurt as well as angry when their children confide in other people.

Adults have very unrealistic ideas and expectations about a child's reactions to sexual misbehaviour. When parents attend school information sessions on matters relating to child protection, they often exhibit a great deal of complacency. Parents can be heard making statements such as: 'I don't really need to be here. My children are safe. It isn't likely to happen to anyone in my family. We live in a respectable neighbourhood. And I trust all of our friends. We don't know anyone who would abuse kids. And we always know where our children are when they go out. We taxi them everywhere. And if something did happen, I'd know. They'd tell me straightaway. They tell me everything'.

When parents are asked, 'Could you have confided in your parents if someone had misbehaved sexually with you when you were seven or eight years old?', the answer is invariably, 'No'. But today's parents have convinced themselves that they are making a much better job of parenting than their predecessors. They maintain that they enjoy 'open and honest' relationships with their children. Some have even given warnings to steer clear of strange men who offer rides in cars, gifts of money or lollies! They are then convinced that they have done all that is necessary to provide protection. As a consequence, parents are invariably shocked and unprepared for the news that their child has been abused, especially if the offender is not a stranger but a family member, neighbour, priest, teacher or other trusted adult.

If parents took the trouble to talk to their children and, more importantly, to listen to them, they would soon discover that the inhibitions which deterred previous generations of victims from reporting sexual offences are still prevalent. Furthermore, these inhibitions, learned from parents, teachers and other caring adults, are the ones which enable sexual offenders to entrap children into long-term abusive relationships with little fear of being caught, prosecuted and punished. To understand why children are so vulnerable to entrapment, parents need to understand how difficult it is for children to recognise, reject and report sexual misbehaviour, especially when the offender is an authority figure. We have to step back and examine our own approach to child rearing.

From infancy, we teach children that to receive approval, affection and rewards from adults they must be 'good'. To be good means to be obedient, not to argue and not to engage in rude behaviour. Children define 'rude' as talking about or doing things involving excretion, nudity, 'bottoms' or genitals. Rude children are naughty and naughty children are reprimanded, sometimes even punished. When we remember what our children have been taught about obedience, their bodies and 'rude' behaviour, we can begin to understand why they are so reluctant to report incidents of sexual abuse.

## What children learn about their bodies

Young children learn about gender differences from the attitudes and behaviours of their parents and their interactions with other children. When five-year-olds were asked how to tell the difference between boys and girls, the children referred only to variations in male and female behaviour, physical abilities, dress, hairstyles, toys and interests. They did not refer to differences in genitals (Goldman and Goldman, 1988).

There are three possible explanations for this. First, five-year-olds have already been taught that it is rude and, therefore, naughty to refer to genitals. Second, few five-year-olds have been given the vocabulary to communicate about genital differences. Third, these differences are not important to young children. Babies and toddlers explore their genitals in the same way as they investigate ears, toes and other protruding parts. When children find that genital touching is pleasant, they may repeat it for comfort in much the same way as they resort to sucking their thumbs. Unfortunately, many parents suffer deep-seated, irrational fears relating to children's sexuality and they overreact. Children are repeatedly told either directly or indirectly that there is something 'bad' about sexuality and it is not unusual for parents to draw attention to the genitals in a very negative way, for example by smacking or threatening to smack children's hands if the touching continues.

By the age of three or four years, most children 'know' that it is socially unacceptable to exhibit the 'private' parts of their bodies. This message is taught by both subtle and direct intervention. Young children who have previously been allowed to run around naked, suddenly find, with no adequate explanation, that the rules have changed: when visitors appear, they must not show their bodies or their underwear. One day, they are suddenly told that they are now 'too big' or 'too old' to share a bath or a bed with siblings of the opposite sex. They learn that there is something very rude, naughty and secretive about the lower parts of the anatomy, something that makes adults very cross when the new rules are disregarded.

When children attend preschool, boys and girls use the same toilets, sometimes without doors. At school, however, they discover not only that boys and girls have separate toilet blocks but that teachers 'go mad' when boys try to find out what is now happening that was not happening before that warrants this new level of secrecy. Children's curiosity increases and this includes the desire to know whether they are constructed in the same way as everyone else. Despite this curiosity being harmless, ageless and universal, adults panic, banning the investigative play and the players in an attempt to insulate children from their own sexuality.

Bright children soon recognise that adults have double standards: by watching television, looking at the covers of adult magazines and watching or eavesdropping on the sexual antics of parents and older siblings, they soon learn that 'rude is only for grown-ups'. Children assume that parents become annoyed because they want to keep this kind of behaviour to themselves. They know that exhibitionism and sexual touching are 'rude' and therefore wrong but, lacking age-appropriate sex education, they do not understand why this is so (Briggs, 1991).

### *Genitals are unmentionable*

Children soon learn that parents cannot cope with genitals which somehow become invisible, untouchable and unmentionable. As a result, most prepubescent girls are unaware that they have three openings between their legs. If they knew, they might enquire why they needed a third opening and that would embarrass adults who cannot cope with human sexuality. Some parents encourage children's ignorance by referring to the entire buttock, anal and genital area as the child's 'bottom'. The author's informal survey of children in the first three years of primary school produced an average of twenty different names for penis in each class. Some were easily decipherable substitute words such as 'wee-wee' and 'pee-pee'. Some were family 'pet' names such as, 'Jimmy-riddle', 'John Henry' and 'diddle'. Some were the names that children were not allowed to use in adult company, such as 'prick' and 'cock'. Ethnic children had been taught to use ethnic names so that only their parents would understand what they were talking about, thus reducing the risk of public embarrassment. Some families had gone to great lengths to provide their own secret code word for penis, such as 'golf set . . . you know . . . two balls, a stick and a bag'.

What becomes clear is that, while parents teach the correct names of other body parts, avoidance of teaching the correct biological names for genitals is almost universal. Apart from transmitting the message that there is something bad about children's bodies, the lack of vocabulary makes it very difficult for victims to seek help in stopping sexual misbehaviour. If, for instance, a boy complained that someone had touched his golf set, no-one outside his immediate family would know what he was talking about.

### *Rude behaviour must be kept secret*

When parents are asked, 'What have you told your children to protect them from the risk of sexual abuse?', the vast majority admit to have said or done nothing. The two most common reasons given for this negligence are: first, 'I don't know what to say . . . I don't want to put ideas into their heads or make them afraid', second, they want to preserve their children's 'innocence'. In this context, parents confuse ignorance with innocence (Briggs, 1987).

Even five-year-old children know something about unacceptable sexual behaviour. They have all encountered 'rude' boys and girls. Most have already either been reprimanded themselves or have witnessed the punishment of other children for doing or saying something 'rude'. They know that adults react emotionally when children behave 'rudely': 'They shout . . . they growl . . . they smack and send children to bed'. Parents are known to 'freak out', 'blow a fuse' and say, 'Don't ever let me catch you playing that game again'. At five years of age, children have already been banned from playing 'mothers and fathers' and 'nurses and doctors'. Most adults can recall the exact moment at which their parents showed panic about their early sexual curiosity.

This makes it all the more confusing when adults behave rudely. 'Why would a grown-up do rude things to me when adults tell kids off for being rude?', victims ask themselves following the first abusive incident. Confusion gives power to the offender. The child thinks, 'I must be mistaken . . . a grown-up wouldn't do that'. The child then feels embarrassed and guilty for having supposedly misjudged the offender. Unless children have been taught and know from experience that their parents can cope uncritically with information of a sexual nature, victims keep all 'rude' behaviour secret, whether they are asked to do so or not. This is because they have learned that:

- rude is naughty;
- naughty means that you are bad, you have done something wrong, adults will be angry and will blame and possibly punish;
- bad means that you are not worth loving and love will be withdrawn;
- if rude behaviour occurs, it must be your fault.

British, Australian and New Zealand five to eight-year-olds told the author that, if someone behaved rudely to them, they could not 'tell' because they would feel stupid, embarrassed and blame themselves for what happened, even if they had rejected the behaviour and escaped. Teachers were viewed as unable to help because they lack authority outside the classroom. At six to seven years or age, children added that they could not confide in teachers because other children might overhear and taunt them with jibes, such as: 'Guess what he did! He's yucky! He must be stupid to let that happen'. (Briggs: 1991)

Children from Asian, West Indian and Pacific Island cultures also disclosed that anxieties about problems within their own families could not be shared with 'outsiders'. Furthermore, the hierarchical family structure ensured that, if the offender was a grandparent or older relative, their own parents would be powerless to intervene.

Reporting sexual abuse only becomes possible for child victims when trusted adults have participated in education for child protection and *they have already demonstrated their ability to receive, uncritically, information about the human body*. If parents have done neither of these things, their children feel unable to confide in them. It is important to note that, when children have undertaken school-based child protection programmes and know about their rights, they will not disclose what happened unless they are convinced that parents can and will help. Some children said that they would tolerate unwanted 'rude' behaviour that they knew to be wrong rather than risk the wrath of loved parents. Others knew that their parents would be unsupportive. For example: 'It would depend on whether mum was drunk. If she was, she'd say, "Oh, just piss off"'; 'My mum never listens to me. I've already tried to tell her about my uncle'; 'My mum would tell dad and he'd be mad. He'd say, "Why didn't you hit him"' (Briggs, 1991).

## Offenders use tricks, threats, bribes and blackmail to gain the compliance of victims

Sex offences against children sometimes begin in infancy. If no-one notices and reports the signs, then the abuse continues and becomes more damaging. As victims grow older, they usually protest about the behaviour and the abuser reassures them that people who care for each other normally behave in this way. As a result, some victims reach adolescence before they realise that the abuse should not be happening. As one survivor said, 'My dad did a good job of teaching me to avoid dangerous strangers. He even said that I mustn't let other people touch my genitals . . . but it was alright for him to do it'.

When the preschool child is used for sexual activity, the offender may create a special, trusting relationship in which sexual touching would be difficult for the victim to resist. Young children are not very good at hiding problems, however, and it is no coincidence that the under five age group is the one most frequently featured in reports.

Children are confused by the first abusive incident—it has never happened before and they sense that it should not be happening now. They become afraid because the offender's physical appearance, eyes, voice and demeanour change when sexually aroused. This confusion is increased when offenders assure them that what is happening is normal and yet so special that it has to be kept secret. Most children have been taught by teachers and relatives not only that secrets must be kept but also that there will be terrible consequences if adult conversations are repeated. Unless parents have participated in a child protection programme which emphasises the importance of adopting a 'no secrets' family policy, children are convinced that they will get into serious trouble for revealing adults' secrets. The threat is particularly great when the secret involves 'rude' behaviour.

Multicultural British, Australian and New Zealand children were asked the question, 'Suppose that a grown-up person did something rude and told you to keep it secret, would you have to keep that secret? Could you tell your mother?'. The children responded that they would have to comply because their mothers:

- reprimand them for telling secrets;
- become very cross if they talk about something rude;
- would not believe them;
- would tell the offender and they would 'get into big trouble'—'adults stick together'.

In other words, children who had not participated in child protection programmes with their parents did not accept that they would either be believed or supported if they reported sexual misbehaviour involving adults.

Unfortunately, if victims do not reveal their secret immediately, they become trapped in the abuse, the offenders then feel safe and increase the frequency and range of their sexual activities—their perverted view of events constructs a situation whereby, to them, their victims become willing and equal participants because they have not reported the abuse. When children protest, they are told, 'It's your own fault. You could have stopped me and you didn't. You're just as bad. Police take bad children away. I'll tell them that you liked it . . . that it's your fault'. This threat is especially effective in silencing male victims of homosexual abuse.

Children who enjoyed some aspects of the relationship with the offender may have ambivalent feelings about the abuse: on the one hand, they may want to maintain the relationship; on the other hand, they want the abuse to stop. They may have enjoyed being 'my special girl . . . my little princess'. They may even have enjoyed the first sexual caresses. Children's genitals are highly sensitive to tickling and sexual touching can be exciting. Enjoyment of any kind often results in life-long guilt and shame.

In cases of father–daughter incest, offenders convince their victims that they have to maintain silence to 'keep the family together'. Female victims are often already in subservient roles, performing personal and menial tasks for the offenders. They are conditioned to believe that family survival depends upon their self-sacrifice. In other words, children experience role reversal: child victims are expected to protect their parents instead of their parents protecting them. Both boys and girls trapped in incest exhibit a form of pseudo-maturity and accept the abuse as their punishment in life. This is extremely damaging to their emotional and social development.

Some victims are trapped in incest for years. The tricks used by offenders are identical throughout Western society. Some tell their victims that what they are doing is normal and even beneficial for their education. Others blame the victim's mother saying either that 'she isn't looking after me properly . . . which is why I am having to do this with you' or, worse 'it's no good complaining to your mother because she knows about it and says it's OK'. As mothers often give children the impression that they are omnipotent and know everything that their offspring think and do, incest victims accept these explanations without question. They are then very angry with their mothers and feel psychologically orphaned.

Even when children reject abuse, they are made to feel guilty and foolish with comments such as, 'There's nothing wrong. Nothing happened. Forget about it. It's no big deal. If you make a fuss, you'll cause a lot of trouble and it will be all your fault. Nobody will believe you anyway'. When children show confusion, offenders reassure them with, 'Remember . . . I'm your dad . . . I love you. Would I ask you to do something wrong?'. The secret is then justified on the grounds that, 'other people wouldn't understand'. In family abuse, secrets are usually accompanied by threats that something terrible will happen to the victims, their pets or other family members if they reveal what is happening. The secret then becomes both a trap and a necessity for the future well-being of victims.

Father–daughter incest is often revealed at adolescence. Victims hear their friends talking about 'petting' experiences with boys. When those friends try to conjecture what sexual intercourse would be like, victims suddenly have to confront the fact that 'this is what dad has been doing to me all these years'. Victims realise that they have been tricked and deprived of their childhood and they become justifiably angry. This is the time when abusive fathers and father figures try to increase their power over their victims. They become excessively restrictive and authoritarian, banning personal freedom and normal socialisation at a time when other teenagers are gaining more independence.

At this stage, adolescent victims who rebel have only two alternatives: they may tell their mothers, trusted teachers or school counsellors or they can run away from home. Unfortunately, this is the age at which victims are least likely to be believed and helped (Bentovim, 1991). If they disclose abuse to trusted friends, the secret will usually be maintained; if they disclose father–daughter incest to their mothers, they are likely to be told, 'You can't expect me to believe that! I would have known. You're making it up! How could you be so wicked'. Those victims who decide to leave home seldom disclose their reasons for doing so. Young and untrained for the workforce, early school leavers may live on the streets and seek sympathy and shelter from those who frequent city cafes and amusement arcades. Such young people are then at high risk of drug and alcohol abuse, prostitution and further sexual abuse.

Sometimes, young victims are taken home by police without close questioning. Abusive parents then claim that their children left home to avoid reasonable family discipline which was imposed for their own protection. Adults tend to sympathise with parents of difficult teenagers and offenders consequently remain free to continue the abuse.

If victims report abuse by family members, strong family pressures may be used to enforce a retraction of the allegations. Some victims only want the abuse to stop—they do not seek retribution and find it difficult to handle the family upheaval that follows disclosure. It is not uncommon for mothers to refer to their financial dependence on the offender and for other relatives to accuse victims of lying and bringing disgrace on the whole family. They all predict that, if the victim persists with the allegation, the family will become homeless and penniless and be rejected by the community—'and it will be all your fault'. In other words, families tend to confirm what the offender has been saying about the consequences of disclosure. Relatives may assure victims that all will be well if they just tell the police, 'I made it up'. Retraction is presented as an easy and logical step which will resolve all the family's problems. In the meantime, offenders may continue to threaten their victims with, 'If I'm sent to jail, I'll only be there for a few weeks and when I get out I'll kill you. Don't imagine that you can escape. I'll find you . . . wherever you are'.

Isolated, friendless and helpless, most unsupported victims bend to such threats and withdraw their statements. They are led to believe that, if they tell the police that they were lying, life will return to normal and the abuse will stop. Sadly, there is no going back. When victims withdraw their statements, the police may prosecute them for making false accusations. Courts take these matters seriously: two Melbourne victims were given substantial jail sentences for such offences while their abuser went free.

Apart from the risk of prosecution, retraction brings ostracism. The adult world is sympathetic to men who are wrongly accused; victims who retract are branded as vicious and dangerous people who are prepared to lie to jail innocent men. After retraction, offenders continue their offences with greater confidence than before, knowing that their victims have lost credibility. The next cry for help is likely to take the form of a suicide attempt.

Ironically, 'caring' parents who teach their children that genitals are rude and unmentionable and do nothing to equip them with personal safety skills, expect even the youngest of children to recognise sexual misbehaviour when it occurs, escape and report it to them immediately. Most parents teach their children to keep secrets and obey adults yet simultaneously expect them to disobey authority figures and reject their demands for secrets when sexual abuse occurs. Parents's expectations of their children are clearly unrealistic.

Sometimes, offences only come to light when children are found to be pregnant or suffering from sexually transmitted diseases. It should be remembered, however, that most victims of sexual abuse never reveal their secret and offenders remain free to continually damage young lives.

## When boys are abused

In the early 1980s, women's organisations exposed the problem of child sexual abuse by known and trusted adults, discarding the myth that the 'stranger' presented the greatest danger to children. Because there was no supportive response from men's organisations, child abuse became labelled as a 'feminist issue' and even a 'women's problem'. This enabled men to distance themselves. While women created Rape Crisis Centres, 24-hour telephone counselling lines and incest support groups for female survivors, men continued to pretend that there was no problem. Even when it became more widely known that most male offenders were child victims, no-one appeared to be interested. Government agencies relied on male myths to explain the lack of crisis and support facilities for male victims. As a result, it was not until 1989 that the first Rape Crisis Centres for males were established in Melbourne (Australia) and England. This was more than a decade after the establishment of Rape Crisis Centres for females. It is important to note, however, that the Melbourne centre was initiated and serviced by a female social worker.

In his book, *Abused Boys: The neglected victims of sexual abuse* (Fawcett Columbine, New York, 1990), Mic Hunter shows that male therapists are so uninformed about male victimisation that many find it impossible to empathise with their male clients, telling them to 'Snap out of it! Be a man! Stop feeling sorry for yourself! After all, it was a long time ago'. Such attitudes add to the psychological damage already done to male victims. Males are expected either to heal themselves or find benefits from their sexual experiences; they are not allowed to complain. In these circumstances, it is not surprising that adult males attempt to be strong and brave by either denying the abuse or responding with, 'I don't know what the fuss is all about. It happened to me and I'm alright'. In desperation some men turn to parent support groups for help.

In 1990 an organisation was created by Australian men to tackle the problem of child sexual abuse. With support from artists in the musical, *Les Miserables*, 'Men Against Child Sexual Abuse' organised nationwide marches and opened resource centres for males in State capitals. This action, although commendable, touched only the 'tip of the iceberg' and there remains a worldwide lack of support and empathy for male victims. The masculine culture has not yet given men permission to report sexual abuse and to understand why we need to look closely at male stereotyping.

### *Male sex-role conditioning*

Despite equal opportunity legislation and a non-sexist curriculum in schools, differences still persist in the perceptions that adults have of what is 'male' and 'female' and this is reflected in the way that boys and girls are reared: girls continue to be admired for being neat and pretty while boys are commended for being assertive, strong and active. Adults have different behavioural expectations of children according to gender. When girls are bullied, they are encouraged to escape and seek help. Boys, on the other hand, are told to, 'Stand up for yourself' and 'Hit back'—they have only two choices of action: retaliation or silence. Our definition of masculinity is the antithesis of victimisation and helplessness. As a consequence, it is extremely difficult for male children to admit that they have been abused. As they grow up, boys learn that they should be able to handle their lives without assistance from other people. This message was firmly fixed in the minds of five-year-old New Zealander boys who, when asked what kind of things made them feel scared, responded, 'Nothing ever scares me . . . silly. I'm a boy!' (Briggs, 1991).

One consequence of this type of conditioning is that if males are not self-reliant, then it becomes impossible to talk about sexual abuse because it diminishes their sense of masculinity. Male victims suffer enormously from this 'self-reliance' ethic. They are in a no-win situation: either they can convince themselves that they were not abused, that they were actually in control and that they enjoyed the sexual experience (even if it was painful) and thereafter, feel ashamed, guilty and anxious because of their participation; or they can accept that they were victims and suffer the humiliation of admitting that they were not in control. Of the two options, the first is the one most frequently chosen because it does not emphasise personal weakness. How could a male victim confess that he had been chosen for sex involving another male given societal taboos on homosexuality?

An additional discouragement to the reporting of abuse is that the dominant male culture accepts the early sexualisation of males as at least beneficial if not as a 'rite or passage' to manhood. Films and books have reinforced the belief that sex with older women is the ultimate educational experience. In such an environment, it is difficult for a male victim to admit that he did not enjoy a sexual experience with an older female. If he cannot stop it, he has to tell himself that he enjoyed it.

### *Myths surrounding the abuse of boys*

We can now see that our cultural myths surrounding what we perceive to be 'masculinity' prevent male sexual abuse victims from receiving the help that they need. For example, we believe that:

- boys initiate and enjoy sexual activity with adults;
- it does them no harm;
- sexual activity with older females is advantageous (it changes boys into men);
- boys cannot be raped by females.

These beliefs have probably contributed more than anything else to the under-reporting of sexual abuse in males.

### *Boys are denied information about child sexual abuse*

Parents are being constantly reminded by the media that it is girls who are used as sex objects and who are vulnerable to exploitation by devious adult males. Caring parents are naturally protective of their daughters' innocence and impose limits on their movement and behaviour which they do not impose on their sons. Boys are encouraged to take risks, seek adventure and enjoy their freedom. The myth that boys are not vulnerable to abuse leads parents to deprive them of information relating to the dangers of sexual assault (Monaco and Gaier, 1988). In particular, parents are unlikely to discuss the taboo subject of homosexual abuse.

> The absence of specific teaching about the nature of sexual assault and strategies for being able to seek help and tell, being directed specifically at boys, leaves them vulnerable and unsure what they should do if they are victims (Armstrong and Hollows, 1989).

*The mateship factor*

An additional factor that concerns abuse for boys is that they are more likely to be seduced in the company of others, for example as members of a class, scout group, sports team, camp, school dormitory, choir. In such situations there is often more than one victim and sometimes more than one abuser. It is much more difficult to resist and report abuse if your 'mates' are presented as being co-operative. Peer group pressure is extremely important and there is a stigma attached to being different to others. Offenders take advantage of this and ridicule boys who resist: 'You're weird . . . See . . . everyone else does it! It's fun!'.

## Boys are probably as much at risk of abuse as girls

For a long time it was thought that boys were at less risk of abuse than girls—fewer cases were reported and, when men were interviewed, fewer admitted that they had experienced abuse. Only recently has it been realised that researchers were asking the wrong question. When the same men were asked about early sexual experiences with someone four or more years older than themselves, a large proportion admitted that they occurred. In other words, early sexual experience is socially acceptable to male culture; sexual abuse is not (Dube and Hebert, 1988).

There is now every reason to believe that boys are as vulnerable to sexual abuse as girls. A study by the Canadian Government and Canadian Gallup Polls (1984) interviewed two thousand people of various ages and found that a third of the males had experienced some type of sexual abuse in childhood. Boys with disabilities are at greatest risk, with 54 per cent of deaf males reporting that they had been sexually abused (Mount and Fetterman, 1989; Kennedy, 1989).

There are variations in the sexual abuse of boys which relate to the social class of victims. Working-class boys tend to live in unrestrictive environments and hence are more likely to be abused by strangers—this type of abuse usually involves one very violent offence. Parents feel comparatively comfortable about reporting such abuse because it does not threaten family status (Dube and Herbert, 1988). Middle and upper-class boys, on the other hand, are more likely to be abused by professionals, relatives and family friends. Even if their parents become aware of these offences, they are rarely reported—well-educated parents are likely to conceal or rationalise offences and attempt to act as amateur psychologists.

Fewer boys than girls are victims of father–child incest but those who are may also be victimised by older brothers and sisters and may be forced to participate in multiple sex with their father's friends.

## The stigma associated with admitting victimisation

Canadian research (Dube and Hebert, 1988) shows that, despite high levels of sexual violence and the physical and emotional damage involved, two thirds of the 511 Canadian male victims interviewed denied that their abusive sexual experiences constituted abuse. Denial was most likely either if they experienced pleasure from any part of the act or if the abuser was female. Victims blamed themselves and suffered enormous guilt and damage to their self-esteem.

Finkelhor (1984) also found that males were unable to talk about their victimisation because it increased their sense of shame. Although a third of offences occurred before the age of six, males could not accept that they were too young to make informed decisions about participation in sexual acts. Student counsellors at the University of South Australia find that male survivors consult them about a wide variety of health and relationship issues but they seldom disclose that sexual abuse is at the root of their problems until the seventh or eighth visit.

The effects of abuse on male self-esteem are especially damaging if there is a homosexual component. Victims worry about their sexuality and the possibility that they might become homosexual. Boys are fearful of the stigma associated with homosexuality in their peer group. When insensitive handling results in offences becoming public knowledge, victims are often victimised yet again by cruel 'poofter' taunts from peers. Even after they marry and become parents, male survivors continue to worry about their sexual leanings. Publicity relating to the cycle of abuse has increased anxieties for male survivors, some of whom confide to their counsellors that they dare not have children because they fear for their safety. Fear of homosexuality and the offender can generalise to a fear of all adults, and males in particular, with victims withdrawing from all social relationships. This is worrying because some turn to children for their emotional satisfaction, thereby increasing the risk of repetition.

Male victims are the ones most likely to experience problems with school authorities and employers—dropping out of tertiary education either because they are failing or because, feeling bad and worthless, they cannot cope with success. Self-punishment often includes frequent suicidal thoughts: they are twice as likely as other men to attempt suicide. In addition, male survivors of sexual abuse suffer more emotional and physical ailments than other males. And, many years after the abuse, 50 per cent of survivors are still taunted by vivid flash-backs of their abusive experiences.

## Sibling incest

One of the most under-reported and misunderstood forms of child sexual abuse is the abuse of children by (usually older) brothers or sisters. Very little is known about sibling incest because, until recently, few cases were reported. This is beginning to change as information is now coming from adolescent and adult survivors who seek help for emotional problems which stem from offences by their brothers or sisters. Sibling incest may have been ignored, first, because of mistaken assumptions that it constitutes normal curiosity (irrespective of the difference in the ages of participants) and, second, because it was thought to be harmless.

Sibling incest occurs across all social classes. Abusers are mostly male but the proportion of female abusers (about 20 per cent) is higher than the reported number of female offenders in sexual abuse statistics as a whole. Furthermore, female offenders abuse their young sisters as well as their brothers. In a survey of sibling abuse in Colorado, USA, one third of offenders assaulted a sibling of the same sex. The average age of the perpetrator was 4.1 years older than the victim (Smith and Israel, 1987).

When sibling incest occurs, it is often an indicator that the perpetrator has already experienced sexual abuse. There is also a strong possibility that the offender's parents were also abused in childhood. It is therefore necessary to work with all family members when providing help for victims of sibling incest. Parents are likely to have emotional attachments to both the victim and the perpetrator. The parents' common reaction is to defend the offender and accuse the victim of causing problems for the family.

Incestuous sibling abuse is just as damaging as other forms of sexual abuse, leaving victims feeling dirty, worthless, guilty and angry.

# 2 The disclosure of child sexual abuse

## How child sexual abuse is revealed

Occasionally, child abusers are caught 'red-handed' by someone who enters a room unexpectedly. Offenders provide innocent explanations for their behaviour, making the observer feel guilty for 'thinking dirty thoughts'. Sometimes, abuse occurs while the child's mother is in the next or even the same room. The more bizarre and more daring the offence, the less likely it is that the victim will be believed and protected.

The two groups of people most frequently involved in making reports of child abuse (of all kinds) are the victims' relatives and teachers. These two groups of people are in the best position to observe any changes in children's behaviour. When abuse is confirmed, mothers often admit that they had 'sensed that something was wrong' but that they 'hoped it was just a phase' and the child would 'grow out of it'. Parents rarely consider the possibility that child sexual abuse might be the cause of the problem. When adults do not expect abuse, they fail to identify the most explicit cries for help.

Many different behavioural signs are exhibited by young victims of sexual abuse. These include:

- frequent sleep disturbances, nightmares, bed-wetting, soiling, night fears and the refusal to get undressed;
- attempts to avoid contact with the offender;
- unexplained sadness, crankiness and irritability;
- re-enactments of what the abuser did, using dolls or other children;
- an obsession with 'rude' matters in play, conversation and artwork;
- frequent masturbation;
- evidence of sexual knowledge beyond the norms for their age;
- the onset of anxiety symptoms such as thumb-sucking, twitching and psychosomatic illness which doctors fail to diagnose;

- social withdrawal and self-imposed isolation;
- poor concentration and regression in school work.

Some young victims make their predicament felt by literally clinging to trusted adults who feel acute discomfort because they have lost their freedom of movement and personal space. When attempting to peel children away from their bodies the children will fight to retain their hold. Without realizing what is happening and why, teachers and caregivers often take a dislike to such children.

*Most victims only give hints about the abuse*

When parents say, 'Why didn't you tell me?', the common response of victims is, 'I did. You didn't take any notice', or 'You weren't listening'. The problem is that, unless children have been exposed to education for personal safety, they are unlikely to possess the language needed to report sexual abuse. Furthermore, unless both children and adults have been involved together, then children remain unsure of their parents' ability to receive information about 'rude' or sexual matters, and dare only attempt communication by giving vague hints that something is wrong, expecting parents to understand. When there is no response, victims feel that they are helpless, hopeless and not worth helping.

Parents are unlikely to realise the significance of such comments as, 'Uncle X hurt my wee-wee (or bottom)', 'The babysitter wanted me to get undressed . . . I don't like the babysitter' or 'The babysitter was mean'. Victims think that they have told their mothers what is happening but that the mothers do not understand (Briggs, 1991). Oral sex is sometimes the problem when a child whines, 'I don't like the taste of his magic fountain/ ice-cream/ magic stick . . . I don't like the way he teases me . . . the games he plays'. Victims also ask, 'Is it alright if (the offender) does funny things sometimes?', 'Mummy, do we have to keep secrets?' and 'Will you still love me if I'm naughty?'.

Unsuspecting parents often affirm that we do have to keep secrets, that we have to learn to tolerate teasing and, yes, it is alright for someone to do funny things if it makes us laugh. When the abuse continues, victims are convinced that nothing can be done to stop it.

*Some victims exhibit sexual and antisocial behaviours*

Having learned to please adults by behaving sexually, victims sometimes attract attention by behaving in a 'promiscuous' way either with older children or adults of the same gender as the offender. The adults instinctively feel uncomfortable and may punish victims for their behaviour. Young victims may act out their abuse with younger children. This is often mistaken for 'normal sexual curiosity' which is distinguishable from abuse in that it involves sharing and equal rights, for example 'You show me yours and I'll show you mine'. Child sexual abuse is likely to be the cause when:

- there is a difference in the age, size and power of the participants;
- force, threats, bribes or secrecy are used;
- the behaviour is adult sexual behaviour, for example involving oral sex, or the penetration of the anus or vagina with fingers or other objects.

Some children play truant from school or run away from home to escape abuse and provide no explanations for their absences. Some become 'street kids' or turn to prostitution, convinced that 'this is all I'm fit for'. Depressed victims may resort to blatant theft, hoping that they will be caught and that their home lives will be investigated. Others resort to self-destructive behaviours such as adhesive and petrol sniffing, alcohol and drug abuse. An American study of depressed preschool children showed that 40 per cent of all child abuse victims exhibit self-destructive tendencies (Rosenthal and Rosenthal, 1984).

*Some child victims express their troubles in their drawings*

Young children draw about the things that concern them and when they cannot talk about their sexually abusive experiences, some victims may express their troubles in artwork. Several common features have been found which should be viewed in the context of the child's behaviour and well-being as a whole. It should be emphasised that the absence of these features does not mean that a child has *not* been abused. For example, the following features have been found after one or more incidents of child sexual abuse:

- drawings may become increasingly 'scribbly' and bizarre—'This is a snake and they're spiders . . . witches . . . creepy crawlies';
- the abuser may be depicted as a monster;
- self-portraits may lack arms even though the artist draws arms on other figures;
- self-portraits may lack a mouth or facial features when other figures are drawn with faces;
- self-portraits may show other deficiencies in the artist's own body image—tiny self-portraits alongside or inside large adult figures;
- large round mouths and exaggerated, pointed teeth often appear in drawings of offenders who demand oral sex;

- self-portraits are often attached to the ground for security while other figures are 'free floating';
- picture content may reveal an inappropriate sexual knowledge or an obsession with 'rude' and sexual matters;
- male offenders are often drawn as phallic symbols or with very large hands and arms, possibly with an outsize, erect penis or third arm;
- artists may choose angry colours repetitively when a free colour choice is available, i.e. red, purple and black (Briggs and Lehmann, 1989).

The drawings of victims of sexual abuse often present onlookers with an uncomfortable feeling which should not be ignored. When artists present strong clues, they should be asked, 'Who is this in your picture? What is he doing? Where do you see him doing this? What do you have to do when he does this? Who else is there when you play this game?'.

When abuse is suspected, victims may be willing to draw pictures about the people and the things that worry them. Some will provide commentaries while they draw and these should be recorded, word by word, dated and signed by the listener. When sexual abuse is suspected, drawings should be photocopied and copies filed safely before handing the originals to child protection services.

## Handling disclosures of sexual abuse

From the moment that abuse occurs, children have to decide whether to tell someone about it or remain silent. The decision will be determined by the:

- nature of the abuse;
- relationship of the abuser to the victim and parents;
- power of the threats imposed;
- children's knowledge about their rights;
- children's ability to recognise sexual misbehaviour;
- children's confidence in their ability to get support from trusted adults.

Few children ever tell their secret but, when they do, the recipients of that information also have a choice to make about whether to respond positively and protect the child or to ignore the cry for help. Most adults are afraid of making false accusations and do not know how to report child abuse. As a result, there is an unfortunate tendency to confront the accused rather than to contact the statutory services responsible for investigations. The confrontation is usually apologetic and offenders then realise that their victims were not believed. They can usually provide innocent explanations for their behaviour which tend to be accepted with a sense of relief. Even when explanations are implausible, few parents know enough about child sexual abuse to challenge them. Victims are then abandoned and the abuse continues.

*When victims become 'survivors'*

Victims of sexual abuse become 'survivors' when they find courage to break the silence and disclose their plight to reliable adults who believe them and who want to help. No matter how parents learn about abuse, whether it is from police, social workers, teachers, friends or the children themselves, their initial reactions are crucial to the well-being of victims. Children who have been sexually molested need to hear caring and trusted adults say:

- 'I believe you'.
- 'Thankyou for telling me . . . it must have been very worrying for you'.
- 'I'm very sorry that this happened to you'.
- 'I want to help'.
- 'I'm glad that you told me. That took a lot of courage. It must have been hard to talk about it. You did the right thing. Grown-ups aren't allowed to do those kinds of things to children. They know it's wrong'.
- 'It's not your fault that he/she did that to you. It's never a child's fault when a grown-up does wrong things'.
- 'It's happened to lots of other kids in your school. Some never tell. They keep it secret. You were very sensible to tell someone about it. We can do something now to stop him from upsetting other children'.
- 'We will have to tell someone else about this. There are people who have special jobs to help children when this happens'.

*Do not cross-examine victims*

When abuse is revealed, the only question that parents should ask is, 'What did (the offender) say would happen if you told me about this?'. Children disclosing abuse are more likely to tell the whole story if they know that the offenders' threats were empty and that parents are not angry with them. How trusted adults behave at the time of disclosure determines how well victims cope in the ensuing months. They need firm, calm, patient handling from protective adults who are in control of their own emotions. Self-control is especially difficult for the mother who learns that the offender is her husband or sexual partner. It can be very damaging for the child if the recipient of the information throws up her arms in horror and declares, 'I don't believe it'. This is a normal adult response to shock but it is viewed by the listener as disbelief and an accusation of dishonesty. Victims then retreat into angry silence or minimise the frequency, duration and extent of the abuse to protect themselves from further strong negative reactions.

It is very tempting for parents to engage in detailed cross-examination about when the offences began and what exactly happened. Such cross-examination is stressful and harmful. The last thing that a child needs after disclosure is to be criticised by parents for not fighting back, or running away and reporting to them. Apart from the fact that children have usually tried many times to tell their parents and their teachers that they needed help, criticism and blame make them feel stupid, weak and guilty and they then wish that they had remained silent. When parents react badly in these early stages of disclosure, there is a high risk that the child will say, 'I made it up'.

Later, when calm, adults must apologise to children: 'I'm sorry I wasn't listening when you tried to tell me what was happening. I didn't realise that it was so important. That was my fault'.; 'I'm sorry I was so cross when you told me. I wasn't cross with you. I was cross because he'd done that to you. I forgot about how you were feeling'. Adults seldom apologise to children but, in abuse cases, it is vital that they do so.

If abusers have threatened children with terrible consequences, those fears will linger long after disclosure and frequent reassurance will be necessary. This is best given when children appear sad and withdrawn, 'I can see that you're feeling sad. I know that you've had a worrying time. You've been very strong. What is it that's worrying you right now?'. It is helpful if victims are encouraged to express their fears, either verbally or through drawings. They also need frequent reassurances that they were not to blame for what happened.

Parents should be referred by child protection workers to parent support services immediately after the disclosure of abuse. Without expert guidance, they are unlikely to know how to help their children and may unwittingly add to their feelings of guilt and shame.

*Explaining to victims why sexual abuse is wrong*

It is difficult for parents to explain why sexual touching is bad. We do not want to alarm children unnecessarily nor do we wish them to develop unhealthy attitudes that will inhibit the development of sexual relationships in later life. Some parents try to explain that the offender is sick or 'sick in the head' and needs help. Children view sickness as being something like chickenpox or vomiting; they know that the offender is not sick by their standards and either disbelieve the explanation or worry about catching the same sickness, especially 'sickness in the head'. Ideally, emphasis should be placed on the offender's bad behaviour rather than on the offender as being a 'bad' person. This is especially important if the child previously enjoyed an affectionate relationship with the offender. If children have admired or modelled themselves on someone who is now perceived as bad, their insecurity increases.

There are many books available to help parents handle this difficult situation. Jenny Hessell's *What's wrong with bottoms* provides a beautifully illustrated story about an attractive Uncle Henry who makes his nephew feel very special. When Uncle Henry makes sexual advances, the child breaks the secret and his mother is predictably cross. 'What's wrong with bottoms?', the child asks. 'There's nothing wrong with bottoms', mother replies. 'But there are things to do with bottoms which are OK and things which aren't OK'. Mother points to the fact that the child romped around naked when he was younger but 'things change as you get older. You wouldn't walk down the street with nothing on now, would you?'. The boy agrees that he would not. 'Well, the same goes for Uncle Henry. He knows very well that he mustn't go around showing off his bottom to children and asking them to do things they don't like'. Mother confirms that Uncle Henry knew that what he was doing was wrong. 'That's why he waited until you were on your own. He hasn't pulled down his pants in the living-room while we're all watching TV has he?'.

One obvious criticism of the book is that Uncle Henry exposed and asked the child to touch his penis, not his bottom. Furthermore, the mother explains societal norms but does not take that extra, more difficult step of explaining why they are necessary.

Another option is to introduce age-appropriate sex education which tells children that: their genitals are good and special parts of the body which must be kept safe and healthy because they will be needed when they are older; genitals are involved in making babies and grown-ups usually take a long time choosing the very special grown-up person with whom they can share these very special parts of their bodies. A wide range of useful publications are available from counselling centres, feminist and educational bookshops, schools and community libraries.

*Prognosis for the recovery of victims*

Despite the fact that child protection publicity continues to focus on dangerous strangers, suffering is likely to be greatest and therapeutic needs most extensive when:

- the offender was a parent or someone known and trusted by the child;
- the offence was repeated;
- the child was blamed by the offender;
- the child was made responsible for the safety of the offender;
- the child was made responsible for keeping the family together;
- secrecy was imposed;
- threats or tricks were used;
- the child was not protected by the mother;
- the child was not believed when abuse was revealed.

Unfortunately, children blame themselves all too readily for other people's sexual misbehaviours. They are especially vulnerable to self-blame if they were doing something unusual or banned at the time of the offence, such as using a new route home or taking a short cut through the park. It is this enormous and misplaced sense of guilt that torments unsupported victims for the rest of their lives.

## The value of medical assessment

When sexual abuse is suspected or confirmed, the child should be medically examined at the nearest sexual assault referral centre. Such centres are usually attached to major hospitals and referral can be arranged by child protection services. It is not advisable for parents to take children to their family doctors because general practitioners are not usually trained to perform the highly specialised investigations that are recessary. There have been many cases where family doctors have dismissed classic signs of sexual abuse as being the result of 'too many bubble baths'. Unless anal or vaginal penetration has been attempted, there may be no medical evidence of sexual abuse. It is important to remember that the lack of medical evidence does not mean that abuse did not happen. Suspicions should not be dismissed merely because doctors do not confirm them.

When providing the history of abuse to health authorities, it is essential that parents report previous medical indications, such as:

- blood spots from the anal or genital area;
- anal/vaginal redness, soreness, bruises, tears, infections or discharges;
- urinary infections, bed-wetting, soiling;
- persistent anxiety when underwear is removed to apply medication;
- the onset of medical problems associated with anxiety, for example asthma;
- love-bites, unusual bruises and hand marks denoting pressure alongside the genital and anal openings, on buttocks, groin or thighs.

**Table 2.1 Some typical family responses in the disclosure phase of father–child incest**

| Father | Mother | Child victim | Siblings |
|---|---|---|---|
| Denial: 'I'll lose my job, my freedom, my family, my reputation'. | Denial: 'I would have known—he wouldn't do that—my child would have told me—I'm sure it won't happen again. I've got to keep my family together. We can sort it out. Children exaggerate'. | 'I'm not lying—it really happened. Please believe me'. | Denial: 'My mum and dad wouldn't tell lies'. |
| Anger towards the victim: 'Because of that kid, I'll go to jail. She had no right to tell. I'm her father. No-one can tell me what to do with my own kids. It's nothing to do with anyone else. I'd like to kill her for this'. | Anger towards the victim: 'Why didn't she stop him? Why didn't she tell me? How could she do this to me? Dirty little bitch'. | Anger towards self: 'I am stupid, bad, deserve to be punished. It's all my fault'. | Anger with victim: 'Nothing will ever be the same again and it's all your fault'. |
| Self destructive tendencies: 'No-one understands. No-one cares about me. I feel terrible. I'd be better off dead'. | Self destructive tendencies: 'I am a hopeless mother. I can't cope with this'. | Confusion and depression: 'I only wanted it to stop'. | Confusion and depression. |
| | Shame: 'What will people say. Everyone will blame me. They'll say I haven't looked after him properly. The police, the court—the publicity. I haven't protected my kids'. | Shame: 'Everybody knows that I'm bad'. | Shame: 'The police came to our house and took dad away'. |
| Fear of consequences | Fear of consequences | Fear of consequences: 'What will happen to me. Mum believes him, not me'. | Fear: 'What will happen to me. I daren't tell what I know'. |
| Uses power to manipulate wife and victim. | Responds to manipulation. Supports abuser, minimises importance of abuse. | Responds to manipulation and says 'I lied. I made it up'. Anger: 'Nobody will help me. I'm not worth helping. It's all my fault. I must be bad'. | |

**Table 2.2 Circumstances needed to restore the victim's emotional well-being in cases of father–child incest**

| Father | Mother | Child victim | Siblings |
|---|---|---|---|
| Did not put responsibility/ secrecy onto the child | Believes the child and says so | Is believed | Honest explanations |
| Admits responsibility for the offences when reported | Supports the child | Is not blamed | Personal counselling |
| Apologises to the victims | Takes the child for therapy | Realises that it is alright to love the abuser but not the behaviour | |
| Leaves the family home but supports the family | Obtains counselling for self | Counselling by a therapist who specialises in working with children in cases of sexual abuse | |
| Joins a treatment programme for sexual offenders | Assertiveness training as necessary | Assertiveness training and a personal safety programme | A personal safety programme |
| Family Counselling | | | |

If the abuse is recent, the offender's hair or body fluids may have been left on the victim's body or clothing. Neither the child nor the clothing should be washed until after the examination. Samples of seminal fluid can be helpful for confirming the identity of an abuser.

Many parents resist taking children to a sexual assault centre because they fear that the medical examination will distress the child. In specialist hands, a diagnostic examination for sexual abuse is no more alarming than any other visit to a doctor's surgery. Furthermore, the paediatrician examines the child as a whole and older victims in particular find it reassuring to hear that their bodies are undamaged.

# 3 Who are the offenders?

Beliefs about child sexual offenders are as varied as the cultural myths surrounding their victims. It is important that both parent counsellors and support workers be familiar with relevant research findings so that they can help parents of victims to make wise decisions about the support or prosecution of offenders.

## Adult male offenders

Very little has been written about child molesters. We do not know exactly how many there are in the community. No-one has been able to find reliable differences between child rapists, paedophiles and 'normal' people who do not view children as sex objects. This is because child sexual abuse is the most commonly denied crime in the world and few offenders are convicted.

Offenders are not easily recognised—they look and, in public, behave in the same may as everyone else; they are found in every suburb, organisation and walk of life; some are married and have sex with their wives and/or other adults as well as with children; others (paedophiles) gain satisfaction only from sexual contacts with children. Offenders may be well educated or not, rich or poor, married or unmarried, employed or unemployed. They are social workers, child care workers and teachers; church leaders, politicians, judges and doctors; our friends, neighbours and relatives. In March 1988, the international press reported that sixteen staff from UNICEF (Brussels), including the Director, had been jailed for using UNICEF's headquarters for the procurement of children for pornography. UNICEF is the United Nations organisation created specifically to protect the world's children. At about the same time, a specialist in children's diseases at London's prestigious St. George's Hospital was convicted of similar offences (Armstrong and Hollows, 1989). In July 1986, the US Child Protection Report confirmed that a prominent Alabama Judge had been accused of raping the grandson of a fellow judge who was the occupant of the next hotel room at a Rhode Island conference. Paradoxically, the conference was called to discuss the judicial aspects of dealing with the growing number of child sexual abuse cases in the USA.

These cases are mentioned because, if we cannot trust judges, medical specialists or senior staff at UNICEF to protect our children, who can we trust? If child sexual offenders are in positions of power, how can we expect protection and justice for child victims? The sad truth is that no-one can be trusted on the basis of either their position in society or their kinship to children. It would obviously be harmful to teach children that society is totally untrustworthy—we must find a balance and help children to recognise and avoid potentially harmful situations rather than identify and avoid dangerous people.0

*Sexual interest in children is not uncommon*

When male students were surveyed at the University of California, 10 per cent said that they were paedophiles and had already used children for sex. An additional 21 per cent said that they were sexually attracted to small children and 7 per cent thought that they would have sex with children if there was no risk of being caught. It is important to note that those who reported the greatest sexual interest in children and who also used child pornography most frequently for sexual stimulation and masturbation were those who had suffered bad sexual experiences in childhood. Given the social stigma of making such admissions, the researchers feared that the actual rate of child-focused interest was much higher (Briere and Runtz, 1989).

## The progression from child victim to child abuser

Most children engage in some form of sexual activity with others in childhood. This is usually normal sexual curiosity and a passing phase. The question is, why do some people remain at this stage and continue to choose child partners? And why do some people use children in addition to their wives and/or other adults? What is even harder to understand is why those who suffer sexual violation in childhood choose to repeat it and damage other children. Many explanations have been offered.

As most parents know, young children commonly act out their fears as a way of working through them. When children undergo surgery in hospital, for example, they engage in hospital play long after their return home. Similarly, some victims of disturbing sexual abuse re-enact their abusive experiences with other children, stopping only when they are either no longer afraid or when the activity is no longer pleasurable. If there is no therapeutic intervention, such children may become habitual offenders, continuing into adulthood.

We know that all child abuse results in psychological disturbance. It affects the way in which victims perceive themselves and others. This has serious implications for the relationships they create in adulthood and for the way in which they protect their own and other people's children. Older victims fantasise about acts of revenge against their abusers but they lack opportunities for fulfilment. Because of the repetitive nature of sexual activity, abusive sexual acts become habitual and addictive and offenders need to seek more and more deviant behaviour in order to provide excitement. They gain sexual satisfaction from reminders about what they did to children; they fantasise about future encounters and gain thrills from secrecy, danger, planning and stalking victims. It is thought that they overcome their feelings of powerlessness by engaging in sex with younger and weaker victims who cannot resist them (Kreps, 1987). By overpowering, manipulating, controlling, hurting and gaining sexual domination over others, former victims overcome the sense of weakness associated with their own victimisation. The need to regain a sense of power and control in relationships combined with sexual satisfaction outweighs the possible negative consequences of deviant behaviour and the victimisation becomes re-enacted with the former victim now acting the role of abuser (Lane, 1985, quoted in Ryan et al, 1987).

## The conditions which lead to sexual offences with children

Not all male victims of sexual abuse become child molesters; not all molesters were victims of abuse. Several conditions have been identified as being conducive to child molestation by male sexual offenders, for example:

- arrested emotional and sexual development (often caused by abusive experiences in childhood);
- desire for male dominance in sexual relationships;
- desire to feel powerful and capable of controlling others;

- desire to re-enact childhood trauma in an effort to reduce the sense of hurt;
- capacity to see children as sex objects.

Child molesters are likely to experience difficulties in creating normal, sharing, caring sexual relationships. Married life will then be unsatisfactory for both partners. Prior to the onset of incest child victims may already be in the role of caregiver due to the physical or emotional withdrawal of the mother. Mothers in such families are often incest survivors themselves who, accustomed to male domination, feel incapable of protecting their children. Sometimes, there are unusual sleeping arrangements in the house or the offender is left in charge of children. In addition, incestuous fathers may control their families so that their wives and children are deprived of support networks and feel powerless. (See Figure 3.1 which shows the process of child sexual abuse.)

When offenders suffer from feelings of low self-worth, they tend to behave badly towards other people, being argumentative, making impossible demands, becoming aggressive and excessively critical and authoritarian. No matter how this scenario is acted out, offenders always end up feeling that no-one understands them and they then turn to children for comfort. The situations most likely to trigger child sexual abuse relate to poor family and work relationships—these may be self-induced or imaginary. Alcohol is sometimes used to overcome inhibitions about using children for sexual purposes. It is important to note that alcohol is never the cause of sexual abuse.

## How offenders choose victims

As part of their therapy, jailed child molesters have revealed how they choose victims. The most frequently selected children were their own. The second most vulnerable were troubled and lonely children who had no other significant males in their lives (Budin and Johnson, 1989). In a British Channel 4/Australian SBS TV programme (1990/1991), child molesters confessed that they had joined 'Parents without partners' specifically to meet unsupported mothers and gain access to their young children.

There is often a planned, lengthy 'grooming' process of seduction during which offenders pay attention to children's likes and dislikes. If necessary, the 'grooming' process includes the victims' parents. Trust is developed so that when children complain about the offenders' behaviour, parents do not believe them (Conte, 1986). When parents trust

**Figure 3.1 The process of child sexual abuse by known adolescents or adults**

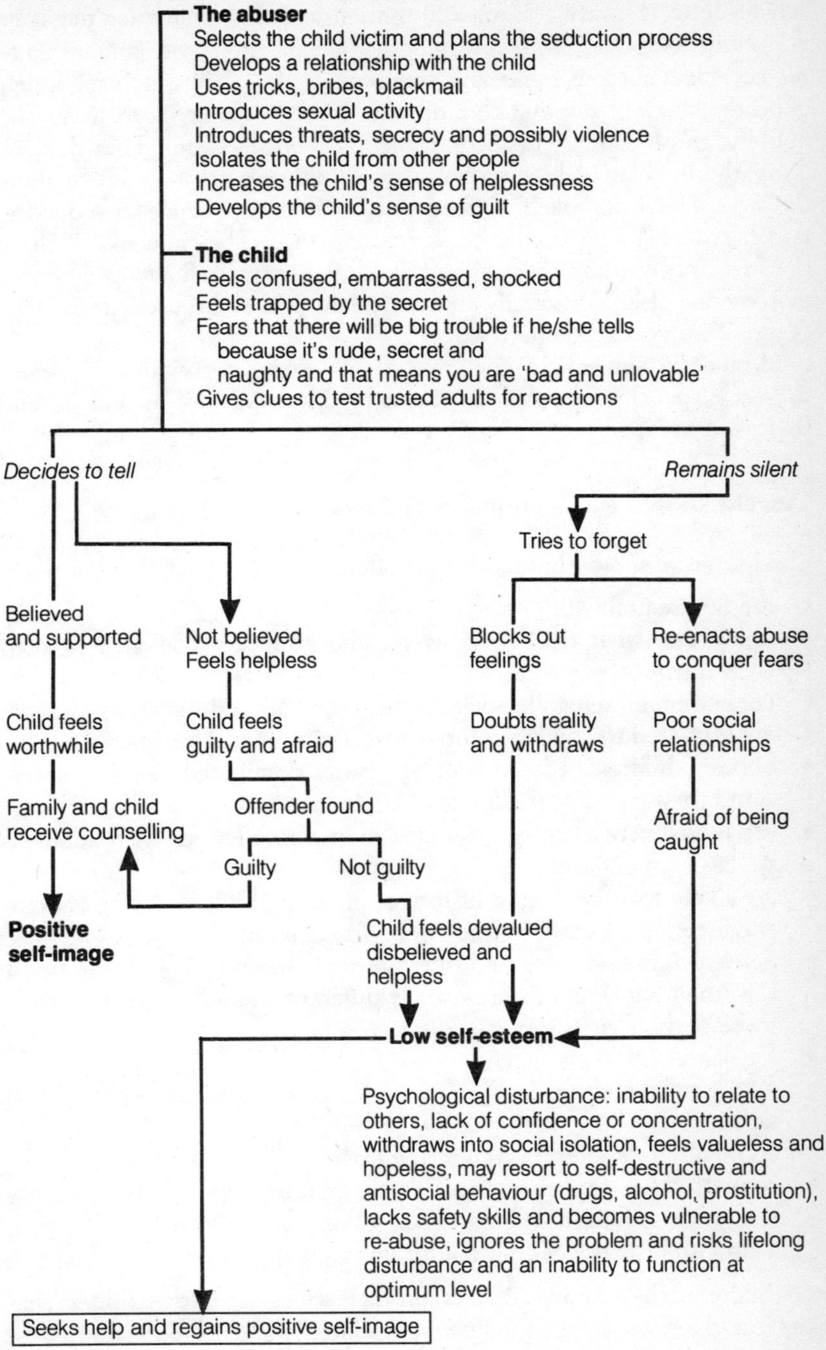

other adults, they are seldom willing to accept that their trust might be misplaced. Offenders who seek victims outside their own families go to public places such as parks and shopping malls. They watch for lonely children who will respond to kindness. They frequent sports areas and befriend those who are unaccompanied and unsuccessful. They develop sympathetic relationships and nurture children's trust before making the first sexual approach. Offenders plan every sequence of seduction and gain satisfaction from success at each stage. They may also include the friends of victims and seek out children known to have been abused by someone else. Non-family abusers are most likely to use flattery, gifts of money, toys and edible treats.

Most child abusers do not have to go looking for victims however; they use the children who are most readily available, in and around their own homes.

### Current knowledge about male offenders

The literature shows that most male offenders:

- are not mentally ill;
- know that what they do is wrong and go to great lengths to keep their offences secret;
- come from all religious, social, educational and ethnic groups;
- are attracted to children's innocence, softness and freshness;
- choose children because they are easily dominated, do not understand their rights or the limits of adult authority;
- are most likely to be heterosexual men who have sex with adults as well as with children;
- are likely to have a long history of abusing children dating back to adolescence (or earlier if they were also abused);
- deny or minimise the seriousness of their behaviour with the result that their explanations are usually different to and less reliable than those of their victims or witnesses;
- are distressed when caught;
- are often immature, lack empathy for others and have poor social skills;
- abuse other children as well as their own;
- commit other sexual offences, such as rape with adults, bestiality (sex with animals), exhibitionism ('flashing'), voyeurism ('Peeping Tom') and the use of children for pornography.

Children trust adults. Adults protect them from the things that frighten them most, such as fears associated with the dark and being alone in the house. Trusting children are easily duped and manipulated. The distorted thinking of offenders enables them to view victims as being equal, informed partners who want, invite and even enjoy being sexually assaulted. They conveniently forget the imbalance of power and the threats, bribes and force used to gain control. This ensures that they have few guilty feelings about what they do. Their concerns centre entirely on themselves and their fears of being caught and jailed. These anxieties may result in self-pity and trigger another cycle of abuse (see Figure 3.2).

In order that adult offenders stop offending, they must feel sufficiently uncomfortable about their behaviour to want to change it; they must admit and confront the details of all their offences, however painful. When possible, they must apologise to victims and accept responsibility for the harm they have done. The reluctance to admit offences was well demonstrated by 558 incest offenders who joined a treatment programme at Great Ormond Street Children's Hospital, London. On admission, only 15 per cent of the men admitted committing any offence; by the end of treatment, the same group had confessed to a total of 291 737 offences—an average of 522 crimes per person (Bentovim, 1991). Similar findings have emerged from treatment programmes in the USA. It is essential that this kind of information be given to those non-offending parents who remain loyal to offenders, convincing themselves that 'it only happened once in a moment of weakness and it won't happen again because he's learned his lesson'.

Abuse could not occur if child molesters were not sexually aroused by children. This is the most difficult aspect of their behaviour for 'normal' adults to understand. Offenders look at ordinary family photographs and find them seductive. Little girls are perceived as being miniature Marilyn Monroes. Offenders fantasise about children's nakedness, miniature buttocks, tiny vaginas and little penises and these fantasies result in erections and orgasms. Arousal becomes habitual. Every contact is sexualised and normal hugs and cuddles are viewed as seductive. Offenders are then only a short step away from acting out their fantasies.

As with most undesirable human behaviours, offenders justify their actions to themselves. Like smokers who should not smoke and dieters who should not eat chocolates, child sex offenders turn to children for comfort, rationalising that 'just one more won't do any harm'. In all three situations, the reward is addictive and the participants want more.

Similarly, motorists who exceed the speed limit know that they are committing an offence but they rationalise that they are in a hurry, are harming no-one and there is little risk of being caught.

**Figure 3.2 The cycle of sexual abuse**

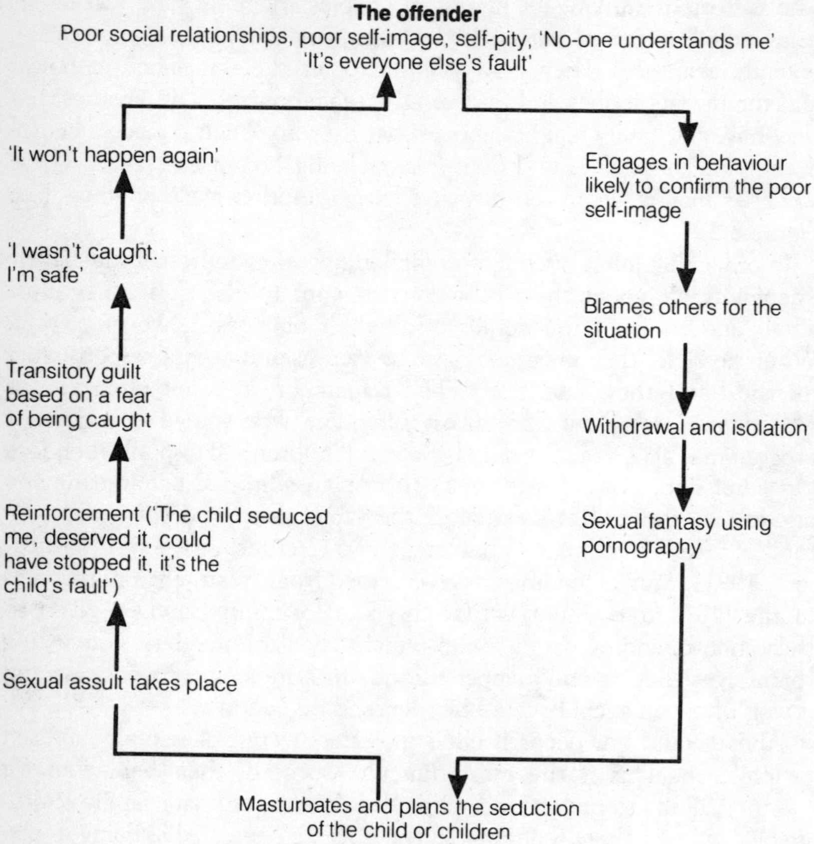


*Source*: Adapted from a diagram by Ryan, Lane, Davis and Isaac, 1987, 'Juvenile sex offenders—Development and Correction' *Journal of Child Abuse and Neglect* 11, 3, p. 390.

Child molesters also tell themselves that they are doing no harm: 'Children like it. They could stop it. And, after all, it's happened lots of times and I haven't been caught'.

Fear and concerns for self preservation slow down offending behaviour but only temporarily. When the speeding motorist sees an accident or a 'speed trap', he brakes and behaves responsibly until the danger is over. When the smoker develops a cough, he worries about lung cancer and reduces or even stops smoking for a time. When the cough is cured and the anxiety decreases, the habit returns.

Similarly, when a child molester fears apprehension, he panics, stops the behaviour and assures himself that it will never happen again. If he is caught but not prosecuted, he is likely to become complacent and even arrogant: 'The police know and they haven't done anything about it. Nobody will help you. I can do what I like. I'm safe'.

## The treatment of male offenders

When offenders join treatment programmes, their abusive behaviour may diminish. They feel more self-disciplined and tell therapists that they are cured and 'don't need to come here any more'. Without psychological support and the attitudinal changes which come from long-term therapy, however, child molesters find that temptation increases, resistance weakens and abusive behaviours return. There are conflicting views about the value and effectiveness of treatment for male sexual offenders. Success seems to depend on the age of the abuser, the length of time that he has been offending, the seriousness and frequency of his offences and his desire to change. In family abuse, it is essential that the offender leaves the home and has no contact with victims until therapists have evidence to suggest that children will be safe.

During treatment, offenders learn how to identify risky situations and break the behaviour pattern at the first sign. A re-education programme attempts to replace deviant thoughts with pro-social ones and to develop self-esteem, normal family relationships and social skills. Simultaneously, there must be counselling for all relevant members before the family is reunited. Not all adult sex offenders are treatable. Those who have spent most of their lives obtaining thrills from sex with children are unlikely to want to change. Some must be isolated for a very long time to protect children from harm.

## Adult female offenders

Until recently, allegations of sexual offences involving women offenders constituted between only 1 and 3 per cent of all reports throughout Western society. This gave the impression that child sexual abuse revolved around the male desire to dominate females and children. At the European Conference on Child Abuse and Neglect in Prague (1991), international reports showed a significant increase in reported offences. Many were committed by women under the domination of male co-offenders. Some mothers know that their children are being molested but do nothing to protect them; some present their children for molestation, for example for money (prostitution and pornography) or when they join satanic cults which include child sexual abuse as one of the rituals.

International conclusions are that reports involving women offenders have masked the size of the problem. Several reasons have been given for this under-reporting:

1 Sexual offences by females are viewed by society as being less damaging than offences by males. This is because people tend to think only in terms of the physical damage and not the psychological damage to victims. The fact that a female offender does not have a penis, cannot make a victim pregnant and seldom uses violence leads society to underestimate the damage caused by female offenders.
2 Boys do not usually report sexual abuse by females. Male conditioning tells them that sexual initiation by older females is beneficial. With such conditioning, it is very difficult for boys to complain that they either did not want it or enjoy it.
3 Women can conceal sexual motives more easily than men. Females expect and receive a lot of physical intimacy and body contact with children.
4 Most offences by women are incestuous. Victims are unlikely to report their primary caregivers.

Like her male counterpart, the female offender does not belong to any single social, racial or ethnic group. Both male and female offenders are likely to have suffered abuse of some kind in childhood.

When reports of mother–son incest are made to police, they are often not taken seriously. These cases come to notice again when the male victims sexually abuse their younger sisters or other children in school. Police in Australia, New Zealand and the United Kingdom have investigated complaints involving both mothers and maternal grandmothers. Few prosecutions have occurred but a number of treatment programmes have been quietly set up for female offenders.

Various explanations have been given for the reasons why women abuse young children. Early literature suggested that offenders were psychotic single parents who placed sons in the husband role. This is not true and does not explain the abuse of female children. Half of reported offenders in an American study (Krug, 1989) lived with their husbands and had no psychiatric problems. Some mother–son relationships were triggered by the mother's wish to dominate males (rather than gain sexual satisfaction); others are searching for emotional satisfaction (Finkelhor, 1984). Whatever the reasons, it is important to remember that all sexually abusive behaviour causes long-term psychological damage and this will be discussed at greater length in a later section on issues for survivors.

## Juvenile offenders

Outside the United States, the problem of child sexual abuse by juvenile and adolescent offenders has not yet been taken seriously. In Britain, Australia and New Zealand, teachers and parents who report sexual abuse by juveniles are often concerned to find that their complaints are not investigated by child protection authorities. Sexual abuse is often mistaken for 'normal (albeit early) sexual curiosity' or explained away, for example 'he's probably seen blue movies at home'. Apart from the fact that exposing children to pornography is, in itself, a form of sexual abuse, failure to take the behaviour seriously ensures that young offenders are deprived of treatment. Without professional help, there is a high risk that they will become habitual offenders, damaging hundreds of lives.

In the mid-1980s, American authorities responded to the information that most adult offenders were once juvenile offenders and that adolescents are responsible for 20 per cent of all rapes and up to half of all reports of child sexual abuse. Substantial funds were allocated for juvenile and adolescent treatment centres, catering for children from three to four years upwards. There were over 500 such centres in 1988.

Most information about young offenders has come from the support programme set up by the Children's Institute International in Los Angeles in 1985. Child offenders are defined as those who act in a sexual way with other children, using force or coercion to obtain the victim's participation or choosing victims who are too young to understand or resist their behaviour.

In families where several children are involved and each child blames the other for being the initiator, all the children are included in treatment. Boys in these families have been found to be excessively sexual and have no understanding of the inappropriateness of their behaviour. Some of the offenders in the Los Angeles programme had begun to abuse other children when they were only two years old. The juvenile offender problem is not associated with any particular social class, race or religion. It was noted however that the Los Angeles clients were most likely to come from single parent households headed by mothers who had histories of drug or alcohol abuse. Most juvenile offenders were victims of father–son and/or grandfather–grandson incest.

Because young offenders are less mobile than adolescents, their victims tend to be family members (70 per cent), neighbourhood children (16 per cent) and school friends (14 per cent). Offences include vaginal and anal penetration with penis, finger and objects, simulated intercourse and genital touching. These activities replicate the sexual abuse they had previously experienced. Furthermore, when the adult offenders used threats and tricks to gain their victims' compliance, their victims adopted the same tactics with younger children. Adolescents are likely to use violence to achieve their ends.

Four to ten-year-old children admit their offences and respond to adult concerns. By eleven to thirteen years, however, denial creeps in as perpetrators fear the punitive consequences of disclosure. The high level of incest offences by disturbed juvenile victims points to the need for community education about the extent of the problem and the need for child protection and treatment programmes. Parents of offenders should be warned not to leave them alone with younger children until therapists feel that they are able to respond to children appropriately.

# 4 Child victims in the justice system

> Where children are caught up in the gladiatorial contest between parties . . . which is our adversarial method of trial, they are bound to suffer (McEwen, 1988).

> Cross examination is that part of court proceedings where the interests of the child are most likely to be ignored and sacrificed (Brennan and Brennan, 1988).

> Do the ends of justice really require that a child of eight should be grilled to the point of tears in the intimidating surroundings of a packed courtroom? (*The Times*, London, 29 March, 1983)

## Children as witnesses

When parents report that children have been sexually abused and offenders are known, they expect the justice system to act swiftly to protect their children and to isolate the perpetrators. To the outraged parents, the reporting of sexual abuse constitutes an emergency which requires immediate attention. They take it for granted that offenders will be confronted, apprehended and remanded in custody until the case is heard. The first lesson that parents have to learn is that the justice system moves extremely slowly and the second lesson is that, in criminal courts, the rights of the accused take precedence over the rights and safety of victims. This is very hard for parents whose children have been violated. They assume that justice will not only be done but will also be seen to be done. They are often frustrated and disappointed.

Until comparatively recently, there were rules which forebade children below a specified age from giving evidence in criminal courts. In some States and countries, the limit was fourteen years of age. When child victims were allowed to appear in court, judges were obliged to warn juries that all children's evidence had less credibility than that of adults. This ensured that sexual molesters who pleaded 'Not guilty' had few fears of being convicted and jailed.

Public concerns brought changes to the rules. In Scotland there is no age limit and children as young as three years of age have appeared in court (Blagg, Hughes and Wattam, 1989). There is no logical reason for any age restriction: some very young children are competent and articulate witnesses while many adults commit perjury. Nevertheless, limits persist. In 1992, police in Western Australia did not prosecute offenders if key witnesses were under twelve years of age. Police in Victoria and South Australia set a limit of eight years. There is unlikely to be any prosecution if victims are deaf, suffer speech impairments or intellectual disabilities. These restrictions relate to the unwillingness of the legal profession and judiciary to adapt court procedures, practices and questioning to meet the needs of children.

Proposals to permit the use of interpreters for young and disabled witnesses were strongly opposed by Western Australia's powerful Law Society. The result is that child molesters have been given what amounts to a licence to rape the most vulnerable section of the population with little fear of apprehension or punishment. Neither magistrates nor judges are under any obligation to test a child's competence to give evidence. Parents are (understandably) angry when the person who violated their child escapes prosecution because the child is considered to be too young or insufficiently articulate to testify and be exposed to the often inappropriate and insensitive cross-examination techniques commonly used by lawyers.

## The legal machinery

In England, Wales and Australia, all prosecutions begin in the local Magistrates Court. In New Zealand and Scotland, they are held in the District Court. In New Zealand, this court is presided over by a judge who is a lawyer nominated by the legal fraternity and employed by the government. The Australian magistrate fulfils the same role. In Scotland, cases are tried by a Justice of the Peace. In England and Wales, some courts have two or three 'lay' (non-professional) magistrates who are advised by a clerk of the court who has a legal background. Offences are graded according to severity. The least serious cases are decided in the local court while offences of a serious nature are heard in a higher court.

In New Zealand, the defendant can elect to be tried in the District Court with a judge and a jury. The third level of court machinery is the High Court. This is equivalent to the Crown Court in England and Wales, the Supreme Court in Australia and the Sheriff Court in Scotland. Despite different names, court procedures are much the same in all five countries. In cases of sexual abuse, child witnesses usually have to appear at the local court on the days of the hearing. There may be several adjournments before the case is heard. If the magistrate or judge decides that an offence has occurred and there is evidence to suggest that the accused person is the offender, the case goes on the waiting list for the court at the higher level. The waiting time can be as long as eighteen months (and very much longer if there are adjournments, appeals and retrials). During that time, the abuse remains uncomfortably at the forefront of the minds of victims and their parents.

In Scotland, the prosecutor is a barrister known as the Advocate Depute. In Australia, England and Wales, the prosecutor is a barrister who has been instructed by the Crown prosecution service. This service falls under the authority of the Attorney General who is usually a lawyer as well as a politician. Because of the small population in New Zealand, prosecuting lawyers are selected locally.

Criminal proceedings in all five countries are founded on the same adversarial tradition. The trial involves a contest between two opposing parties, each of which presents their case. The court decides between the two. If the jury finds the defendant guilty, the judge decides the punishment within the limits of the law. When the case goes to the higher court, child witnesses must attend unless otherwise instructed. Children and their parents are placed in positions of uncertainty because they do not know what they will be asked, when they will be called to give evidence or how long it will take. Long waits and fear of the unknown can be extremely stressful for children. Glasgow Sheriff Court appears to be the only court with a creche facility (Blagg, Hughes and Wattam, 1989). In others, children are kept waiting in corridors and public areas where they are no toys, books or play materials to help them to fill these stressful hours.

## The cross-examination of child witnesses

Courts were designed by adults for adults. They work on the principle that all participants and contracts are equal, but children can never be equal to adults in the court system. The long delays involved in court proceedings are always advantageous to offenders and disadvantageous to victims because they allow the time for defence lawyers to create confusion in the minds of young children who do not keep diaries and seldom know the precise dates or times of offences. Children are unlikely to remember the postal address of the house in which the abuse occurred. They may know that it happened before or after tea or during a certain television programme, that it was on a birthday or during a holiday and that they were in a certain person's house in a particular room. They will remember who did what, whether it hurt and what the offender said. Defence lawyers are able to confuse child witnesses by expecting a level of knowledge that is beyond their developmental capacity. Those who were abused on a daily basis over many years are unlikely to remember whether the offender sought oral, vaginal or anal sex on a specific date. Defence lawyers then suggest that there is no case to answer because the victim's memory is unreliable.

Parents are angry and frustrated when a persistent offender is released because witnesses could not recall the exact date or time of the offence or what they were wearing two years earlier. The fact that most adults in court would not know yesterday's date (without reference to a calendar) and could not recall what they wore a week ago, least of all a year ago, demonstrates the inappropriateness of this kind of questioning. Defence lawyers have been allowed to use a wide range of tricks to discredit children's evidence. They have asked children whether they believed in Father Christmas or the 'tooth fairy' and when the child said 'Yes', the defence argued that the child was unreliable because he or she could not tell the difference between fact and fiction. Without the evidence of the key witnesses, there is no case to answer and offenders are released.

When children give evidence in a criminal court, they are subjected to the same kind of questioning as adult rape victims. Defence lawyers often accuse them of being vicious liars and seductresses in the hope of breaking them down. In some cases, children have become so distressed that they could not continue their evidence—judges have stopped trials and offenders have been freed. There is clearly a strong incentive for defence lawyers to reduce children to tears. Judges have the power to stop unsuitable questioning but they rarely exercise it. Sometimes, the prosecutor tells the jury that a particular question was inappropriate, but usually after it occurred when the child is already confused or distressed. An awareness of the appropriateness of questioning for specific age levels requires an understanding of the dynamics of child sexual abuse and child development, neither of which are included in legal training.

Similarly, regardless of the normal concentration span associated with childhood, young witnesses are kept in the witness box for hours or days on end. They are asked about the same detail again and again in the hope that they will become confused and contradict themselves. These practices can cause enormous psychological damage to child victims. Some courts allow the child witness to sit close to an adult friend while giving testimony but there are rules which forbid communication. If the child becomes distressed, the adult may not speak or comfort the child. When parents are to be called as witnesses, they may not be present in the courtroom while their children are giving evidence. With funding from the British Government, psychologists from Leicester University monitored 544 trials involving child witnesses (Davies and Noon, 1991). They found that the average delay between the arrest and trial of the accused was ten and one half months. Such a delay always increases the defence lawyer's opportunities for confusing the child about insignificant, small details which may have nothing whatsoever to do with the offences but which are used to demonstrate that the witness has a deficient memory.

In the British courts, more than half of the lawyers (for both the prosecution and the defence) asked questions which were inappropriate for child witnesses. They failed to adapt to children's language, using double negatives such as, 'Am I not right in thinking that you are not telling the truth'. They began their sentences with the customary 'I put it to you that . . . (you are mistaken)', 'I suggest to you that he . . . (did not do the things you say he did)', 'I am about to put it to you that . . . (this is what really happened).' In the British cases, such inappropriate questioning ensured that child witnesses were unable to answer more than half of all questions put to them. They exhibited a wide range of emotionally disturbed behaviours both before and after the trial and symptoms of stress were apparent during the trial.

Child protection agencies and support services have long complained about the emotional abuse of children in the justice system. In response, members of the legal profession justify their practices with, 'The accused has more at stake than the victim' and 'The court cannot heal the damage that has already been done to the child'. Seemingly ignorant of the long-term psychological harm inflicted on children, lawyers convince themselves that 'children soon forget'. And, of course, they are wrong.

## The 'professional witness'

In the 1980s, increasing numbers of professional men were accused of child sexual abuse and incest. With their reputations and livelihoods at stake, they were prepared to pay substantial sums of money for expert testimony by witnesses claiming expertise in the reliability (or unreliability) of children's evidence. A leader in this field was American Ralph Underwager. In the period to 1990, he is claimed to have made hundreds of court appearances on behalf of adults charged with sexual offences against children. He was so successful that he achieved international media publicity and was invited to appear in cases overseas. In 1989, he conducted seminars in Australia and made television appearances. He told audiences what they wanted most to hear: that most accused adults are innocent and the evidence of children is always unreliable. He argued that children have a basic need to please the adults who care for them. That, in turn, makes them 'too open to suggestion' and ensures that their evidence is always 'contaminated' by the adults involved in the interviewing process.

Underwager appeared as a witness for the defence in the Glebe (Sydney) 'Mr Bubbles' kindergarten case. After hearing his evidence, the magistrate ruled that there was no case to answer because the evidence of nineteen children had inevitably been 'contaminated' by the questioning of police and social workers. The magistrate was asked to interview the children to check their reliability for himself but he refused, concluding that the children were 'too young to understand their duty to tell the truth' and 'not competent to take an oath' (*The Australian*, 11 August 1989).

Underwager's success faltered in 1990 when an American Court refused to allow him to give evidence because he was a 'researcher who did not have bona fide qualifications'. The Washington State Superior Court was not satisfied that Underwager's claims relating to the unreliability of children's evidence were accepted by the scientific community nor was it satisfied with the reliability of his research methods (*State* v *Swan*). The State Supreme Court confirmed the trial Judge's decision, saying that Underwager's testimony had been 'properly refused' both because it was not established that Underwager's views were accepted in the scientific community and because his evidence did not meet minimum standards for admissability (Court transcripts 55393–9, 114WA2d613, 790P.2d 610–1990).

In the meantime, the New England Commissioners of Child Welfare Agencies were alarmed by increasing defence claims that children's evidence was always unreliable because of contamination by questioning. It was noted that a book by Underwager and Wakefield was used as an authoritative source by the defence in child sexual abuse trials. With funding from the Commissioners, Dr Anna Salter investigated the book and published her findings in 'Accuracy of Expert Testimony in

Child Sexual Abuse Cases: A Case Study of Ralph Underwager and Hollida Wakefield' (1991). The National Centre for Prosecution of Child Abuse reported that, after reviewing over 500 of the books and articles cited in Underwager and Wakefield's book, Salter claimed to have found hundreds of errors (Update, Vol. 4, 3, March 1991).

While Underwager's success attracted a great deal of media attention, the Washington Supreme Court and Salter's findings were not so widely publicised and some defence lawyers continue to use Underwager's arguments relating to the 'contamination' and unreliability of children's evidence. The message for (non-offending) parents, child protection and support services is clear. When the defence is using professional witnesses, ensure that prosecuting lawyers have read Salter's publication. It contains a list of questions for the cross-examination of these witnesses in child sexual abuse cases (p. 53). This is useful because such witnesses often quote from literature which they do not take into court. By the time the prosecution can obtain the articles or books through inter-library loan, the trial is over.

Information relating to American professional witnesses can be obtained from the National Center for Prosecution of Child Abuse, American Research Institute, 99 Canal Center Plaza, Suite 510, Alexandria, VA 22314, USA.

## The outcome of legal proceedings

When an offender is convicted, judges sometimes assess the seriousness of the crime on the basis of physical damage only. If there is no psychologist's report to show the psychological effects of the abuse, the offence may be trivialised with statements such as, 'The child is young and will forget', or 'No real harm was done. It only happened three times'. The offender is likely to receive a good behaviour bond which neither satisfies outraged parents nor resolves the abuser's behaviour problems. Judges who appear to know nothing of the dynamics of child sexual abuse may also apportion blame to young victims on the grounds that they did not say, 'No', scream, fight back or run away, albeit from their own bedrooms in the middle of the night. Some offenders are reassured that they are 'more to be pitied than blamed' because they allowed themselves to be 'seduced' by their seven-year-old sons and daughters. Reports of such conclusions still occur but, thankfully, with better community education, they are becoming less and less frequent.

However, even when a judge makes a powerful speech on the abhorrence of the crime and imposes a harsh sentence for the protection of society offenders are often released (without treatment) after a few weeks or months because of remission for good behaviour. Convicted offenders also often successfully appeal on the basis of seemingly unrelated matters.

The problem for the community is that while there is no incentive for offenders to seek voluntary therapy and when no treatment programme is imposed by the courts, nothing happens to change their attitudes, behaviours and sexual preferences. Abusers are therefore likely to renew their powerful hold over their own and other people's children on their release.

## The need for change

It has long been accepted that the present system of justice neither stops child abusers from offending nor provides protection for children. Few child molesters are prosecuted and even fewer are punished. Furthermore, a prison sentence is unlikely to change attitudes or sexual preferences.

Child protection authorities have considered the introduction of a 'treatment alternative to jail' for first-time offenders who plead guilty to offences within the family, accept responsibility, apologise to victims and provide financial support. The 'treatment alternative' has long been available in the USA where a 'guilty' plea ensures that child victims are spared the trauma of cross-examination in court and offenders receive intensive treatment. There has not been any widespread international movement to adopt this approach however. Its introduction necessitates legislative changes which are opposed by lawyers who have a vested interest in maintaining the present system of trials, retrials and appeals. Trials are much less time-consuming (and hence lawyers' fees are reduced) when child molesters plead 'guilty' and without a treatment option there is no incentive for offenders to admit their guilt as admission invariably results in a prison sentence. Parent support groups often find that, when offenders express regret and admit their offences, their lawyers persuade them to plead 'not guilty' when they appear in court. The recipients of the confessions are debarred from giving evidence and defendants are released.

All support agencies confirm that substantial changes are needed to protect children from emotional abuse within the justice system. They point out that it is not necessary for justice that child witnesses should:

- have to sit facing, and in eye-to-eye contact with, those who have harmed and probably threatened them. Sex offenders have already exerted a great deal of power over victims and, by using threatening body language, can continue to control them in court;

- be grilled by adults who, in the 1990s choose to dress up like performers in Gilbert and Sullivan operas and use a form of language which is only understood by the legal fraternity;
- have to tell their story a dozen times to a dozen different people when there are alternative methods available.

Most child protection authorities have sought law reform. In most States and countries, change has been fought by the legal profession which is the profession best situated to influence the politicians who are responsible for legislative changes.

## The video link

The United States has been at the forefront in improving conditions for child victims in court. In 1983, US courts introduced the video link which enables children to testify from an adjacent room in which there is a video camera and screen. The television picture of the child is relayed to the courtroom. If cameras are appropriately placed, child witnesses only see the television image of a judge or lawyer when questions are asked. They never see the accused. This interview method has been used successfully with victims as young as four and five years of age. In 1991, it was used in twenty-nine American States.

New Zealand's High Courts and some Australian Supreme Courts are also equipped with close circuit television equipment for use with child witnesses. Recent legislation in Western Australia will make the facility available to all vulnerable witnesses and victims of violence. Elsewhere there are age limits, varying from ten years in California to eighteen years in the Australian Capital Territory.

The video link was introduced to fourteen Crown Courts in England and Wales in 1989 and provision was extended to thirty additional courts in January 1991 to provide a comprehensive geographic coverage. The evaluation (Davies and Noon, 1991) shows that children were more confident and less stressed when they did not have to appear in the courtroom. Furthermore, 74 per cent of the judges and 83 per cent of the barristers expressed a preference for the system. Wigs were removed in 62 per cent of cases when children were giving their evidence. An application to the judge was sufficient to trigger these arrangements.

During the same period, Dr Judy Cashmore of Sydney's Macquarie University evaluated the effects of closed circuit on child witnesses in the ACT Magistrates Court, Canberra. The legislation decreed that the court could only make an order to permit a child witness to use CCTV if the child was 'likely to suffer mental or emotional harm if required to give evidence in the ordinary way or the facts would be better ascertained' by its usage. This led, predictably, to legal arguments about what constitutes 'mental or emotional harm' and whether common sense was sufficient or whether expert evidence was needed to show that harm was likely. Legislation also decreed that the Court must not make an order to allow a child to use CCTV if usage 'would be unfair to a party to the proceedings' (and, of course the defence has long argued that any procedure which stops eye to eye contact with the accused is unfair).

The draft report of the Law Reform Commission, 'The use of closed-circuit television for child witnesses in the ACT', October 1992, shows that when the system was made available to child witnesses:

- there was a reduction of stress *if* children wanted to use it and were allowed to do so;
- lawyers were more supportive and magistrates intervened more often during cross-examination;
- children found it easier to testify than if they had to face the accused in court;
- respondents viewed CCTV as fair to both the defendant and child;
- children benefited from having some measure of control over the process.

However, because the court was left to make the decision about whether a child should have access to CCTV, there was no consistency in its availability. The report recommended that, in accordance with Australia's international obligations under the United Nations Convention on the Rights of the Child, Article 12 (1990), child witnesses should have the right to use CCTV unless *they* did not wish to use it.

Davies and Noon's report also shows that few child witnesses were given appropriate preparation for their appearance in court. Some had not been introduced to the equipment prior to its use. This would clearly disadvantage those witnesses.

## Evidential video interviews

The United States also took the initiative in using video cameras to record police and social worker interviews with young victims of sexual offences. Video evidential interviewing provides accurate records of children's statements and reduces the number of interrogations. Video evidence is extremely powerful and, when shown to offenders, substantially increases the number of 'guilty' pleas. It provides no magic cure, however, because technology provides more opportunities for lawyers to argue about technical issues. Video interviews demand specialist skills which require specialist training and this is not widely available.

Evidential video interviewing is used in some countries outside the USA, but change is slow and inconsistent. Most Family Courts will accept video evidence when there are allegations of sexual abuse in custody and access disputes. Some courts will view video evidence when child protection services seek orders to remove children from unprotective homes. Some Magistrates Courts will accept children's video evidence in criminal cases, but others will not. The Ministry for Justice has provided evidential video units for sexual abuse investigation teams throughout New Zealand but video evidence has not been accepted by all High Courts. Australian authorities have discussed the use of evidential video interviews in criminal courts for the past seven years but, in 1992, some are still procrastinating.

Changes to the justice system requires changes to legislation and that involves politicians, politics and parliament—all of these are notoriously slow in responding to the needs of children.

For further information on child witnesses and the close-circuit TV-video link, see Professor Graham Davies, and Elizabeth Noon's report, 'An evaluation of the live link for child witnesses', HMSO, London, November 1991, available from Home Office Library, 50 Queen Ann's Gate, London, SW1 H9AT and Davies (1992).

## Child victims and parents in battles for access and custody

There may be little chance of rescuing young victims from intrafamilial abuse unless mothers separate from offending partners and obtain court orders depriving offenders of access to victims. It follows that the court which is experiencing the most dramatic rise in reported cases of child sexual abuse involving young children is the court involved with family law. This is the Divorce County Court in England and Wales, the Court of Session and Sheriff Court in Scotland and the Family Court in Australia and New Zealand. Divorce courts in England and Wales are being 'phased out' in favour of Family Courts.

Increasing numbers of contested custody cases involve allegations that children have been molested by their fathers' or their mothers' new partners. In allegations of father–child incest, the offences have usually contributed to marital breakdown or they may have come to light after separation. When father–child incest is revealed, the mother often takes immediate action to prevent the father from having further contact with her children. Complications arise when the accused father denies the behaviour. The court is then placed in the unenviable position of having to decide whether or not the child will be at risk of abuse if contact with the accused person continues.

As in other courts of law, the judges, lawyers and counsellors involved in family disputes are not required to possess any expertise relating to child development. They may have no understanding of what is normal or abnormal child behaviour or how normal children react to sexual abuse. And yet they are required to make decisions which have serious implications for a child's safety and long-term emotional and physical wellbeing.

When a decision is necessary about a victim's future, the court may seek independent advice from a family counsellor. In England and Wales, this may be a Child Welfare Officer employed by the court. Australian and New Zealand Courts tend to use counsellors in private practice. Child protection workers complain that these counsellors have diverse backgrounds which seldom include professional qualifications in child development or professional expertise with young children. Furthermore, there is often no consultation between the counsellors and the therapists who have been working with the children since the disclosure of the abuse. As a result, the counsellor's report tends to be comparatively superficial and this superficiality has resulted in some very strange and unsatisfactory decisions being made relating to the care of child victims.

Child sexual abuse allegations result in bitter custody battles in which children are both the pawns and the sufferers. Cases are complicated by the fact that the abuse of young children usually involves oral sex, genital touching or masturbation which may leave no scientific or medical evidence. Furthermore, victims do not give evidence in these courts. Another complicating factor is that the person receiving the disclosure and making the report is usually the mother. Even if she witnessed the abuse, she is not viewed as an impartial witness but as one who has ulterior motives for accusing or discrediting the father.

In custody and access battles, the accused father's lawyers may discredit the social workers, therapists, child psychologists and paediatricians who decided that abuse had occurred. Even when there is medical evidence to show that a child has been raped, it may be disregarded. Proof of rape does not always provide evidence that the father was the rapist. Mothers who begin proceedings may find themselves placed in much the same position as the rape-victim of old. They find themselves answering questions about matters which have no bearing on the allegation of incest. They are cross-examined about their private lives, associates, employment and even their political leanings to make them appear to the court as either incompetent mothers who have exposed their children to other abusers or as having been influenced by left-wing man-hating feminists who are opposed to traditional family life. This line of questioning has been used most effectively when women have found it necessary to seek help from women's refuges.

Caring parents who turn to courts for help are often surprised to find themselves facing counter-allegations—that they maliciously instructed their children to report abuse as an act of revenge, that they abused their children or that their friends or relatives were the real offenders. When mothers actually witness the abuse and seek psychological help to cope with the trauma, their action is likely to be used against them in court. Through their lawyers, fathers argue that their former wives had long been psychologically disturbed and the allegations of abuse were the result of the disturbance rather than the cause of it. Fathers then seek custody of the children on the grounds that their wives are 'unfit' parents.

When mothers are incest survivors, offenders are also likely to use this information against them claiming that their wives were obsessed with abuse and saw signs of it where none existed. When these mothers become distressed by the frustration of their powerlessness in court, their distress is viewed as further evidence of their emotional instability. They, too, are then at risk of losing the custody of the children that they were trying to protect.

Sinister motives are also attributed to fathers who seek custody of their young children after the disclosure of offences involving step-fathers or other men involved in relationships with their former wives. Accusations rarely involve the mothers themselves.

When custodial fathers learn that their young children have been abused on access visits to mothers, they, too, turn to the court for help. The mothers then face the dilemma of whether to support their new partners or their children. When leaving their families for new partners, women made a tremendous emotional commitment and may (rightly) fear that if they support their children they will lose their homes, financial security and means of support. To protect their new partners, some mothers agree that their children have been sexually abused but they lodge counter accusations, claiming that the person who committed the offences is their own father, not their current husband or lover. To strengthen their case, mothers then feel obliged to seek the custody of their children through the courts. When they win, the children are the losers because such mothers are likely to turn a blind-eye to further abuse in order to maintain their own status quo.

### When parents are dissatisfied with court decisions

Until comparatively recently, the Australian Family Court had no history of conceding that child sexual abuse and incest constituted sufficient grounds to stop a father's access to his child victims. The general approach of the court to mothers' concerns about child sexual abuse has been one of scepticism, disbelief and the desire to protect male parents from 'spurious changes' (Scutt, in Hetherington, 1991, p. 118). Although legislation in 1975 required the court to act in the best interests of the child, no Family Court in New South Wales deprived a parent of access on these grounds until 1985.

Allegations that Australian Family Courts were failing to provide the necessary protection for children led the Attorney General to issue an instruction that courts must act in the interests of a child's safety and access should cease if there are risks of sexual molestation (1988). Recent reports suggest that this directive has had little impact on court practice because judges still have to assess whether or not the risk is real and that decision depends on the honesty of the conflicting adults and a sound knowledge of the problem of child sexual abuse. Some authorities and professional associations have provided seminars on 'Child Abuse and Family Law' for court personnel but attendance is, of course, optional and those who attend are usually the ones least in need of education.

If a parent is dissatisfied with the level of protectiveness in a court ruling and fails to hand a child over to his or her abuser, as required by the court, the parent is deemed to be 'In contempt of court', an offence punishable by imprisonment. The abuser is then likely to gain custody of the child while the protecting parent goes to jail. The best publicised 'contempt' case in recent times was that involving Dr Elizabeth Morgan, who served a record 759 days in an American prison after refusing to disclose the whereabouts of her daughter, Hilary. The court had heard evidence to the effect that Hilary's father had sexually molested her and her half-sister on visits to his home. He responded with counter-allegations and the court decided that access should continue. Dr Morgan refused to hand her child over to her ex-husband and she was arrested. She said that she would remain in jail indefinitely rather than subject her child to the risk of further abuse. Dr Morgan was released in October 1989, only because President George Bush intervened and changed the law to limit the penalty for 'contempt' to a maximum sentence of one year in jail. Accompanied by considerable media publicity, the accused father mounted a worldwide search for his daughter and traced her to New Zealand. Upon her release, Dr Morgan continued her fight, this time in the Family Court in New Zealand.

In Australia, Family Law is the responsibility of the Federal government and child protection laws are the responsibility of the States. Because Australian State laws supercede federal laws, it is possible for Australian parents to seek protection for their children from the Children's Courts if they are endangered by a Family Court decision. In New Zealand, there is no children's court: the Family Court judge who makes the decision about access is the same judge who makes decisions about children. Furthermore, the 1989 New Zealand child protection legislation is widely viewed as disadvantaging children by replacing the former emphasis on children's needs with an emphasis on family responsibility. Critics point out that Family Court judges have no history of involvement with children and, when there is doubt, they tend to err on the side of the adults.

Parents can go to an Appeals Court if they are dissatisfied with the technical aspects of a custody or access decision. The process is lengthy, extremely expensive and something that mothers with young children can rarely afford. It is a matter of public concern that innocent parents who have committed no offence pay heavily to protect their children from erring partners. Australian and New Zealand support services report that mothers who receive legal assistance are required to pay the full costs after the property settlement which follows divorce. Mothers have incurred legal fees of up to $A72 000 (32 000 pounds) in their attempts to provide protection for their children. In some cases, this has necessitated the sale of possessions and the family home.

Kee MacFarlane (1986) summed up the access and custody hearings well:

> Few circumstances are less conducive to evaluating allegations of child sexual abuse than those associated with these cases. Frequently such allegations are dismissed or lightly regarded by the courts as yet another weapon in an ongoing battle over a lost marriage. In some cases the abuse allegations remain unresolved while the custody disputes rage on for months and even years at great financial expense to the parents and often at great emotional expense to the children.

## Do mothers make up false allegations of sexual abuse?

Mothers who seek changes to access or custody arrangements on the grounds of sexual abuse are commonly accused of concocting false allegations, first for revenge (for example when ex-husbands have found new partners or when they fail to provide maintenance for their children) and, second, to avoid expensive travel costs when either parent has moved to another locality. American research shows that, although one fifth of divorced mothers try to make access visits unpleasant in the hope that children will refuse to visit their fathers, they do not deliberately make false accusations of abuse (Wallerstein and Kelly, 1980; MacFarlane, 1986).

Mothers are most likely to try to upset children's visits to those fathers who remain financially stable and support their new partners and their children while neglecting their own financial responsibilities. Newly impoverished mothers also become disgruntled when fathers who showed no previous interest in their children now spend access weekends providing lavish treats. Access is also resented when children 'play-off' one parent against the other, viewing their mother as a mean ogre who disciplines them, sends them to school and makes them go to bed early while their weekend father presents himself as an eternally benevolent Santa Claus.

Divorce can be so bitter that some participants will go to great lengths to hurt each other. False allegations of sexual abuse by mothers are very rare however (MacFarlane, 1986, p. 123) and they should not be difficult to detect in the interviewing process. If stories of abuse are fabricated, the supposed victims are unlikely to be able to respond to the wide range of questions that are usually put to them by paediatricians, police and social workers. Coached children can only repeat what their coach has told them to say. They cannot add the significant detail of what happened before and after the alleged abuse, i.e. the detail which provides authenticity. And if interviewers ask, 'Did mummy tell you to say that?', coached children will usually respond affirmatively. When asked 'What did mummy tell you to say?', the answer may confirm that the parent merely told the child to use the word 'penis' instead of 'pee-pee'.

Because false allegations can be detected by experienced interviewers, they are unlikely to reach courts of law. It should be emphasised that any attempt by one parent to damage a child's loyalty to another is likely to cause long-term psychological harm. Children suffer from severe emotional trauma when they are openly exposed to parental warfare and are drawn into taking sides. Involving children in fictitious allegations of sexual molestation is only marginally less damaging than sexual molestation itself.

Genuine concerns are often raised by mothers who feel uncomfortable about their children spending large periods of time in the company of men who are no longer trusted. An increased awareness of child sexual abuse will contribute to the state of anxiety and this, in turn, may be transmitted to the children. Highly anxious children may show some of the traits exhibited by molestation victims. To mothers who have divorced violent men who are hated and feared, any unusual behaviour which appears after an access visit may be noted and interpreted with suspicion. As a result, some mothers are convinced that their children have been abused when the most conscientious interviewers and examiners have found no evidence. For further reading on this subject, see Chapter 7 of MacFarlane (1986).

# 5 Children's behaviour problems and their management

## Issues for non-offending parents

### *Unwanted behaviour*

Parents often complain that after sexual abuse their child's personality and behaviour 'changed for the worse': 'She's a different child . . . I could strangle her . . . She's driving me round the bend' cry despairing mothers. Parents commonly complain of the following distressing behaviour in their child:

- bedtime problems—fear of going to bed, refusal to get undressed, nightmares, bed wetting, soiling, wanting to sleep in the mother's bed;
- sexually explicit behaviour—exhibitionism, re-enactment of the abuse with other children or dolls, frequent masturbation, sexual behaviours with older children or adults of the same sex as the offender;
- risky behaviour—flirting, inappropriate touching or attention seeking (especially with visitors and strangers of the same sex as the offender);
- constant clinging;
- stealing, lying, aggression and destructiveness;
- wilful disobedience;
- temper tantrums and expressions of hatred for the non-offending parent or caregiver;
- anxiety traits—such as nail biting, twitching, loss of appetite or over-eating, sadness, fretfulness, asthma attacks;
- withdrawal.

Such behaviour problems come at a time when parents are most distressed and least able to handle them in a caring and sensitive way. When child sexual abuse results in problems such as these, parents must take a close look at their parenting methods and be prepared to make changes. This process can be very painful. At the best of times, few of us care to acknowledge that our parenting may be inadequate. A useful place to begin is to fill out a behaviour checklist such as that shown in Figure 5.1.

## Strategies for managing difficult behaviour

### *Analyse the sequence of events surrounding the behaviour*

Most unwanted behaviour relates to a child's feelings of insecurity, loss of trust, confusion and the belief that he or she is unwanted and unloved. Support workers can help parents to find the cause of misbehaviour and, once understood, parents can plan prevention and management strategies. The first step is to examine what happens immediately before the misbehaviour. What are the triggers? How do others respond? How does the parent respond? What happens afterwards and what are the outcomes for the child? Does the child gain more adult attention by behaving well or by behaving badly? The sequence of events should be recorded on a chart (see Figure 5.2).

Discussion can then focus on prevention, for example, if siblings argue and fight as soon as they arrive home from school, we need to consider the possible reasons for their irritability at that particular time. Are they tired, hungry, thirsty, vying for their mother's attention or all of these? Does the problem improve if mother meets them at the door with a big hug and steers them to the table for a drink and a snack? Do the fights and arguments stop if mother helps the children to 'unwind' and talk about their day?

### *Involve children in creating family rules*

The changes that occur to families after the disclosure of sexual abuse make it necessary to have round-the-table meetings involving all household members for discussion and revision of family rules. Parents who do not normally talk to their children may feel uncomfortable and make excuses to avoid this process, but it is extremely important.

Parents must be honest with their children and say openly that they have been worried by what happened and now, more than ever, they want to be sure that everyone is safe. Ask children if they know why rules are needed. What might happen if there were no rules? Let them

**Exercise 5.1 Child behaviour checklist**

Parents need to identify which troublesome behaviours they wish to change (group leaders and support workers can help with this). Tick the most troublesome behaviour.

| Behaviour | How often does it happen? | | |
|---|---|---|---|
| | Frequently | Occasionally | Never |
| Inappropriately affectionate | | | |
| —with strangers | | | |
| —with family friends/relatives | | | |
| Angry | | | |
| Aggressive | | | |
| Attention seeking | | | |
| Bad tempered | | | |
| Bed wetting | | | |
| Bedtime problems | | | |
| Clinging | | | |
| Destructive | | | |
| Disobedient | | | |
| Fearful | | | |
| Fretful | | | |
| Fights with siblings | | | |
| Fights with peers | | | |
| Flirts with adults | | | |
| Irritable | | | |
| Jealous | | | |
| Lacks concentration at school | | | |
| Masturbates | | | |
| Moody | | | |
| Phobias | | | |
| Sexual behaviour with | | | |
| —dolls | | | |
| —children | | | |
| —adults | | | |
| Soiled pants | | | |
| Stealing | | | |
| Tells tales about others | | | |
| Temper tantrums | | | |
| Toilet avoidance | | | |
| Whining | | | |
| Withdrawal | | | |
| Violent | | | |
| Others: | | | |

List behaviours for immediate and urgent attention:

**Exercise 5.2 Changing my child's behaviour**

This is one of the behaviours that I wish to change: ........................

..............................................................................

This is how I behave when my child does this (*tick as necessary*)

| | |
|---|---|
| I get angry | I get frustrated |
| I shout | I scream |
| I smack | I feel sorry for myself |
| I threaten my child | I shake my child |
| I send him / her to bed | I lose control of myself |
| I ban privileges and treats | I tell my child I hate him/her |
| I say he / she is stupid | I say he / she is naughty |

I let my child know that I love him/her but cannot allow the behaviour to continue

Others: ......................................................................

..............................................................................

1. When does this behaviour occur?
2. What is happening immediately before this behaviour occurs?
3. Who does it affect the most? Why?
4. Does anybody else complain? Why?
5. What happens after you have handled it in the usual way?
6. What message does this give to your child?
7. Can you think of a reason that this behaviour should happen at this particular time? (For example, is your child tired, hungry, thirsty, in need of attention or approval, being taunted?)
8. Does your child receive more attention when he/she is misbehaving?
9. Think of two ways in which this behaviour might be avoided? (Try them both out and record the results.)
10. Consider other ways in which the situation could be handled. Try them out. What happened?

know that some members of the family have already been hurt by adults who broke the rules. The family can now discuss what rules are necessary to provide protection for all members while at the same time allowing for individual rights and responsibilities. Each child should be encouraged to contribute his or her own ideas and others must listen respectfully. Parents must remember to thank each contributor in turn. If ideas are impractical or unsafe, children should be asked, 'Would that be possible? Would that be safe? Can you think of something safer?'. We must do everything possible to develop the self-esteem of vulnerable children, and so parents should be warned that, on no account, should any family member be denigrated if inappropriate suggestions are made.

Children who have agreed that rules are necessary and who have been involved in their making, are more likely to keep them, hence reducing the likelihood of resistance and argument. Misbehaviours increase when rules are changed without discussion. Attempts to break the rules can be met with reminders of why they were considered to be necessary in the first place.

After abuse, some parents panic and go to extremes, banning children from all social events with the mistaken notion that the only way to protect children is to keep them within sight. Parents cannot supervise children for twenty-four hours a day and attempts to do so result in resentment and rebellion.

*Discipline must be consistent*

When children have experienced the betrayal of trust by an abuser, they need patient, consistent handling with predictable routines in order to provide a sense of security. They need to know that, even when they behave badly, someone will keep them safe. Furthermore, when they are naughty they need to hear that they are still loved, even though parents may be disappointed with that behaviour. Unfortunately, parents who are obsessed with their own problems or who blame or dislike their own abused children are unlikely to meet any of these needs. When parents of abused children distance themselves both physically and emotionally they increase both the level of the child's anxieties and the range of their disturbed behaviours.

All children need consistency in their lives but victims of abuse need it most of all. The breaking of rules, especially ones involving the rights and safety of others, must be addressed firmly, quickly and calmly. Unfortunately, calmness is seldom a feature of parents who have experienced the trauma of sexual abuse of their child. The most damaging kind of discipline is that which varies according to the current feelings of parents. When they are either in a 'good' mood or a 'couldn't care less mood', activities which were forbidden yesterday are permitted; when in a bad mood, new rules apply without reason or discussion. When the question 'Why won't you let me play at Darren's?', receives the reply 'Because I said so', this fails to satisfy a child who has previously been allowed to visit Darren. Typically, the child argues, whines, nags, screams, proclaims that 'It's not fair' and continues to be troublesome until the parent either smacks or capitulates. Similarly, we find that an inconsistent parent will participate in an argument with a child who does not accept the first 'no' and who persists with, 'Please mummy . . . mummy . . . mummy. Just this once mummy . . . Go on, let me mummy'. After saying 'no' a dozen times in various ways, the exhausted, inconsistent parent says, 'Oh, alright . . . just this once'. (See also Figure 5.3.)

**Figure 5.1 Bedtime problems**

1 Brainstorm the problems that parents encounter at bedtime.
2 Think about (or role play in a group) the following sequence;

Scene: Mother and child are watching television. It is 9 p.m.

*Mother*: 'It's time you went to bed. It's long past your bedtime'.

Child ignores mother. Mother continues to watch TV.

*Mother*: 'Come on, get ready for bed'.

Child and mother continue to watch TV.

*Mother*: 'Did you hear me? I told you to go to bed. It's nine o'clock'.

*Child*: 'Just let me see the end of this. It's my favourite programme'.

*Mother*: 'I' ve told you twice. Go to bed'.

Child continues to watch TV.

*Mother*: 'If you aren't in bed by the time I count three, I'll . . . '.

*Child*: 'I'm hungry. I want a biscuit. Can I have a glass of milk?'.

*Mother*: 'Oh, alright. But hurry up'.

Child returns to the television and drinks the milk slowly.

*Mother*: 'Hurry up and go to bed. You have to go to school in the morning'.

*Child*: 'I haven't finished my drink'.

*Mother*: 'Bed!'.

*Child*: 'It's not fair. Everybody at school watches this programme'.

*Mother*: 'I don't care who watches it. You're going to bed'.

*Child*: 'I've just remembered. I have to do something for school tomorrow'.

*Mother* (screams): 'Bed! Now!'.

*Child* (moves away slowly muttering): 'I hate you. I wish I lived somewhere else'.

*Mother*: 'And I wish you lived somewhere else, too'.

3 Questions:

- Did the mother give the child adequate warning that it was bedtime?
- Is it reasonable to interrupt a child in the middle of a programme?
- How could this situation have been avoided?
- How did the child irritate the mother?
- How did the mother irritate the child?
- How did they both feel when the child went to bed?
- How could this have been avoided?

Parents should ensure that, when a request is refused, a good reason is given for the refusal, indicating that the decision has nothing to do with the mood of the day.

### *Give children some responsibility for improving their behaviour*

Children need to develop the realisation that they have *choices* about how they behave. If they behave in a dangerous or unacceptable way, they should be told that their behaviour is not acceptable and that they will be deprived of specified privileges if they *choose* to repeat it.

Unacceptable behaviour is that which causes distress to other people, is unsafe or likely to damage property. If the child ignores the warning, he or she should be removed quickly and calmly with the reminder that he or she chose to repeat the behaviour with full knowledge of the consequences. If the child throws a tantrum or cries protesting, 'Just let me stay and I promise I'll be good', the parent must remain consistent and continue with the removal. The adult who gives in to the child's wishes ensures that the behaviour will be repeated. When the child is composed, he or she may be invited to choose another activity. Eventually, the opportunity to return to the problem area can be offered again but only after the child shows that the rules are understood.

This approach takes a little more time than either yelling or smacking but it is more effective. If the child returns and repeats the behaviour, the ban should be extended to half a day or longer. 'You knew that if you did that again, the result would be . . . You chose to do it again and this is what happens . . .'.

It is clearly much better for everyone if misbehaviour can be avoided and punishment be used only as the last resort. Punishment used unwisely can give children the impression that adults have lost control and are not coping. A message that says, 'I don't care what has happened to you or how upset you are. I'm going to show you who is the boss round here', adds to the distress of those who already feel powerless.

Desperate parents often send children to their bedrooms as a punishment for being troublesome. The culprits do not sit on their beds regretting their behaviour, as parents hope—they become resentful, rebellious, self-pitying and lament the unfairness of the world. If 'time out' is used because children are quarrelling, the parent should say, 'I can see that you need to rest and calm down for a few minutes. When you're not so angry, we can talk to work out how you can both . . . *and I'll help you if you need me*'.

Many potential behaviour problems can be spotted and nipped in the bud with a stern glance, a gentle pat on the shoulder or by removing the hazardous object. Clearly, prevention is better than punishment.

### *Acknowledge and respect children's feelings*

To support a child's social growth, the home environment needs to be characterised by respect for children's feelings. This may be a new and difficult concept for mothers who are complaining that no-one has given any consideration to *their* hurt feelings. For example, children need cosy bath times and bedtimes with one-to-one attention to help them to sleep without nightmares. Bath time should be a fun time during which children feel safe, can relax and ask questions and talk about their problems; bedtime should be a time for safe cuddles, picture books and stories about assertive children who remain safe and solve their problems without adult help. Many parents have never read a story or taught a nursery rhyme to their children. Parent support groups usually stock appropriate books for home loan and, when necessary, show parents how to use them.

When children are being unco-operative, parents often nag or issue commands—children dig in their heels and start a tug of war. Quite often, the issue is not worth fighting about. It is important that a child's feelings are acknowledged without suggesting that those feelings are appropriate: for example, '*I can see that* you don't feel like joining us right now. When you're ready, let me know'. In matters which are not critical, this approach can be used to protect a child's sense of autonomy and increase the likelihood of co-operation (Katz and McClellan, 1991).

Family life becomes strained when children treat every minor setback as a major tragedy. It is not good for young children to get everything that they want when they want it. When they whine, it is again useful to refer to their feelings, 'Yes, *I know that you're disappointed* because you would like to have that right now but you can choose something else . . .' or '*Yes, I know it's annoying for you* when . . . but you can . . .'.

*Reinforce the desired behaviours*

Whenever possible, parents should ignore or minimise minor unwanted behaviours—a spilt drink is best handled with the reassurance that, 'Everyone has accidents. Let's get a sponge and you can help to mop it up'. To make real progress, parents should concentrate on praising children for making an effort or succeeding in something that is desirable. Positive comments should be made when they help others, show kindness, tidy up or exhibit other desirable behaviour. Abused children need a great deal of reassurance and they respond favourably to healthy attention, affection and approval. Children tend to repeat behaviours which attract praise. However, parents should be advised not to give edible or monetary rewards to children for being helpful—recipients soon expect them and then demand them for doing minor chores, thus creating more problems.

Unfortunately, many parents rarely praise their children. They think that they do but when asked about the last occasion on which praise was given, they cannot remember. It requires little effort on the part of the adult to say, 'I noticed that you put your toys away tonight', 'You did a good job making your bed this morning', or 'Thank you for setting

**Exercise 5.3 What I like about my child**

Name of child: . . . . . . . . . . . . . . . . . . . . . . . . . . . . . . . . . . . . . . . .

1 My child (please tick):

- has a nice face
- has nice eyes
- has a generous nature
- responds well to praise
- helps in the house
- looks angelic when asleep
- is kind sometimes
- likes to please me
- has a nice smile (when he/she smiles)
- likes cuddles
- has an affectionate nature
- is good at school
- is obedient at times
- loves surprises
- other qualities and strengths . . . . . . . .

. . . . . . . . . . . . . . . . . . . . . . . . . . . . . .

2 Things that I enjoyed doing when I was a child . . . . . . . . . . . . . . . . . . . . . . .

. . . . . . . . . . . . . . . . . . . . . . . . . . . . . . . . . . . . . . . . . . . . . . . . . . . . . . . . . . . . . . . .

3 Things that I would have liked to have done when I was a child (and could not)

. . . . . . . . . . . . . . . . . . . . . . . . . . . . . . . . . . . . . . . . . . . . . . . . . . . . . . . . . . . . . . . .

4 Things that I enjoyed doing with my child in the past . . . . . . . . . . . . . . . . . . .

. . . . . . . . . . . . . . . . . . . . . . . . . . . . . . . . . . . . . . . . . . . . . . . . . . . . . . . . . . . . . . . .

5 Things that I would like to do with my child this week. . . . . . . . . . . . . . . . . .

. . . . . . . . . . . . . . . . . . . . . . . . . . . . . . . . . . . . . . . . . . . . . . . . . . . . . . . . . . . . . . . .

6 How I plan to do this with my child this week: . . . . . . . . . . . . . . . . . . . . . . . .

. . . . . . . . . . . . . . . . . . . . . . . . . . . . . . . . . . . . . . . . . . . . . . . . . . . . . . . . . . . . . . . .

the table . . . it was a big help'. Few parents actually talk to their children. Researchers using tape recorders have found that parents' communications with children consist mainly of instructions, threats, criticisms and complaints. When parents focus on misbehaviour, the relationship with their children becomes locked into a struggle for power. Children become less troublesome when parents spend more time with them doing things that everyone enjoys. Parents who have not been accustomed to spending time with their children may find it difficult to make this adjustment. Disgusted with the human race and feeling inadequate, non-offending mothers readily slip into the frame of mind where they see their children as perpetually troublesome and their own future as hopeless.

The exercise shown in Figure 5.4 can be used to help parents to re-establish contact with their disaffected children.

*Learn to listen*

If few parents actually spend time talking to their children, even fewer listen to what they have to say. The parents of sexually abused children need no reminders that they have not been listening. Most learn the hard way that, unless communications within the family are open and honest and unless people listen as well as talk, to one another, children either communicate in code or else they remain silent.

For a healthy recovery, children need to be able to talk about their feelings relating to the abuse and their abuser to a listener who does not interrupt, criticise or argue and tell them that it is they who are wrong. Few parents possess these listening skills and that, of course, is why so few child abuse victims disclose their experiences and innermost thoughts and fears to their parents. When children bottle up their feelings and become upset, they behave in ways that aggravate their parents.

*Develop a sense of justice*

When children fight each other, it is often a futile exercise to attempt to work out who started what and why. It is more profitable to discuss whether the individuals had the right to engage in unsafe misbehaviour involving other children. When the parent indicates that hurting a brother or sister is not allowed, it is useful to add, 'And I don't want anyone to hurt you either'. This message tells the child that the rule which prevents his or her aggression will also provide protection.

It is always helpful if parents explain their actions to unhappy children. Sibling rivalry and jealousy can be tackled in this way, for example , 'Your brother has had a really bad day today and needs some special help to feel good again. *When you have a bad time, I cuddle you too*'. Because children's needs, dispositions, experiences and behaviours vary, we cannot treat them all alike. In a just and fair household, children understand that their different needs are taken seriously (Katz and McClellan, 1991).

*Appeal to children's good sense*

When parents endow children with the capacity to approach social conflicts and problems sensibly, children are more likely to see themselves as being sensible and responsible and therefore behave accordingly. When parents see their children as being nothing but a nuisance, the child takes this as being confirmation of their low value as a person.

Parents often label their unpopular children as 'the noisy one . . . quiet one . . . clumsy . . . stupid one'. Children who are rejected at home are often rejected elsewhere, not because they do not know how to behave with others but because their expectation of rejection prevents them from using their social skills appropriately. If we are able to confirm in children a sense of being well liked, their behaviour becomes more confident and they will actually become well liked (Rabiner and Coe, 1989). Parents should understand this concept—many mothers and fathers function well in their own social groups but, when they return to their parents' homes, they are often treated like children and find themselves behaving according to the expectations of their parents.

*Be loyal to child victims*

Even the best of parents waver in their loyalty to their abused children, especially when the offender was trusted and they are now being swayed by convincing arguments from both him and his articulate supporters. It seems that parents long for evidence to show that their children were mistaken so that order and security can be restored to their own lives. Children know intuitively when they are not believed and become frustrated and distressed. They often withdraw into sullen and angry silence feeling unloved, unworthy and helpless and they become uncooperative and unattractive. Parents then withdraw affection, increasing the child's sense of isolation and emotional and behavioural problems. When children have been abused by their mothers' sexual partners, the mothers sometimes confess to feelings of hatred for their children, perceiving them as competitors who may have deliberately set out to destroy the relationship and steal their partners from them.

*Discourage sexual behaviours*

Although it is difficult to teach survivors of abuse that they have the right to be safe when their experience has always been otherwise, it is essential that all children in the victim's or caregiver's family are taught protective behaviours and personal safety skills as soon as possible. Most parent support groups amass a lending library of books and kits for this purpose. No-one likes to be told that their behaviour is unacceptable. Criticism is sufficient to make us feel rejected, worthless and frustrated. It is difficult for parents and caregivers to provide guidance on changing unacceptable, sexual behaviour without this damaging their relationship with the child.

Adolescents' unconscious 'Come and get me . . . I'm available and know what it's all about' messages are the hardest to change, especially if they have become well established. Children are genuinely confused when they constantly attract unwanted sexual attention and ask, 'Why is this always happening to me? It doesn't happen to everyone else. Why am I different? What's wrong with me? I can't take any more of this "shit"!'. Most abused children despise their bodies and want to be as unattractive as possible to avoid further molestation.

When children are old enough to understand, they should be told that they must take some responsibility for changing their own behaviour. They also need constant reinforcement of the idea that they no longer need to be sexual in order to gain affection and approval—they can come for a safe hug at any time as long as they are appropriately dressed. These rules protect both children and adults. If we can explain, uncritically, what happens when they either dress or behave provocatively and how some males respond, there might be some incentive for survivors to identify and control the unwanted behaviour. When adolescents are willing to learn and co-operate, they should sit down with their parents or caregivers to work out mutually agreed, private signals, such as a wink or raised eyebrow, to indicate that it is time to stop and change whatever they are doing.

It should be borne in mind that children's behaviour regresses when they become anxious about their new perception of themselves—honest, open, caring communications are essential to reduce these fears. Children need to know by words and actions that they are wanted and liked because they have qualities that are unrelated to sex. The long-term aim should be to concentrate on helping them to create good relationships with responsible young people of their own age. This helps to promote self-confidence and higher self-esteem which, in turn, provide a foundation for self-protection. A withdrawn, unhappy, isolated child who continues to feel a 'victim' is the most vulnerable to further abuse.

It is important to note that, when children are already abusing others, the help of skilled professional therapists should always be sought. Parent counsellors are not equipped to undertake such sensitive work.

### *Strategies for coping with bed-wetting*

Although bed-wetting is a common symptom of emotional disturbance, sufferers should be medically checked to ensure that there are no infections or other reasons for the problem. Young sufferers can be assisted in many ways. For example, drinks should be banned after the evening meal and children should be toileted when the adults go to bed. The most effective treatment, however, is a reduction in anxiety levels. It is all too easy for parents and caregivers to become angry when they are faced with daily laundry, bed-making and urine stained mattresses.

(Caregivers could ask the responsible agency for a water-bed which does not absorb urine stains.) Children as young as five or six years of age can receive praise from adults for removing wet bed linen after accidents.

The most exasperating behaviour is when children are awake but choose not to go to the toilet. This occurs when they are anxious or angry. The most effective way of handling the problem is to remain unruffled and say, 'OK. You know where the clean sheets are. I know you can do a good job of making your own bed'. During the day, adults should watch for opportunities to praise the child for desirable behaviours. At some time, it might also be useful to say, 'Look . . . I know that you're worried. Let's talk about it. Maybe I can help. I hate to see you sad'.

Parents and caregivers should be made aware of the availability of 'bed-wetting programmes' from psychologists attached to family services. These can be effective when children understand their problem and are motivated to change. Caregivers who care for abused children on a regular basis need an industrial washing machine and tumbler dryer to reduce the stress commonly associated with this behaviour problem.

### *Develop parents' confidence in parenting*

When parents feel helpless and hopeless and view their own lives as failures, it is very difficult for them to encourage self-confidence and help promote self-esteem in their children, let alone motivate them to change inappropriate behaviour. Building parental confidence is the primary goal of support groups and the importance of such groups in the establishment and maintenance of healthy family relationships is discussed in Chapter 8.

Often it is the inability to accept that things can change that inhibits the process of emotional healing so necessary for abuse victims. Parents need to understand that, in order to change their child's behaviour, they must be prepared to examine and change their own. For example, it is unrealistic for parents to complain about violence or shouting if they are either violent themselves or shout at their children. Both verbal and physical violence provide further confirmation that the strong can hurt the weak. If change is to be made possible there must be:

- strong bonds of affection and mutual respect between parent and child;
- explanations and reasons for rules which are mutually agreed;
- firm but kind handling.

When parents complain about their children, they often present themselves as being ideal in every way. They live in a world of fantasy and self-deception. When questioned, few can recall giving their children a cuddle. Few have ever said, 'I love you lots and lots'. Some confess that, since the abuse, they have found it difficult to touch, hug or kiss their children because of their disgust about the abuse itself. Parents assume (mistakenly) that children know that they are loved by the many things that are done for them every day. Parents are often too embarrassed to put tender feelings into words, especially if they were reared in affectionless households where the display of emotions was perceived as a sign of weakness.

## Issues for caregivers

### *Children's reactions to family separation*

Child victims are likely to be taken to a place of safety when the abuser is either the father or stepfather and he either remains in or persists in returning to the family home thus leaving children unprotected. The move is often sudden and without warning, occurring immediately after the disclosure of abuse. When children arrive at their new residences they present a sad sight, with their worldly goods in a plastic bag and usually in a state of shock following a family crisis of unprecedented proportions. Deprived of their homes and perhaps relatives, such children experience all the symptoms of grief that occur with the loss of loved ones through death. They do not understand what is happening and why it is that they must leave home. After all, they have done nothing wrong; they merely told someone about the abuse. They did not expect (or want) their world to fall apart as a result of the disclosure. The emotional turmoil experienced by child victims is greatest when the abuser is the mother's sexual partner and she chooses to let him remain in the family home while her children are forced to leave. It is often difficult for the new caregivers to understand that, no matter how violent or unsupportive their families may have been, most children go into a state of grief when they leave home. Parent support groups are often approached for help by step-parents, foster parents and relatives who, having taken abused children into their homes, find it difficult to cope with their behaviour.

#### *Shock*

Children may appear to be calm, composed and almost indifferent to events when they first arrive at their new residence. In a state of shock, they show no emotion and may seem to adapt quickly to their new surroundings. But they worry about practicalities; they complain about the clothes that were packed for them—their underwear is dirty, the jeans do not fit, the shoes are odd or the socks belong to someone else. Usually they have left home in a hurry and no-one thinks to pack their favourite toys, family photographs and other special things that would make them feel more comfortable in their new surroundings.

*Denial*

The children sense that by being removed from home, it is they who are being punished and they begin to have misgivings about reporting the abuse. They feel particularly helpless when the offender denies his offences, is not charged and continues to receive the mother's support. Victims conclude, rightly or wrongly, that their abusers were believed while they were not. There is no justice in the child's world and this has a devastating effect on their self-esteem. It is easy for them to slip into thinking, 'I'm stupid. I may as well go back home. These folk are alright but they're not my real family. This isn't *my* home'.

When reality becomes too difficult to handle, children deny their situation and begin to distance themselves or minimise the gravity of the abuse saying such things as 'He only did it a few times . . . it's no big deal. I don't know what all the fuss is about'. From there, it is only a short step to accepting some, if not all, of the responsibility for what happened. Many victims were told by their abusers that, if they revealed the secret behaviour, they would be 'taken away and put into a home'. When this actually happens the victim can see that the offender was right and takes the blame—'it's all my own fault for telling'.

In sibling and step-sibling abuse, the offender is often protected at the expense of the victim. When one child has to be removed to protect others, parents often discount the seriousness of the abuse and choose the one who is of most material value. For example, a youth was reported for raping his young sisters. The parents placed the girls in foster-care and allowed the offender to remain at home arguing that they had bought their farm with the expectation that their son would ultimately inherit it. They could manage without the girls but they needed the youth for his labour!

*Retraction*

Not surprisingly, some children become so distressed by the lack of family support that they retract their statements as this offers an attractive alternative to emergency care and court appearances. Retraction is especially likely when children find themselves under pressure to: 'Just say you made it up and put an end to this trouble. Look at what you've done to your family! You're just selfish! If you carry on with this, he'll go to jail and where will that leave us?'.

Survivors need to know that retraction will not return their world to normal (see p. 9). They need a tremendous amount of reassurance that they behaved properly when revealing the abuse, that the abuser deliberately *chose* to commit an offence and that he *knew* that it was wrong. Assurance is essential if survivors are to gain strength and confidence.

### *Depression*

When the shock wears off victims are likely to become depressed—life seems purposeless and empty and they wonder what they have to live for. Young people might neglect their health and personal hygiene by drinking too much coffee or alcohol, smoking too many cigarettes, forgetting to bathe. Lacking any interest in eating a well-balanced meal, they often become vitamin and mineral deficient and very tired. At the same time, they are often unable to sleep. Caregivers become irritated by the refusal of adolescents to help around the house complaining that they either lie in bed listening to depressing rock music all day or gaze blankly at the television. If such behaviour continues, the help of a competent therapist (preferably one experienced in child abuse cases) should be sought.

### *Anger and self-blame*

Child and adolescent survivors have good reasons to be angry, especially if they have no family support. Those in care vent their anger on the safest people in their environment—usually their caregivers: 'I hate you, I hate this place. I want to go home' is a normal reaction. Feelings tend to be ambivalent—there may be love and hate for the abuser and mother coupled with absolute confusion about themselves. Caregivers find it hard to accept that children often retain fond thoughts of their abusers. It is advisable not to agree with children when they talk about their natural parents in a hostile way. It helps to assure them that no-one is either wholly bad or wholly good and that it is alright to care for someone who has behaved badly towards them. They need to know that they can care for the person but hate what he or she has done.

Caregivers need to know how to handle anger in a healthy way, assuring children that their anger is justified but it needs to be talked through and understood. Caregivers can help by encouraging children to talk openly about their angry feelings, interrupting only to clarify specific issues such as, 'Am I understanding you correctly? This is what I hear you saying . . . . You are really cross because . . .'. This gives a sense of logic to children's very confused emotions. Adolescents are often less angry about the sexual abuse than about their betrayal by their parents, who did nor act as 'real parents' and who did not love and protect them as they should. The grief that survivors experience is a mourning for their lost childhood and the loss of a loving family relationship.

Anger directed at themselves is the most dangerous of all grief-related behaviour and it can result in self-injury, for example by stabbing with cigarettes, scissors, needles or other sharp instruments, or the abusive use of alcohol, drugs, glue or petrol. Children in care rationalise that, if their mothers loved them, they would have found some way of keeping them; if they are unloved, it must be because they are bad. Survivors of abuse have to learn, from their relationships with others, that they are worthwhile people who can be respected, praised and liked. They need to learn that they can have fun and be hugged without sex. They need to learn to trust others in safety to gain confidence in themselves. Unfortunately, this is a slow process. In the meantime, depressed adolescents often place themselves in dangerous situations which merely confirm their low self-worth. They may not intend to die but care so little about life that they fail to protect themselves and engage in risky or even dangerous behaviour. They need continual confirmation that they are loved for themselves. Risky behaviour should be curbed with a firmness that says, 'I care about you too much to let you do this to yourself'.

*Anxiety and fear*

Grief is usually associated with feeling of anxiety and fear. The sufferer thinks, 'Why has this terrible thing happened to me? What did I do to deserve this? What other horrors are in store? I can bear no more'. Victims of sexual abuse mistrust all adults and the fear of males may be extreme. They may also develop additional fears relating to being in the house alone, undressing or going to bed (if the abuse took place in the bedroom). Such fears will only diminish in the safety of a stable home. Again, if they continue, a competent therapist should be consulted.

When children are anxious their behaviour can alternate between being morose and being angry and destructive. Some run away from home or school with no idea where they are going and end up in cafes and amusement centres in the company of other youngsters with similar problems. Complaints about all kinds of aches and pains, bowel and bladder troubles, headaches and menstrual problems are commonly heard from anxious survivors of sexual abuse. These relate to both the abuse and the resultant strain and tension during the crisis. Some children become so disturbed that they withdraw into silence, bottling up their anxieties to such an extent that they suffer from a myriad of psychosomatic illnesses. American studies have shown that when child victims are placed in care, they suffer and continue to suffer more physical and mental illness and developmental and educational delay than others of the same age (Schor, 1982; Kavaler and Swire, 1983). The probable source of poor health at the time of entry to residential care is their family history as well as the abuse. Aspects of well-being are worsened as a result of the uncertainties they experience from day to day. Survivors may be terrified of meeting their abuser in the street or in court and that the threats of violence will be carried out. One day, they worry that he will go to jail and, the next, that he might not.

*Loss of reality*

Caregivers often feel that they are hated by their charges, taken for granted by social workers, resented by the natural parents and inadequately rewarded for what they do. One of the most aggravating experiences for caregivers is the tendency for abused children to fantasise about their natural parents and home lives. Rejected children often talk about their families as they would like them to be rather than as they really are: 'My mummy will buy me a pony (or some other expensive gift) for my birthday' when mummy does not even send a card.

Children proclaim that their natural mothers are better cooks, provide better clothes and better everything than their caregivers. These outbursts help them to survive the reality that many of the important things have been missing from their lives. They know that they are fantasising. It is hurtful to be reminded of the truth and caregivers should not attempt to correct them. This apparent parent-worship is irritating for those who know that the natural parents have done nothing to merit their children's loyalty. It is especially disturbing when the parents' behaviour causes continuing distress for the child and that distress results in difficult, emotionally disturbed behaviours for the caregiver to handle.

*Coping with inadequate parents*

Caregivers become angry when mothers make promises which they never fulfil. The following scenario is not uncommon. An arrangement is made to collect children for outings and as departure time approaches, excited children sit near the door asking, 'Is it nearly time yet? When is she coming?'. Time passes slowly when you are only six years old. Some children may remain there for the entire afternoon. No-one arrives and no-one telephones. Eventually, they creep back to their bedrooms to cry, emerging later with a brave face, pretending that they 'don't care' and that they 'didn't want to go to that dumb place anyway'. Some children release their disappointment by lashing out at their caregivers or others in the house.

When children go home for weekends or holidays, they sometimes return infested with vermin. Others tell horrendous stories of what happened while they were at home. When mothers have taken in new partners who 'don't like kids', the children are often made to feel like unwanted visitors who are 'in the way'. Again, caregivers have to pick up the pieces and provide reassurance to repair children's damaged self-esteem and confidence. It is not surprising that caregivers often dread children's home visits, loathing the parents for what they do to their children.

It is appropriate to empathise with children in their disappointment but it is vital that caregivers do not show their own negative feelings about children's relatives. Some children will pretend to hate their parents to please their caregivers but the hatred is often contrived. It can be damaging for children to be taught that their families are inadequate, especially if social workers are attempting to reunite them.

*Unhealthy attention*

Children who have been the victims of misused power, later find themselves at the centre of attention but this can often be unhealthy. They realise that, for the first time in their lives, they are very important people. Numerous professionals seek their opinions and attend to their needs. The professionals have meetings about them. Astute children learn to use and abuse their new found power, manipulating carers and causing chaos at a time when they need stability. When they do not get what they want, they tell sympathetic caseworkers that they do not like their new homes or their caregivers. Young and inexperienced social workers then rush off to see what can be done to make these young people happy.

*The risk of re-abuse*

The most troublesome behaviour problems are those exhibited by adolescent girls who were sexually abused in their own homes for many years. Caseworkers are often very sympathetic and agree that adolescents should now have the freedom to attend rock concerts and discos along with other youngsters of the same age. This can be a recipe for disaster, however. With no experience in problem solving, no history of self-protection, no social skills with peers and a long training in sexual behaviour, they are at high risk of further sexual exploitation. This provides further damaging confirmation that their own needs and feelings are unimportant.

Adolescent survivors often look much older than their years and, in the company of older men, they give the impression that they are worldly wise. When they go out with boys, their unconscious, learned sexual responses ensure that they attract those who are only interested in using them for sex. Naively, they imagine that men who buy them drinks are kind. They want to have fun and when boys offer to take them for rides, they go. The boys may be drunk or drugged, the cars may be stolen and the girls may be raped when they only want fun. When they protest, the girls are often 'dumped' miles away from home. A telephone call in the middle of the night sends anxious caregivers out to their rescue.

Children who have provided sex for older men relate comfortably to others of the same kind. Their vulnerability is worrying to caregivers. When they attempt to provide protection, they are accused of being old-fashioned and restrictive. The girls complain to their caseworkers who are sometimes only a little older than their clients. They sympathise with adolescent struggles to gain independence and, behaving as a third parent, may counter the caregiver's instructions.

Adolescents want freedom without responsibility. Survivors of sexual abuse adopt an air of confidence to hide the frightened child inside. They swing from extremes of wanting to be treated as women of the world and behaving like children who need very basic protection. The result is utter confusion for themselves and their caregivers.

## Caregivers' strategies for avoiding behaviour problems

### *Rules for housekeeping*

Children who have been sexually abused need rooms of their own to provide opportunities for privacy, but their chaotic lives are often reflected in the state of their rooms. Caregivers often complain that children store stale food and uneaten school lunches in drawers alongside dirty underwear, used tissues, used tampons or sanitary towels. In general, their standard of cleanliness relates to how they feel at the time and personal hygiene is worst when the children are feeling depressed and anxious. Caregivers often feel very sorry for their new arrivals and that makes it difficult to introduce discipline.

It is important that rules be created and agreed from the very beginning because they become more difficult to introduce later when children have already engaged in undesirable behaviour. The children should be invited to contribute to this process so that housekeeping becomes a co-operative effort. It helps if drawers and shelves are labelled so that children know exactly where to put socks, shirts, underwear and toys. It also helps if a specific day is chosen for bedroom tidying and cleaning. However, children should have control over their 'space'—remember, they may never have experienced the privacy or even safety of their bedroom or body before.

*Dress*

When children arrive ill clad, it is useful (and often necessary) for caregivers to provide a special treat (at the agency's expense) by taking the children shopping to buy new clothes. As children from authoritarian, incestuous homes have usually had no personal freedom, their involvement in the choice of clothing provides a good introduction to decision making. It is unlikely that children in residential care will want to buy school clothing; in emergency placements, they are uncertain of where their future lies. Adolescent children are also unlikely to select clothing that caregivers would like them to have. Girls often insist on buying the worst of trendy gear, such as already too-tight black jeans and tops. Caregivers can ask questions about the quality of the fabric, its washability or when it will be worn, but they should not criticise; they must grin and bear it as an exercise in diplomacy while children learn from their own mistakes.

Girls who have been abused should also be given the opportunity to choose pretty underwear and night-clothes. Most survivors of abuse have negative feelings about their bodies and attractive underwear helps to restore a positive body image.

*Hygiene*

Some survivors of abuse neglect personal hygiene because they have never been taught cleanliness at home; others neglect themselves because they are depressed and lack the necessary energy and self-interest to take a shower and shampoo their hair. Alternatively, young people who have been raped feel unclean and may spend excessive periods of time in the bathroom, irritating other members of the household. It will then be necessary to make arrangements to ensure that bathroom needs do not clash.

Children from negligent homes are likely to be attracted to bathing if they are provided with cosy bathrobes, huge, warm towels, their own choice of good quality shampoo, soap, talcum powder and cologne. Special things can help to make them feel worthwhile again.

*Food*

Eating disorders among abused children are common either because the children are emotionally disturbed and this affects their attitude to eating or their digestion or because they have been accustomed to different kinds of food. Most people have strong likes and dislikes and caregivers should not press children into eating unwanted food as this tends to increase their anxiety levels and further reduce their food intake. At the opposite extreme, some children over-eat for comfort. Do nor impose diets on children or adolescents, however. It is best to consult a medical practitioner if weight is a problem.

It is useful if children can be involved in planning menus and helping with the preparation of meals. Even young children enjoy mixing cakes, licking the spoon at the end of the operation, beating eggs and watching cakes rise. These are the everyday homely treats that many abused children have missed. Such occasions also provide opportunities for caregivers to praise children for their efforts and help so that they begin to feel needed and useful. There is also an enjoyable end-product to share at the end of the activity!

*Health*

When children are in residential care, the most frequently diagnosed health problems are, not surprisingly, those of an emotional nature. These are also the most difficult for caregivers because not only do they affect the lives of other family members in a very profound way but also adolescent mental health services are in short supply.

The complexity of health problems suffered by child and adolescent survivors suggests that there should be a referral network of medical and psychological support systems readily available to non-offending parents and other caregivers. In particular, there is a need for prompt testing for pregnancy and sexually transmitted diseases, family planning, AIDS education and help for drug and alcohol avoidance. Services should be provided by child welfare agencies which are sympathetic to and comfortable with adolescents and issues of ethnicity, culture and language. Embarrassed adolescents will only consult low-key, accepting agencies that provide a non-threatening environment.

The emotional and educational growth of survivors should also be monitored as part of their routine health care and evaluation. Anglican Community Services in Adelaide, South Australia found that abused children in foster care were, on average, four years behind their peers in basic literacy and numeracy skills. Such retardation was attributed to a lack of encouragement and attention in children's own homes and high anxiety levels relating to the abuse. The agency provided a teacher to give two hours of personal attention (in school) to each child each week. Confidence and concentration improved to such an extent that, within two years, these gaps had substantially reduced.

Clearly, survivors of abuse benefit enormously from healthy one-to-one attention. Group therapy can also be useful for small groups of children who have suffered similar experiences. While it is useful for parent support groups to initiate new groups for child victims, the therapeutic work should be in the hands of trained and experienced therapists who have skills in this area. Support groups can help by putting caregivers in touch with the appropriate services.

## Child protection and self-protection

The information that caregivers and step-parents need is how to manage children's inappropriate sexual behaviour and how to develop protective, safe behaviour in *all* members of the household. Caregivers and step-parents must ensure that they do not place themselves at risk of being accused of abuse, either by children or by their vindictive parents. Father replacement figures have to discipline themselves to step back in a professional way when children and adolescents behave sexually. This is necessary, not only to protect the children but also to protect themselves. What starts off as an innocent game of chasing and tickling or 'hide and seek' can end with the child behaving seductively, not because the child *wants* sex but because the sexual response has been well and truly learned by repetition and reward.

For everyone's safety, caregivers and their families must become more sexually aware. The sad thing is that other children in the family lose some of their personal freedom. Rules about nudity and the use of the bathroom and bedrooms have to be introduced to ensure privacy. Bathrooms and toilets should be fitted with locks if there are none there already. Small precautionary steps should be taken to ensure that there are no misunderstandings about what is acceptable or unacceptable behaviour.

Even those caregivers who are not encountering problems still need to be aware of why survivors are vulnerable to re-abuse and how they can help. The main challenge is to find a balance between controlling inappropriate behaviour without rejecting the children or making them feel guilty. Formal boundaries must be set at the first sign of seductiveness. Adolescent girls who come into the living room in revealing nightwear should be asked to wear a dressing gown and, if necessary, pants. Caregivers find that suggestive, flirtatious behaviour is most likely to occur after children have seen the offender, attended an interview or had some other reminder of the abuse. Girls who have been taught that they have to be sexual to please their fathers or father-figures need a great deal of help to understand that sex is no longer necessary for approval.

### Parent support groups bring improvements to child–parent and child–caregiver relationships

In a study of the effectiveness of support groups funded by the State Department of Health and Rehabilitative Services, Orlando, Florida, Winton (1990) found that group participants reported decreases in children's disturbed behaviours while they attended group sessions. The groups met for one session of two hours each week for thirteen weeks. Group members had already demonstrated their ineffectiveness in dealing with their children's unwanted behaviours. Therapists confirmed that parents' ineffective and unsuitable methods were, in turn, the result of their inappropriate emotional responses to the sexual acts involved in the abuse. Parents often had unrealistic expectations of their children and some had already sabotaged or were trying to sabotage their children's treatment. This damaging behaviour related to the parents' own desire to avoid dealing with the reality and implications of the abuse itself. It was also noted that the parents who stopped treatment had not been involved (by therapists) in the treatment process.

All the parents said that support groups were successful in their aim to provide parent education. Leaders were judged to be knowledgeable and supportive. Sessions and handouts were helpful and easy to understand. Most parents gave high ratings to sessions on parenting skills, children's emotional and sexual development and the management of children's behaviour. Sessions on stress management and improving child–parent relationships were also well received. Parents valued and enjoyed group therapy sessions, mutual support, guest speakers and the parent library incorporating books on parenting skills and activities for children.

When parent participants were asked, 'What have you learned?', the most frequent response was that they had learned how to become better parents—they were more patient, less volatile and had acquired valuable coping skills. The only complaint seemed to be that they needed more sessions to deal with stress factors. They suggested that a minimum of thirteen sessions should be allocated to learning about their children.

Clearly, parent support groups can provide a valuable service in helping participants to create more supportive relationships with their abused children. The prognosis for recovery is then much greater than if parents were left to resolve their own problems without assistance.

# 6 Why parent support groups are necessary in cases of child sexual abuse

## The need for family intervention

There have long been services to help parents who physically abuse and neglect their children. Local authorities, social services departments and non-government agencies such as the NSPCC (National Society for the Prevention of Cruelty to Children), Children's Society, National Children's Home (NCH) and Barnardos provide family support programmes in disadvantaged areas throughout the United Kingdom. Some Family Centres are multipurpose and offer a wide range of neighbourhood resources; others only cater for families in crisis. Similar centres are operated in Australia by the Uniting Church and other religious organisations—the State of Victoria has an additional service provided by the Children's Protection Society, a counterpart of the NSPCC. In New Zealand, the largest care agencies are Parent Help and Parentline, both of which began with child maltreatment in mind.

Groups for the parents of child victims of sexual abuse only evolved in the mid-1980s when the increase in reported cases exposed a new community need coupled with the lack of professional services for victims and their families. Child protection workers cannot spend the substantial amounts of time needed by distressed parents after the disclosure of abuse. Other support services are necessary because parents experience powerful emotions when their children have been violated (see Chapter 10). These emotions often prevent them from providing sound protection and psychological support for child victims. The risk is especially high if parents were also victims of sexual abuse in childhood.

Parent support groups operate from the premise that child abuse is a public concern because it has major consequences for society. Much of the trauma suffered by parents and victims stems from the community's response to sexual abuse. The community has, then, a responsibility to be actively involved in child protection and all that it entails. All support agencies recognise that, to help child victims, it is necessary to help parents to help themselves. This can be a lengthy process.

## The services needed

Parent support groups offer most if not all of the services listed below. At the time of the disclosure of sexual abuse they provide:

- a twenty-four hour telephone crisis line manned by trained counsellors;
- immediate support to help (non-offending) parents to cope with the trauma—this is especially necessary in the cases of abuse by fathers and father-figures;
- assistance in the provision of emergency care when mothers have to leave home to provide protection for their children;
- introductions to other relevant agencies;
- support for parents reporting offences to child protection authorities;
- face-to-face counselling in the family home or at the centre;
- moral support and practical help when children go for medical examinations.

After the initial disclosure they provide:

- group support for parents and foster parents caring for children who have been sexually abused;
- parent education relating to child sexual abuse;
- parent guidance through the assessment and justice process;
- assistance with the preparation of children for court;
- introductions to competent therapists to provide treatment for child victims and parent-survivors of sexual abuse;
- assertiveness training programmes (especially needed for victims and their mothers when the abuser is a family member);
- parent effectiveness and re-parenting programmes (most needed by mothers who are incest survivors and who lacked sound protective parenting models in childhood);

- mutual support, available through drop-in centres and group sessions;
- assistance for handling children's emotionally disturbed behaviours.

In addition, parent groups engage in community activities which include:

- developing public awareness of the high incidence of maltreatment;
- developing good relationships with other support agencies such as police, schools, preschools, child protection services, clinics for mothers and babies, counsellors and therapists who have special skills in working with child and adult survivors;
- representing the needs of abused children in government, the social services and other relevant agencies;
- seeking changes to legislation and the justice system process to ensure adequate protection for children;
- actively discouraging the sexual exploitation of children.

## Parents do not know where and how to report abuse

Occasionally, children disclose abuse to trusted parents. More frequently, however, young children reveal their abuse by accident. Most (non-offending) parents lack accurate information about child sexual abuse and are not aware of the role and location of child protection services or how to report abuse. In a moment of panic, they use the emergency telephone number and request police assistance. Uniformed patrol officers may arrive in marked police cars, terrifying those victims who were threatened by the abuser with, 'If you tell, the police will come and take you away'. Uniformed police seldom have the special skills needed for handling suspicions of child sexual abuse. In large towns and cities, there are usually sexual assault or child protection units to assist with investigations, but in country areas, police and social workers may have responsibility for handling the whole range of community needs.

The quality of service varies substantially from time to time and place to place. Some professionals are naturally responsive to children and can talk quite comfortably about sexual abuse. Inevitably, there are those who are still grappling with their own attitudes and problems relating to sexual offences and their responses are likely to be less supportive. One of the strengths of a parent support group is that staff quickly learn to identify efficient and empathic police and social workers and develop support networks to introduce clients to them when help is needed.

## The need for guidance through the assessment process

Quite frequently, police officers and/or social workers have the unenviable task of going into a home to break the news that a child in the family has been sexually abused. It is like dropping a 'time bomb' on the family. The investigating agents do not wait for the bomb to explode. At this stage, social workers are only concerned about the safety of the child. They need to know whether the child has been abused, whether the offender has access to the child and whether there is a risk of re-abuse if the child remains in the home. If the victim's safety is assured, the case will be regarded as less urgent than one in which the child is living with the perpetrator. Unless the situation is carefully explained to parents, they are likely to be upset by the fact that the abuse of their child is not considered to be top priority.

Sometimes, two social workers visit the home to interview the victim: one questions the child while the other records the conversation. This ensures a higher level of accuracy than when there is only one interviewer. At other times a social worker and a police officer interview the child together. This helps to reduce the number of times that victims have to tell their painful stories. Where evidential video units are available, children may be invited to visit the units so that their statements can be recorded on video. Most children enjoy this novel experience but it is important to reassure them that the offenders will not see them on the six o'clock news.

Social workers collect the information necessary for their reports, make whatever arrangements are needed for the safety of children and move on to the next case. Their reports usually go to child protection committees which accept responsibility for the management of cases.

Police officers want to know whether there has been a breach of the law and, if so, where, when and by whom. Police collate information and send forensic evidence, such as stained clothing, pubic hair and blood samples for scientific examination. Police prosecutors examine the combined reports and consider whether to prosecute the offender. In making this decision, they will have to consider whether the witnesses are sufficiently articulate and confident to withstand detailed cross-examination in the criminal court. Police, too, collect their evidence and move on, leaving the family to cope with the impact of the news.

Following the disclosure of abuse, children may be exposed to a range of health professionals who specialise in the assessment of sexual abuse and the treatment of victims. Each professional has a different focus. Sexual assault assessment centres are staffed by both male and female doctors who specialise in child health. These centres are often attached to large hospitals. Arrangements should be made for country children to be taken to the centres to ensure that they are in expert medical hands. Because such journeys can be time-consuming and troublesome, parents often refuse to allow their children to attend for medical examinations. Parent group counsellors can provide both moral and practical support. They will emphasise the importance of medical assessment, accompany parents and provide transport when necessary. Most child protection teams employ child psychologists to interview very young victims who lack the vocabulary to explain what happened. Psychologists' reports are important in criminal trials and their recommendations are useful in access and custody disputes.

In all of these interviews, it is important that children be questioned in a room where they cannot be overheard by parents or other relatives. Parents expect to be present during interviews and they become apprehensive when they are excluded. Most children are not embarrassed to talk to strangers about sexual matters if those strangers make it obvious that they are comfortable with the conversation and are there to help. If parents are present, however, children censor their statements to avoid mentioning things that might distress them. Interviewers do not hear the whole story of what happened and this seriously hampers the investigation. It is inappropriate, though, for distressed mothers to be left alone with their anxious thoughts in the corridors of hospitals, child protection units and police stations while their children are being questioned. Parents who feel excluded are the ones most likely to withdraw their support from both professionals and child victims.

Parents soon learn that child protection is a highly complex, confusing multiprofessional concern. Mothers who have never discussed sexual issues with anyone before, suddenly find themselves talking about embarrassing sexual matters with strangers. Also, when professionals focus attention on the abused children this can cause resentment when there are other children to be cared for and mothers themselves are in a state of crisis. When offenders are fathers and father-figures, mothers want to cry out, 'What about me? Who is going to help me? What do I do now?'.

The assessment process is slow and time-consuming. Children may be required to give several interviews before any decision is made about the prosecution of the offender. Parents become impatient. Grappling with their emotions, they become exasperated with the system and direct their hostility towards its representatives. In a state of shock and panic, parents are apt to forget or misinterpret what has been said by police or social workers—repetition is often necessary. Again, the support worker is ideally situated to clarify the parents' understanding of the reporting procedures and provide a sense of stability after the professionals have gone. The support worker performs a valuable role in encouraging parents to talk about what the professionals said to ensure that their perceptions of professional intervention are accurate. All too frequently, parents feel 'let down' by the various agencies because they misunderstood the powers and limitations of their authority.

## The parents' need for emotional support

In the crisis following the disclosure of child sexual abuse, it is important, especially for victims, that (non-offending) parents receive immediate emotional support. Often, the most effective help is that provided by other parents who have experienced the sexual abuse of a child and survived. In the supportive company of other parents they can talk freely and in confidence, knowing that listeners will not be shocked by what they hear. Child protection workers who have never been in the parents' situation, are apt to become impatient with their confusion, their lack of concentration, forgetfulness and distrust. Parent support groups are in the best position to provide assurance that parents' experiences, emotional responses and feelings are normal.

Parent support groups aim to help parents to regain control of their lives so that they can provide their children with the stability and reassurance that *they* desperately need. For a healthy outcome, parents and children must feel that they are neither being punished nor blamed. Parents needs a positive, safe environment in which they can explore their feelings and receive empathy from people who are willing to listen to their anguish, rage and repeated attempts to clarify their confusion.

## Support workers wait for the 'time bomb' to explode

When support workers visit families for the first time, they are often puzzled by the behaviour of parents. In a state of shock, mothers may continue their household chores as if nothing has happened and fathers may bury their heads in the newspaper and ignore the social workers' presence. Such behaviour is commonly exhibited when parents cannot cope with their feelings and are trying to maintain control. Rudeness and unco-operative behaviour from both parents is most prevalent when the abuser was a trusted friend, partner or relative and the crisis has far reaching implications for the whole family.

Support workers find themselves talking for four of five hours with mothers before they are able to acknowledge that there are problems to be faced. Delay is especially likely if the abuser is the victim's father or father-figure and the family is financially dependent on him. Mothers talk about the weather, the shopping, anything to postpone dealing with the problem. When confrontation can no longer be avoided, the floodgates open with tears of self-pity. 'What shall I do? What is to become of me? I can't cope'. Self-pity is followed by denial and then anger (see Chapter 10). It is unfortunate that, after suffering so much already, victims may now suffer further emotional abuse at the hands of their confused parents. Support workers can help at such times by pointing out to parents that children do not tell because they know that caring parents will make an enormous fuss. And, of course, they are right. Support workers can present the child's perspective to parents in a sensitive way, bearing in mind that young children are incapable of expressing their feelings. Similarly, the worker may have the opportunity to explain to victims why mummy is very upset and that she is cross because she thinks that it is her fault. All parties need regular reminders that there is only one person to blame and that is the abuser.

## Group support helps to break the sense of isolation

Group programmes and drop-in centres provide effective therapy by bringing together parents who have had similar experiences thus helping to break down the intense feelings of isolation that are commonly experienced by the (non-offending) parents of abused children. Parents are often unable to seek help from within their former social networks —sexual abuse is such a secret crime, embarrassment and feelings of shame and guilt make it difficult for them to reach out to family members and friends. Those who do seek help, often find that previously helpful people withdraw; they either 'don't want to know' or they express uninformed, hostile opinions. Mothers are invariably blamed, particularly by family members, and are held responsible if they trusted someone who proved untrustworthy, if they had a sexual relationship with the abuser or if they, unwittingly, helped to give the abuser access to their children. Non-offending mothers sense that they are alone and that, in some way, they must be abnormal for this to have happened. This makes them highly vulnerable to collusion with the offender. Some mothers actually persuade victims to withdraw their statements in an attempt to resolve their own immediate problems.

In the early stages, it may be necessary for support workers to take a firm stance that intrafamilial sexual behaviour of any kind is unacceptable. At the same time, support workers must acknowledge the fears and concerns of all family members. When parents are ready, they should be encouraged to consider realistic options for action. For example, when the abuse involved grandfather–grandchild incest, the perpetrator is often old, lonely, sick and dependent and parents are torn between concern for the safety of their children and loyalty towards the abuser and the family as a whole. They want the abuse to stop but fear that court attendance and imprisonment might shorten the life of the perpetrator, leaving everyone feeling guilty. Sometimes, reporting the abuse does contribute to the death of an elderly offender and young victims then blame themselves for the fatality: 'It's all my fault. If I hadn't told them, he wouldn't have died'.

Parents need to provide frequent assurance to their children. Victims need to be reminded that their abusers had a choice and that they deliberately chose to do something that was both harmful and wrong. Children understand that, when we do very wrong things, we are punished. Victims need to be told repeatedly that children are never to blame for what grown-ups do. Parents are often attacked and ostracised by other family members when they report abuse involving relatives. Families are expected to 'circle the wagons' and protect each other from outsiders to keep shameful behaviour hidden. All too often, the relatives who rise to the defence of the offender discover, many years later, that their own children were also victims but did not disclose it because they knew that they would not be believed.

One of the most difficult situations for families to face is when the incestuous father is reported and takes his own life. People are often callous and say, 'It's what he deserved. You're better off without him!'. This can be intensely damaging and support workers must realise that children remain loyal to their parents and, in such circumstances, their suffering is enormous. Those who reported the abuse believe that they are responsible for the death—children seem to have a capacity to carry enormous guilt and separate, additional bereavement counselling is needed to deal with issues relating to the suicide. Bereavement counsellors can be found in most major towns and cities. If possible, family members should be referred to 'Bereaved-by-suicide' support groups. If suicide counselling is neglected, there is a high risk that all the children in the household will become emotionally disturbed and may adopt antisocial and self-destructive behaviours to punish themselves.

When parents are made aware of the nature and effects of child abuse and where support workers offer realistic support in their decision making, most will find the strength to take whatever steps are necessary to protect their children. It must be recognised, however, that some mothers will continue to respond to their own needs and transfer their allegiance from their children to the offender. If, after a period of about two months, such parents continue to deny the seriousness of offences, it is unlikely that there will be any value in continuing support. Their presence will be a disruptive and negative influence on other group members. Levels of commitment should also be investigated if members attend groups only sporadically.

During the first few weeks in a parent support group, some parents reveal that they, too, were sexually abused in childhood. A decision must then be made as to whether the parents should join a special group for parent-survivors or move into the long-term parents' group. Much will depend on the circumstances of the earlier abuse and whether the parent has had the opportunity to work through the related emotional issues (see Chapter 12).

When the abuser lives with the family, he or she should always be persuaded to live elsewhere. This is now commonly accepted practice in the United States. Ideally, when the father is the offender, he continues to support his wife and children, accepts responsibility for his actions, apologises to his victims and undertakes treatment. Support groups are often instrumental in persuading both parents that this course of action is necessary. It is deplorable that, in the United Kingdom and Eire, Australia and New Zealand, innocent victims are still the ones who have to vacate their homes to stop the sexual abuse. Perpetrators often remain in the comfort of their homes while their wives and children live in emergency refuges, dependent upon social security benefits. With money to spare, offenders take new partners, have more children, abuse them and the process is repeated. Women's refuges have provided care for the second, third and fourth families of persistent offenders who have never been prosecuted.

For non-offending parents, voluntary support groups can provide assistance for all the phases of the recovery process but additional, individual therapy may also be necessary, depending on the circumstances.

## Parents of abused children need a twenty-four hour crisis line

Most parent support groups offer a 'round the clock' telephone crisis line. The night service is needed by both male and female parent-survivors and by unsupported mothers whose husbands or partners are accused of sexual abuse. Unable to sleep, their thoughts turn to the abuse, their own inadequacies and their current predicament. Alone, in the middle of the night, their problems become exaggerated. Feeling helpless, hopeless, friendless, guilty and full of self-pity, they sometimes become suicidal and may even decide to 'take the kids with me'. It is also not unusual for callers on night lines to announce that they are feeling drowsy because they have taken an overdose of some readily available but lethal drug. Night-time counselling services are well used by both male and female survivors. They are impersonal and comparatively non-threatening. They guarantee confidentiality (except when children are at obvious risk).

Although it only provides a restricted service from 9 a.m. to 9.30 p.m. NCH (Leeds, UK) Touchline received 1490 calls for help from 835 clients during the first year of operation. Most repeat calls involved incest; about 30 per cent involved reports of sexual abuse. Abusers were responsible for 2.2 per cent of calls. The service was intended to help victims and (non-offending) parents in the areas of West Yorkshire and Humberside. Records show that the team of 51 trained volunteer counsellors helped callers throughout the country.

In some organisations, volunteers take turns to answer night calls which are diverted to their home telephones. Parent Help (Auckland) uses this system for the operation of a 'round the clock' telephone counselling service. Each volunteer offers a four-hour shift one day per week. In smaller Australian groups, senior workers volunteer for all night rostering. The caller is in control of timing and what is discussed. In some organisations, calls are either free or the counsellor returns the call. The caller may choose to remain anonymous and the counsellor only provides his or her given name. The telephone link:

- breaks down feelings of isolation, letting callers know that they are not alone;
- enables callers to share their thoughts, explore their feelings, review what has happened and assess possible future actions;
- enables callers to gain information about child sexual abuse and where to find other forms of help.

Telephone counsellors are trained and closely supervised for six to twelve months before they are allowed to work independently. Thereafter, there is a system of supervision and debriefing. All groups offer in-service training and encourage conference and seminar attendance. NCH (Leeds) only accepts volunteers who have previously worked on other crisis services. To be effective, telephone help lines must be well advertised and details of services must be clearly indicated in the emergency pages of the telephone directory.

## Support groups introduce parents to professional therapists

Some of the well-funded support groups employ professional counsellors and psychologists to provide therapy for child victims and parents. Small groups cannot afford this and for their advisory role to be successful, group leaders need to locate and make contact with therapists who work effectively with male and female child victims and male and female adult survivors of sexual abuse. This contact is necessary because there is a shortage of good, experienced therapists for both child and adult survivors. Referral to professional help is essential when parents report continuing problems with children's emotionally disturbed behaviours or the acting out of sexual abuse. It may also be necessary for parents who cannot provide adequate support for their own children because they have not dealt with major problems relating to their own childhood victimisation.

Parent support groups may also be contacted by adult male survivors who have been unable to find help from the psychiatrists and psychologists to whom they were directed by their general practitioners. They also receive calls from men who are worried about their child focused sexual desires which put their own children at risk. These callers should be supported and directed, as a matter of urgency, to an offender treatment programme or, if no programme exists, to a therapist who specialises in this work. As children may be at risk, it is also advisable to maintain contact with callers to ensure that their needs are met. Group leaders have the responsibility of deciding if and when to report such callers to child protection services.

Parent groups should have current information about the fees charged for the various services, whether they are available through national health benefits or private health insurance and, if the latter, the extent of the client's contribution. This information is necessary because the level of awareness among general practitioners is not high and they tend to refer patients to the nearest psychologist or psychiatrist who may not only be expensive but also, if unskilled in the treatment of survivors of abuse, can be damaging. Women's and Community Health Centres, Sexual Assault Centres and Rape Crisis Centres tend to know about free and reasonably priced treatment services. State-funded health services are not usually allowed to make recommendations relating to the abilities of individual therapists.

## Support groups and the justice system

Parent support groups have four major roles to fulfil in relation to the justice system. First, they act as guides to non-offending parents when cases go to the criminal courts or when parents seek changes to custody or access arrangements (see Chapter 4). Second, they help parents to prepare child witnesses for their appearance in court. Third, they act as community educators to increase public awareness of the nature of child sexual abuse and the inadequacies of the justice system as it relates to child victims. In addition, they lobby for change.

For their advisory role to be successful, support workers get to know their local courts, police, social workers, prosecuting lawyers and those skilled in family law. They can then inform clients of who to turn to and what to expect in the assessment and legal process.

### *The preparation of child witnesses for court*

New Zealand police now regard the preparation of child witnesses as one of their most important roles. In other countries, the task is sometimes undertaken by prosecuting lawyers but some provide no preparation at all. That is when the parent support worker is of most help. Some groups train individual workers to act specifically as child witness support workers. Their role is to:

- provide information to parents and child witnesses about court procedures;
- help parents to prepare children emotionally for their court appearances so that they feel that they have some control in the court setting;
- explain the remand and bail process and the rights of the accused;
- take the children on a conducted tour of the court, explaining who sits where, what they do and what they expect of witnesses;
- inform children about the kind of questions that they will be required to answer and how to answer them effectively;
- arrange (with court staff) for young children to handle wigs and gowns so that they are not frightened when they see people wearing them in court;
- physically support and emotionally reassure parents and child witnesses during the waiting time in the court building during the trial and at the time of sentencing or acquittal;
- provide emotional reassurance after the trial by explaining the legal conclusions.

It must be emphasised that support workers must never give legal advice or coach children in what to say.

Children need to be told that they should not attempt to answer questions unless they thoroughly understand them. Some defence lawyers deliberately try to confuse child witnesses (see Chapter 4) and it is important that children understand that they have the right to ask questioners to re-word their questions again and again until they know exactly what is meant. It should be explained that, 'Some people use very long words. They forget that children don't understand them. If you don't understand, it's important to say, "I don't understand what you mean. Please try again and use words that I can understand"'. In teaching children about their rights in court, we should never underestimate how difficult it is for child witnesses to challenge adults, especially intimidating adults wearing strange clothes in an unfamiliar environment. When more than one offence is involved, police should check to ensure that children remember the dates, times and places of separate offences.

If courts do nothing to protect victims of sexual assault from contact with their abusers in the courtroom, it will also be necessary to show children where the accused will sit. They should be reminded that their abusers no longer have power to harm them. They also need information about the jury and why those people are there. Child witnesses need to know that judges and jurors are the most important people in the courtroom and they should look at them, not at the accused, when they answer questions. The preparation of children for court requires slow-handed care and patience—it is time-consuming but rewarding work. A comfortable, knowledgeable child is more likely to perform confidently in court than one who is unprepared.

When the prosecution is sloppy and disinterested, parent support groups find themselves preparing parents so that they, in turn, can prepare their children for their appearance in court. The South Australian Child Protection Unit (Adelaide) has made a video for the preparation process.

*Group workers provide moral support at court hearings*

It is often helpful if experienced support workers can accompany parents to court hearings. Parents are usually grateful for the company of other non-judgmental, experienced parents especially during the often very long delays. Moral support is especially necessary when the accused is the former spouse or partner and he fills the public seats with his friends and relatives to intimidate witnesses.

Support workers can also offer practical help—providing transport, accompanying parents for snacks and short walks. The support person's role is to listen, remain silent when silence is needed, answer questions when information is sought and boost morale. With expertise, support workers can point out, if a case is lost, where the prosecution went wrong—this is important because parents tend to blame their children for saying too little or too much or answering questions inappropriately. Similarly, it is important that child witnesses know why the prosecution failed. If they gain the impression that people believed their abuser rather than them, their sense of powerlessness increases and their self-esteem suffers yet another blow. It is very beneficial for abuse victims to know that they were believed by the jury. It is also important for them to hear the judge confirm that the abuse really did happen and that it was not their fault.

*Parent groups lobby for better services for children*

Although child protection services have improved in recent years, we have a long way to go before we can describe assessment and justice as psychologically supportive to victims. Parent groups have an important role to play in lobbying for the improvement of these services. They are well placed to collect information, give praise when praise is due and make complaints when services are under-staffed and/or perform inadequately. Group leaders can lobby for better, multiprofessional education for those who work with children by bringing deficiencies to the attention of Deans of Schools of Medicine, Social and Community Work, Education, Counselling and Nursing. New Zealand support groups have negotiated contracts to provide education on child abuse for local colleges and universities. Groups should not undertake this type of work without payment.

Group leaders make themselves and their organisations highly visible by presenting details of their experiences at local and national conferences and seminars relating to child abuse. They also maintain regular contact with all branches of the local media.

Child abuse is a political issue. Politicians are responsible for the law, for procedures in the child protection and justice system and for the allocation of funds for child protection services. They must respond to their voters and listen to minority groups. (Why else would they have changed the law to permit homosexuality between consenting adults or to permit the viewing of pornography? These changes were not widely sought). Group leaders should make appointments to see the Directors and Ministers responsible for services which fail to serve. If they do not receive a satisfactory response, they are then free to inform their Members of Parliament, Shadow Ministers and the press of what has happened. Publicity generates public debate and increases the pressure on politicians to act. Writing letters of complaint may seem to be an easier option but often letters do not reach the people with the power.

The value of parent support groups is that they are independent—they have no allegiance to any political party, they are not hampered by public service rules and procedures, they can by-pass public servants and professionals who, afraid of jeopardising their chances of promotion, would rather maintain the status quo. Children need strong advocates who are not afraid of being open and honest and who gain recognition for that rare commodity, integrity.

Successful lobbying requires many face-to-face contacts with service administrators, local council members, local politicians and, when necessary, the government ministers responsible for justice, education, health and social services. Such contacts are important, first, to provide information and increase the profile of the support group and its value to the community and second, so that group leaders gain inside information about the service, the people who run it and what it can do to help their clients.

A survey of support services shows that the most successful groups are those which developed strong networks of support early in their formation. The Director of Hamilton's Parentline makes regular visits to New Zealand's Parliament House to see the relevant ministers. Parentline is noted for its success in lobbying for improvements to services. For example, in 1987, the Executive Director (Hamilton) went to Dallas, Texas where she learned the skills of evidential video interviewing for cases of child sexual abuse. Parentline then invited three American experts to tour New Zealand to provide separate two-day workshops on video interviewing, legislative change and offender treatment. The visitors' expenses were recovered from workshop fees. Parentline's initiatives received full media coverage and, following a TV documentary which highlighted the lack of treatment for sexual offenders in New Zealand, the Minister for Justice announced that a seventy place treatment centre would be made available near Christchurch.

### *Parent groups lobby the Prosecutor's Office*

Although support groups receive many complaints about the behaviour and attitude of prosecuting lawyers, leaders are often afraid of tackling this articulate and isolated group of people mainly because they rarely communicate in the same language. Parent support groups, however, can and should lobby for better services when complaints are received. Cases of child sexual abuse are sometimes given a low priority by the public prosecutor's office. Some Australian lawyers admit that they avoid abuse cases because they lack skills in interviewing children. They do not know how children think and communicate and, as a result, they feel uncomfortable when questioning them in the witness box. When children sense that discomfort, their confidence diminishes.

Most lawyers are ignorant of the dynamics of sexual abuse. Failing to understand how normal children respond to abuse, they miss opportunities to challenge defence lawyers who often make wild claims about children's memories or complicity, for example. When cases are dismissed, they lose confidence and job satisfaction and, as a result, it is not unusual to find offenders being represented by a QC while the case for the prosecution is in the hands of a recent graduate. Weak lawyers are in a 'Catch 22' situation. Unless they take steps to develop their expertise in questioning children and unless they make the effort to learn about child abuse, their performance and success rates will remain unrewarding for themselves and their clients.

When parents or support workers are dissatisfied with the performance of prosecuting lawyers, their complaints should be delivered to the administrator responsible for the office of the Crown Prosecutor. In Australia, the State Attorney Generals have that responsibility.

## The role of the parent support group in community education

Parent support groups have a vested interest in developing community awareness in relation to the problem of child sexual abuse. Publicity enables the service to reach a greater number of clients and, at the same time, attract the attention of people interested in becoming voluntary workers. When groups are widely known, it becomes easier to obtain the funding necessary to maintain an efficient service.

All groups engage in community education. They provide information to students and offer opportunities for field experience in community work. Staff present workshops at national and international conferences. They give talks to schools, parent-teacher associations, police training establishments, colleges and universities. When they have been established for a few years, support workers become experts in their own right. They are constantly in touch with the needs of families of abused children and are usually up to date on what is happening in the wider community. Furthermore, volunteer workers have no hidden political agendas: they aim to provide better protection and support for children and caring parents.

Groups are often approached by teachers who suspect that children have been abused but, lacking appropriate training and confidence, they feel the need for another opinion before they make an official report. Parent support groups are staffed by ordinary people who are much less threatening to confused teachers than social workers or their own administrators.

The New Zealand groups have, because of their size and longer history, been more enterprising in community education than their Australian counterparts. Both Parent Help and Parentline employ part-time professional Education Officers whose work includes both volunteer training and community education. In Hamilton, the education team comprises seven workers who provide education on child protection issues for organisations scattered across a large geographic area. In 1990–91, Hamilton's Parentline provided twenty days of seminars accommodating 750 people. An additional twenty-nine talks were provided for police, student teachers, nurses, ambulance workers, social workers, paediatricians, child care workers and foster parents. Parentline also offers education programmes for inmates of the local jail. Courses include parenting skills and child development.

The New Zealand groups offer well-publicised local and national seminars, workshops and conferences, often involving overseas speakers. Visiting experts are perceived as particularly useful because they can be hard-hitting and critical of the country's political and judicial responses to child abuse with none of the inhibitions placed upon local experts. They offer new challenges and make suggestions for improvement without having to worry about upsetting the establishment.

New community education initiatives are carefully researched and planned. Groups focus on one major project a year. For example, in 1986, Parentline (Hamilton) invited Rolf Harris to New Zealand to publicise his child protection video for children and, simultaneously, draw the attention of parents and educators to the need for child protection programmes. All primary schools in the Waikato region were invited to attend sessions in four different locations. Each location catered for eight hundred children.

# 7 Setting up a parent support group

Parent support groups are usually formed at the instigation of one or two individuals who recognise that there are parents in the community who need help. Some initiatives have come from individuals who experienced the trauma of abuse in their own families and suffered from the gap in the provision of social services. Some have come from health and welfare professionals working in assessment and therapy units and family support services. Other groups have had informal beginnings when parents met and shared experiences while their children were attending assessment and therapy units.

When several children from a day-care centre, school or club were abused by the same offender, social workers brought the parents together to discuss troublesome issues. These groups have tended to be temporary, catering for a specific purpose at a specific time.

**Some groups are attached to established child and family services**

The ideal arrangement is for a support group to be formed under the umbrella of an existing non-government agency which already caters for children and families. For example, the National Children's Home (NCH) Leeds (UK) parent support group fitted into an established Family Centre provided by a national organisation which already had a sound reputation and substantial experience in fundraising and the use of volunteer counsellors to operate crisis lines.

To start the Touchline telephone and parent support service, NCH applied for grants to the Department for Health and Social Services (DHSS) and Mental Health Foundation (MHF). Reputable organisations have less difficulty than new ones in convincing funding agencies that their projects are worthwhile. In this case, the DHSS provided

£53 500 and the MHF awarded £10 005 over a three year period. Grants were also provided for telephone costs and staff training. This provision is in marked contrast to the long-term financial struggles experienced by independent, single purpose groups, some of which have operated for up to seven years without any form of government assistance. After funds were received, NCH set up a working party with representatives from local child protection agencies. With the approval of the education authorities and council, leaflets and posters were then printed and placed in schools, libraries and health centres. Media coverage was arranged and a child protection video was commissioned for the education of children.

The success of the Leeds centre helped NCH to become a prime initiator in the national provision of treatment centres for child victims and (non-offending) parents in the United Kingdom. In 1989, an additional £4 million was made available for services for victims of sexual abuse. These services may be provided on condition that local authorities and/or DHSS agree to provide an equivalent amount of funding. Projects opened in Preston and Glasgow and others are planned for Nottingham, Scunthorpe, Sunderland, Port Talbot, Oxfordshire, South-east Kent and West Cumbria. NCH anticipates that sixteen new centres will be provided during 1992, each including parent support groups, parent counselling and family therapy facilities.

Ad hoc parent support groups have been formed by other established non-government services 'when the need arises'. British providers include the NSPCC, Barnardos, Incest Survivors, Rape Crisis Centres and the Children's Society. In addition, some DHSS Child Sexual Abuse Assessment Centres also make provision for short-term groups.

## Single-purpose groups

Some single-purpose, continuous groups have been created to provide a service where none previously existed. British pioneer Jill Trueman found the need for support when her own life 'fell apart' following the disclosure that her young daughter had been abused by her second husband. After she had 'picked up the pieces', Jill Trueman established SAMS (Sexual Abuse Mothers' Support Group) to provide support for other mothers in the same situation (1988). SAMS is now the most frequently quoted parent support group in Britain. Initially operating from the founder's own home, the service grew and now offers a comfortable, centrally situated house at Southend and a drop-in centre at Basildon. Although its main purpose is to support mothers, SAMS also arranges assistance for fathers and offenders. The organisation has the long-term aim of providing drop-in centres throughout the County of Essex. SAMS receives a council grant of £9980 (1991) for rent and the basic running costs of centres. Volunteers then have the task of raising an additional £10 000 a year to 'stay afloat'. Counselling is provided by volunteers with professional back-up.

A 'low-profile' group, 'Sanctuary', provides a similar service in Maidstone and Rainham in Kent and a second group, 'Family Matters', offers assistance from Dartford, Swanley and Gravesend. The latter provides support to the partners of survivors as well as to survivors and non-offending parents. Similar groups are scattered throughout the United Kingdom. They are all dependent upon fund-raising and the use of trained volunteers to provide twenty-four-hour telephone crisis lines and individual and/or group counselling services. Because they operate on shoestring budgets and there is no national coordination of services, they receive little publicity and are difficult to locate. Parents are usually referred by statutory services or by other satisfied clients. The advantage of these specialist groups is that they offer a wider range of personalised services to clients than the agencies involved in multiple family services. Lacking funds, they usually cater for much smaller numbers of clients.

## Provision in New Zealand

One of the first New Zealand groups was Parent Help, initiated in 1977 as a result of concerns by staff at an Auckland Hospital. A public meeting was called which resulted in the establishment of a twenty-four-hour telephone counselling service to cover all forms of child maltreatment. The first voluntary telephone counsellors were trained by Lifeline. The operation then had no paid staff but workers received back-up from members of the advisory committee who were professionals working in the child protection field.

Many callers required in-depth counselling. This presented problems because Parent Help then had no office premises and counsellors worked from home. The demand for face-to-face counselling was such that a social worker was appointed (salaried from trust funds) to make home visits. Home visiting and telephone counselling continue to be part of the Parent Help service. Counsellors are appointed to teams, each team with a coordinator who is responsible to a half-time salaried administrator. There are thirty-five telephone counsellors catering for the city of Auckland alone.

Parent Help has an extensive role in community education for child protection. This includes the provision of lectures, seminars and, with the help of advertisers, the publication of sophisticated educational material for families and professionals. Parent Help (Auckland) now has a central city office as well as a community house. The house, bought at low cost from the Department for Social Welfare, is shared by two other family services. Parents are encouraged to 'drop-in' when they need informal or formal counselling. In 1992, Parent Help employed six part-time staff and had an annual budget of $180 000. Funds came from a variety of sources such as bequests, trusts, industry, commerce and government agencies.

One year after the introduction of Parent Help, a Hamilton social worker, Maxine Hodgson, called a public meeting to investigate the need for a similar service for the Waikato region. Parentline was created (1979) with financial support from the Mayor of Hamilton, Catholic Social Services and private individuals. In the first two years, the director concentrated on developing the visibility and credibility of Parentline in the area. She contacted key people to discuss how Parentline might participate effectively alongside existing statutory services. Gradually the organisation extended its focus to include the primary prevention of child abuse. This included:

- extensive, long-term support for parents with individual counselling, home visits (as necessary) and twenty-four-hour crisis telephone lines;
- a drop-in centre for parents with a playgroup for children;
- education for improving parenting skills, two days per week;
- a foster-care and alternative care programme;
- play therapy and a programme to develop self-esteem and assertiveness in selected children;
- community education;
- participation in family group conferences (which are required by New Zealand's child protection legislation (1989)).

Parentline (Hamilton) is now the largest organisation of its kind in New Zealand with a budget for 1992 of $400 000–half of this came from a government contract for work under the *Children and Young Persons and their Families Act*, 1989. In 1990–91, Parentline received 8012 counselling calls including 780 first calls from new clients.

The provision of purpose-built premises (October, 1991) helped to elevate Parentline's image. This project was made possible by the provision of free labour by the Maori community. The accommodation offers a spacious reception area, play rooms, therapy rooms, counselling rooms, staff kitchen and vast office space for counsellors. The fifteen salaried staff include a full-time director, treasurer, secretary, two senior counsellors and two counsellors. Part-time staff include an education officer, play therapist and foster-care coordinator. In addition, the university uses Parentline for students' field experience.

In 1992, there were ten independent Parent Help and Parentline groups in New Zealand under the umbrella of the Society for the Prevention of Child Abuse and Neglect. Personnel meet three to four times a year and share conferences. None of these organisations cater exclusively for issues relating to child sexual abuse. Other, single focus groups exist. Some operate under the umbrella of the HELP Foundation. HELP centres can be found in Auckland, South Auckland, Tauranga and Wellington. The groups are managed separately and have different aims and philosophies. While most groups concentrate on women and children, the Auckland centre caters for both male and female clients, including the male partners of female survivors. The Auckland management is committed to the payment of staff and, on principle, will not use voluntary female labour for this important work. The South Auckland group emphasises its multicultural service. All have medical expertise available on a twenty-four-hour roster.

Small parent support groups are available in towns throughout New Zealand. Most are informal and attached to community and neighbourhood centres. There is no communication between these groups and they are not affiliated to any national organisation.

## Australia's single-purpose groups

While New Zealand's efforts began in the 1970s with concerns relating to the physical abuse and neglect of children, Australia's groups were created specifically to cater for problems arising from the increase in reports of child sexual abuse in the 1980s. Unattached to other services and focusing exclusively on parents' needs, they operate on shoestring budgets with little or no financial help from government. As a result, they serve fewer clients but offer a much wider range of personalised services than multifocus, wealthier agencies.

Some groups have their origins in the concerns of hospital staff employed in Sexual Assault Centres for the assessment of abuse and the treatment of children. In South Australia (1985), when parents met informally at the Royal Adelaide Children's Hospital, they found commonality in their grievances and frustrations. With staff support, they called a public meeting and invited members of the state government's Task Force on Child Sexual Abuse to attend. It was a very emotional gathering at which Task Force members had to listen to the litany of horrendous experiences endured by child victims in the justice system.

From that gathering, 'People Against Child Sexual Abuse' (PACSA) emerged. The aims of the organisation included lobbying and educating the community on child protection issues and providing support for the non-offending members of families affected by sexual abuse. During the first two years, the group held monthly meetings at the hospital. In 1986, a church congregation fasted and raised $2000 for PACSA. The group was then able to move to premises occupied by a service for the support of single parents. The coordinator rented a desk and a telephone. One year later, the State government provided funds for the renting of separate premises for two PACSA groups. In 1989, the grant was cut to provide one small salary to be shared by two coordinators. One group closed and the rent of the other has since been paid by fund-raising. Staff are assisted by seven full-time and twenty occasional helpers, all of whom are former clients of the organisation who volunteered to undertake in-house training. In 1991, PACSA published a book of poetry written by parents and parent/survivors of sexual abuse.

Other Australian organisations began as the result of concerns by child protection workers. Queensland's PACT (Protect All Children Today) also began its operations in 1985 but it was not until 1989 that it received funding to employ two social worker coordinators. One coordinator is salaried by the Women's Health Policy Unit with both State and federal funds, while the other receives 75 per cent of her salary from government funding and 25 per cent from fund-raising efforts. In 1991, PACT's service was offered from the garage of a house used as a refuge for women and children. The authority did not see its role as a provider of office space, albeit in a domestic garage, and PACT was asked to find alternative accommodation. With some assistance from the Health Department, PACT now occupies a comfortable, rented house and employs thirty-five child witness support workers, ten telephone counsellors, six group therapists plus voluntary office staff, all of whom are trained by the two coordinators. PACT emphasises the value of its specialist child witness support service and its telephone link between new and former clients.

In 1992, Perth, with a population of a million people, had no government funded parent support group. SASHA (Sexual Abuse Self Help Association) was 'in recess' for lack of funds. With money obtained from raffles, PACSA (WA) offers telephone counselling, parent support, community education and lobbying for law reform from the home of its founder, Jan Bennett. Funding has been a source of discontent because, while politicians have praised PACSA's efforts and approved the allocation of considerable government funds for services dealing with domestic violence, child sexual abuse is labelled as 'in another category' for funding purposes.

In Melbourne, Parents Against Child Exploitation (PACE) are also aggrieved. Once again, the group's efforts have been praised by the State's Premier in parliament but no funds have been allocated to the group. As a result, PACE is based at the Glen Waverley home of its founder and president. She is assisted by eleven voluntary workers and finds that 'there are never enough people to meet all the cries for help' in a city of some four million people. In addition to the routine support of families affected by sexual abuse, PACE has provided support to parents and grandparents in cases of child-sex murders and satanic ritual abuse.

In Sydney, Parents Support Network (PSN) aims to provide 'total support', catering for parents' individual needs. Twenty-five trained volunteers provide twenty-four-hour telephone counselling on five-hour shifts. Family and Community Services fund two part-time salaried workers for a total of thirty hours per week and accommodation is provided by the Health Commission. There are many other services which will assist parents but child sexual abuse is not their prime focus. (See Appendix).

In New South Wales and Victoria, ad hoc groups have been formed by parents caught up in the same crisis situations. Parents in both States formed mutual support and lobbying groups when they learned that their preschool children had been victimised in satanic rituals involving their preschool centres. In these cases, a large number of families were involved. Their prime purpose was to lobby for better protection for children from the justice system. Informal meetings began as soon as the abuse was confirmed. Eventually, when no more could be achieved, the groups dispersed.

At Elizabeth, South Australia, a group began as a result of the voluntary efforts of a local social worker who met several mothers in one of their homes. This arrangement soon became too difficult because of the workers' official commitments. She tried to persuade parents to continue meeting but her efforts failed because the women lacked expertise and leadership. Group members then protested that social services had let them down. A second group, Friends of Abused Children Taskforce (FACT) survived without direct professional involvement when mothers maintained telephone contact with each other and with two sympathetic child protection workers. These workers recognised that a trained community worker was needed. They recruited and trained a volunteer. They then convened a public meeting in the Town Hall to draw attention to the high incidence of reported child molestation in the community and the inadequacy of support services for families. They recognised that there were potential volunteers in the area and this potential source of assistance could be tapped.

The meeting was well publicised and well attended, predominantly by parents who were survivors of abuse or whose children had been abused. In addition, foster parents and registered child-minders, daycare staff and early childhood teachers accepted personal invitations to be present. When members of the audience commented, 'This is terrible' and asked, 'What are you doing about it?', the question was returned with, 'You live here. Is this what you want to happen in your community? What are you prepared to do about it? Are you prepared to help? If so, we will do all that we can to assist you to create your own support group'. Ten women volunteered their services. Some were registered community aides working with statutory social services. The remainder were mothers of sexually abused children and their friends.

The social workers provided a short training programme and the service was advertised. The first client group comprised mothers of children who had been abused by their fathers. The mothers had all moved out of their family homes to protect their children. They were all dependent on social security benefits and they had all experienced a marked decline in their living standards subsequent to the disclosure of the abuse. The mothers were resentful about their predicament and blamed their children. They felt that they had lost self-esteem and their lives were out of control. Because the children had suffered abuse, the loss of their fathers and homes and most had experienced changes of school and locality, their behaviour was predictably disturbed and difficult to handle. Forced to move to cheaper accommodation in remote suburbs that lacked public transport and other services, the mothers had stopped taking their children for therapy at the Children's Hospital, thirty-four kilometres away.

Community aides, prepared by case-workers, visited the homes and listened to parents' problems. They learned about the children's nightmares, bedwetting, disobedience and their acting out of the inappropriate sexual behaviour. They heard the mothers describe how they 'freaked out' when their children climbed into their beds and offered sexual touching in exchange for cuddles with the assurance that 'Daddy says this is what you do when you love me'. The community workers heard of the mothers' problems in trying to restore a sense of order to their family lives and, together, they worked out priorities for creating change and resolving problems.

## Continuing education

Most group cater for the continuing education of their trained staff. British groups commonly use teaching materials from the course on Child Abuse and Neglect available from the Open University. British and New Zealand staff also attend lectures and short courses at regional Polytechnics and Colleges of Further Education. Their Australian counterparts are more dependent on in-house training and attendance at seminars and conferences.

# 8 The recruitment, selection and training of volunteer support workers for parent support groups

## Suggestions for the recruitment and selection of volunteers

One of the first tasks in creating a parent support group is the recruitment of voluntary support workers. This can be achieved by advertising in all available local media, shopping centres, schools, clinics, hospitals and other places that parents tend to meet and congregate. As the group constitutes a charity (and should be registered as such), enquire at local radio stations which donate free air time for community announcements of this kind. The advertisement should invite applicants to telephone a group leader for further information when a series of initial questions should be asked. For example:

- What experience have you had with children? Your own? Other people's?
- What contact have you had, if any, with groups for adults?
- What do you know about the work that we do?
- How would you like to help? What do you most enjoy doing?

- Could you attend the training sessions which will start on . . . . day (date) . . . . . . . at . . . . . . . . . . . . . . . . . . . . from . . . . . . a.m. to . . . . . p.m.?
- Do you have a car or other transport available? If not, do you live near the group's premises?
- Do you have any family commitments which would limit your hours of work?
- What would you like to know about the organisation?
- Can you attend for an interview?

This process results in some self-selection and reduces the number of applicants to be interviewed.

From the telephone interview, it should be possible to check the callers' availability, level of commitment, potential for making a contribution to the group, experience with children and parents and their telephone manner. Ideally, volunteers should be selected by an interviewing panel comprising a group coordinator and two members of an advisory panel. A formal interview should establish that the trainee has:

- a telephone, access to private transport (or lives in a central situation) and can fit in voluntary work with other work or family commitments (it might be possible to offer office work or home-based telephone counselling for those without transport);
- an understanding of the expected level of commitment to the work;
- an understanding of the responsibilities of volunteers;
- an understanding of the supervision that will be involved;
- self-awareness, strengths and ideas;
- receptiveness to new information and new ideas;
- an understanding of their own values (and faults) and a readiness to acknowledge different and conflicting values.

Even when volunteers have been clients and are known to group leaders, it is advisable to proceed through a formal interviewing process. Every applicant should be contacted. The reasons for non-selection should be truthfully but tactfully given along with suggestions for the applicant to direct his or her skills into other helping areas.

Some groups place new volunteers on a six-month period of probation, during which time they work under the supervision of experienced staff. During that time, they are given opportunities to participate in the full range of work experiences, including office routines, home visits, educational programmes and meetings with other agencies. An example of a volunteer records sheet is shown in Figure 8.1.

**Figure 8.1 Volunteer records**

*Given name* . . . . . . . . . . . . . . . . . . . *Family name* . . . . . . . . . . . . . . . . . . . . . . . .

*Address* . . . . . . . . . . . . . . . . . . . . . . . . . . . . . . . . . . . . . . . . . . . . . . . . . . . . .

*Tel. no. (Home)* . . . . . . . . . . . . . . . *(Work)* . . . . . . . . . . . . . . . . . . . . . . . . . . . . . .

*Times available for voluntary work* . . . . . . . . . . . . . . . . . . . . . . . . . . . . . . . . . . . . .

. . . . . . . . . . . . . . . . . . . . . . . . . . . . . . . . . . . . . . . . . . . . . . . . . . . . . . . . . . . . . .

*Driving licence* . . . . . . . . . . . . . . . . . *Car available for voluntary work?* Yes/No

*Previous experience of working with parents* . . . . . . . . . . . . . . . . . . . . . . . . . . . . . . .

*As* . . . . . . . . . . . . . . . . . . . . . . *With* . . . . . . . . . . . . . . . . . . . . . . . . . . . . . . . .

*When* . . . . . . . . . . . . . . . . . . . . .

*Other*

*Previous experience of community work:*

*As* . . . . . . . . . . . . . . . . . . . . *With* . . . . . . . . . . . . . . . . . . . . . . . . . . . . . . . . . . .

*When* . . . . . . . . . . . . . . . . . . . . .

*Other*

*References*

*Previous training*

## Orientation programmes for volunteers

An orientation programme should be made available for new volunteers either before they start training or as the first training session. The aim of such a programme is to provide new recruits with an overall understanding of the philosophy of the organisation and how it operates, why volunteers are needed, the types of work available and details about training, rules, procedures and expectations. Volunteers also need information about the responsibilities of individuals, social activities and the relationship of management to staff and clients. Some of this information will have been given at the initial interview but when people are new and nervous, they are apt to forget the detail of what was said. Care should be taken not to overload and alarm new recruits.

Students need to know that it is alright to show emotion and to leave the room if necessary. At the same time, the orientation session should be sufficiently interesting to challenge all participants. Group leaders may use film, video, leaflets, overhead projectors and other visual aids to maintain student's attention. A social event such as a group barbecue is a good idea to help students and trainers get to know one another.

On the first working day, each volunteer should be welcomed by a leader, introduced to staff and shown the facilities. The leader will prepare the volunteer for action by referring to the job description for the work selected, explaining the tasks to be done and introducing the volunteer to a support worker who will provide supervision. This supervision should be carefully explained to reassure new recruits that they will not have to make difficult decisions on their own. Volunteers should always be given opportunities to ask questions before and during each work session. At the end of the day, there should also be an opportunity for feedback.

**Establishing group expectations for trainees and clients**

Whether working in training sessions with new volunteers or in group counselling sessions with new clients, it is important that all group members be given the opportunity for establishing 'norms of behaviour' and group rules at the very first session. Through discussion, all group members will quickly understand the need for rules relating to confidentiality and consideration of other people's feelings. It is helpful for members to discuss effective ways of handling different situations, for example what to do if someone attempts to monopolise a session or interrupts others.

Practical issues also need to be discussed, such as banning obscene language, the need for smoking zones, who should provide and make the refreshments, how frequently and at what times members would like to have breaks and what rules are necessary relating to cleaning up.

Leaders should introduce and discuss the need for the rule that support workers are not allowed to give their full names, addresses and private home telephone numbers to clients. It is also necessary to discuss the reporting of disclosures of sexual abuse and how to handle these reports sensitively to reduce the trauma for children and their families.

## The rights of volunteers

When volunteers are recruited, some time should be spent discussing the values and basic rights of each individual. Each volunteer has:

- a basic right to be treated with courtesy and respect at all times;
- the opportunity to choose from several different work options;
- the opportunity to train and develop skills;
- a need to make a useful contribution to the service;
- a right to positive feedback for effort and a job well done;
- the right to confidentiality about personal issues;
- the right NOT to be exploited.

Individuals should be invited to clarify their values and expectations as well as their responsibilities to the agency and clients.

There is a potential for discord where some staff members are paid and others are volunteers. Care must be taken that the paid responsibilities are clearly identified and that volunteers must not be given work that falls into the paid category. It should be decided early in the creation of the agency whether or not volunteers can be paid for using their motor vehicles to take children and parents to court or hospital. If management agrees that refunds will be made, procedures for claims should be clarified and implemented. Claim forms should be designed and produced to ensure that basic checks can be made on claims. This may seem irksome when groups are small but it is better to reduce opportunities for exaggerated claims from the beginning. Work records should also be kept (see the examples in Figures 8.2 and 8.3).

## Insurance protection for volunteers and clients

Voluntary agencies should take out public risk insurance to cover them in the event of a client or volunteer suing the agency for injuries attributed to negligence. Personal accident insurance should also be taken out to cover volunteers irrespective of the type of accident or the level of fault. When workers use their own cars for carrying clients, the agency should ensure that they are in possession of a current driving licence and that the vehicle is appropriately insured.

## Outline of a preliminary training programme for voluntary support workers

The first training programmes should be planned with and implemented by professionals while group leaders watch and listen with a view to the

**Figure 8.2 Travel claim: sample form for parent support groups**

| Date | Mileage Departure | Mileage Return | From | To | With | Reason for journey | Total claimed |
|---|---|---|---|---|---|---|---|
| | | | | | | | |

**Figure 8.3 Record of work: sample form for parent support groups**

| RECORD OF WORK OF | | | | |
|---|---|---|---|---|
| Date | Time involved from/to | Client | Details of task | Discussed with (leader) |
| | | | | |

provision of future programmes. When volunteers are the parents of abuse victims, they have often had unpleasant experiences at the hands of professional services and do not relate readily to people with professional backgrounds. Professional trainers must not be used simply because they are willing; they must also be skilled at relating to families in crisis. In the ideal supportive environment, there is no superior-inferior status and learning is viewed as a continuous process.

Most training programmes develop from a trial and error approach. Mistakes must be accepted as part of the learning experience. Both teachers and volunteers must be encouraged to both give and receive constructive criticism and feedback after each session. Formal, anonymous evaluation sheets should also be used (see the sample in Figure 8.4).

When planning a programme, it is important not to overload students with too much information. Child sexual abuse is a heavy, emotionally demanding subject and new volunteers may soon feel overwhelmed. The first training programme should extend over a period of twelve to sixteen weeks, by the end of which, students should be competent to relate to any or all of the situations which refer to the

**Figure 8.4 Evaluation of the training session**

| |
|---|
| I would like to know more about .......................................... |
| .......................................... |
| .......................................... |
| .......................................... |
| I was pleased that .......................................... |
| .......................................... |
| .......................................... |
| I was disappointed that |
| .......................................... |
| .......................................... |
| What I found most interesting was.......................................... |
| .......................................... |
| .......................................... |
| I learned most from .......................................... |
| .......................................... |
| .......................................... |
| but could have managed without.......................................... |
| .......................................... |
| .......................................... |
| .......................................... |

organisation and training programme (under the supervision of senior staff). After orientation, basic minimal training should include the following topics.

*Child sexual abuse* The problem of child abuse in the community—who abuses children, signs and symptoms of abuse and children's responses (see Chapters 1–3). Videos are valuable for showing how abusers manipulate their victims into compliance and how parents often miss the cries for help. Preparation is needed before showing such videos to volunteers who are also survivors of abuse. They can be very powerful and cause distress. Summarise and discuss how some children learn to live with abuse.

*How incest affects families* This session involves the use of brainstorming methods, exercises and videos as appropriate.

*Working as a team* Team building, conflict resolution, constructive confrontation, confidence building, how to create a network of support with other agencies such as the police, therapists and case workers.

*What happens after the notification of child sexual abuse* It is useful to involve a forum of relevant professionals in this session and to include visits to other services. Students benefit from learning about:

- the police perspective—what should happen and why (and why, sometimes, it does not);
- the work of the prosecutor—followed by a visit to the criminal courts to observe cases in progress (these do not usually alarm students when they are not personally involved in the cases);
- the family or divorce court at which, by arrangement, counsellors can explain the perspectives and powers of the court in relation to allegations of child sexual abuse;
- women's refuges to meet staff who work with mothers and children after they have left their homes to escape from abusive partners;
- statutory social services and their roles, powers and limits of intervention;
- voluntary services working with children 'at risk' and their families;
- sexual assault referral centres and treatment centres to learn how children are interviewed, how child abuse is assessed and what is involved in treatment;
- how to get legal aid, advice and representation for children in court;
- domestic violence and offender treatment centres to enable staff to explain about the dynamics of domestic violence, how offenders think and the complexities of treatment.

*Developing communication skills*

*Working with families in a multicultural society*

*Behaviour modification* Helping parents to handle children's emotionally disturbed behaviour. Helping foster parents to create safe environments for child survivors of sexual abuse.

*Telephone counselling skills* These are needed for crisis lines.

*Assertiveness and personal safety skills* For example the right to be safe, the need for a personal support network and the importance of debriefing, reporting disclosures, handling angry feelings. While emphasising the need to learn about child abuse, leaders stress the importance of self-protection. At these sessions, volunteers often choose to disclose their own abuse for the first time. Not all volunteers are ready to receive information of this kind at this stage. Those who have not been abused may be shocked. Some survivors have a need to talk continuously about their experiences. This is the cue for a coffee-break to create a tactful diversion and the opportunity for the leader to take the trainee aside for a more appropriate private session. Women survivors and non-offending mothers are often very angry people and a great deal of time and effort is necessary before they can begin to respect other people's feelings.

Ideally these issues will be discussed in greater detail at debriefing sessions and workshops. Until they are proficient, workers should be invited to recall everything that transpires between themselves and their clients. Leaders will ask them whether they were satisfied with their responses at each stage and what they would do if the same situation arose again. This is to check that they are understanding and responding appropriately to cues.

It is very important that trainers:

- ensure that all trainees are introduced to each other and to staff;
- learn all the participants' names;
- provide an atmosphere in which everyone listens respectfully to others;
- emphasise the need for confidentiality;
- provide an atmosphere in which students can express themselves freely without fear of being judged;
- ensure that everyone has the opportunity to speak;
- respect the right of individuals to 'pass' when the subject is too uncomfortable;
- support participants as they confront their feelings;
- help the less articulate participants to put their feelings into words, if necessary;
- check that students' perceptions are accurate;
- learn to feel comfortable with silence;
- plan for everyone to benefit from each session;
- conclude meetings on a positive note;
- provide opportunities for informal socialising.

These 'musts' remain the same when volunteers are working with parent groups in counselling sessions.

## Teaching methods used in training

*Brainstorming*

The teaching method most frequently used by support groups involves brainstorming and discussion. Brainstorming sessions generate the maximum number of ideas in the minimum amount of time with everyone participating. All ideas are valued equally and recorded on a blackboard or large sheets of paper. The rules are simple:

1 Ensure that the task is clear, for example 'What did you feel like when . . .'
2 Write the topic on the blackboard.
3 Invite short responses limited to a single word or phrase.
4 Accept and record every idea that is presented.
5 Give reminders to participants who digress.
6 When members run out of ideas, go through the list, summarise and discuss the responses. For example:
—'Let's look at the variety of conflicting feelings here';
—'Let's look at the feelings associated with . . .'
7 Allow time for general discussion.
8 Summarise findings.
9 Discuss the implications of these findings for the group.
Brainstorming methods ensure that trainees are not 'talked at'. Everyone is encouraged to participate and all ideas are given equal consideration.

*Role-play*

This is a useful educational technique that enables people to explore their emotions, behaviours and attitudes to particular situations and gives opportunities to learn and practice new skills, reflect on these experiences and gain understanding. Role-play is about trying to put yourself in someone else's shoes and to be successful, there must be adequate time for preparation. Some members may be shy of performing and become embarrassed and speechless and even panic. Unwilling people should never be forced into participation. Sometimes, leaders may have to take the difficult roles.

Role-play can be useful for learning and practising child management skills when parents are experiencing problems with their children. Students soon learn the tutor's jargon and this can be misleading. They may say 'I would be supportive' but when asked to demonstrate exactly what they would say to a parent, they often use words, body language and tones of voice that are critical, authoritarian, sarcastic and even hostile. If trainees can practice with others, change roles and then discuss how they felt, they can learn a great deal from the experience.

At the end of each session, time must be made available for individual reflection and evaluation. For example, trainees should tell others what it felt like when they were acting the part of the child or the mother who is trying out new behavioural management techniques. Trainees should also be encouraged to discuss what happened and what they learned from the experience. This should be followed by a period of relaxation. It is the leader's responsibility to ensure that participants do not return home without first discarding their acted roles.

## Training volunteers in communication skills

One of the main roles of the counsellor in a parent support group is to assist parents to free themselves of their inhibiting and rigid patterns of feeling and behaviour relating to the abuse. With precise and well-timed assistance, parents learn to release their pent-up feelings until their experiences no longer affect them in a damaging way. These experiences then become sad memories of an all-too-common life occurrence. With good communication skills, support workers help clients to put their troubles behind them and plan for a new life.

When we are hurt, there is a desperate need to understand why, 'Why me?', 'Why my child?' and 'What did we do to deserve this?'. We all need logical explanations for the traumatic things that affect us. Explanation restores a sense of order and security. Parents and survivors of sexual abuse are often prevented from reaching any deep understanding of their situation because thoughts of the abuse renew the pain. To stop pain, we try to stop thinking and switch off. To avoid hurt, we deprive ourselves of the opportunity to think things through in any meaningful and healthy way.

People rarely begin a conversation by revealing the things that worry them most. We all conceal part of our inner selves from others, especially when we have been badly hurt, and we test people out to see how much they can handle. We assess whether they will be shocked or sympathetic. We watch body language to see if listeners back away or maintain non-judgmental eye-to-eye contact when we talk. This is exactly the way that abused children behave. The things that we really need to discuss are the things we hide from others. People go to the doctor when they are worried but when they walk into the surgery, they often fail to disclose the real reason for being there. Trainees should be invited to consider why this happens.

Similarly, parents often come to groups to talk about serious issues but settle for something quite trivial, lacking the confidence to introduce their real concern. Unfortunately, inexperienced counsellors 'home in' on trivial problems and avoid asking the hard questions. The parents return home convinced that the group is incapable of providing the right kind of help. Adults are conditioned not to show their emotions, especially in the company of others. This makes it difficult for parents of sexually abused children to talk about how they feel.

Adult communications can be very inaccurate because they involve a code. The skill of decoding messages is largely learned by experience with an element of guesswork. We can hear what is being said and see what is happening but we can only guess at the meaning and how that person really feels. The way in which a message is sent and received can be shown as follows:

| *Communicator* | *Actions* | *Listener* |
|---|---|---|
| Thoughts and feelings are known only to self | Body language, words, expressions are disguised according to the circumstances and level of trust | Interprets according to experiences, attitudes and perceptions of the message. |

It is useful for leaders to introduce the importance of acquiring good communication skills to trainee volunteer support workers by brainstorming and taking note of how we each express feelings of sadness, fear and anger. The following exercise may help with this.

**Exercise 8.1 Brainstorm how we commonly express our feelings**

| *Emotional tension* | *How it is manifested* |
|---|---|
| Sadness due to loss | |
| Fear | |
| Slight anger | |
| Severe anger | |
| 'Fed Up' | |
| Distress/sense of hopelessness | |
| Emptiness | |

The exercise continues with four parts:

1 Make a list of the emotional tensions shown above. Brainstorm with students and list manifestations in the right-hand column.

2 Make another list of emotional tensions. Brainstorm how other people expect us to behave when we suffer these emotional excesses.

3 Compare the differences between our normal responses and how other people expect us to behave.

4 Discuss how people's expectations affect the way in which we express our emotions.

*Learning to listen*

The first important training task for support workers is to learn to listen carefully to other people without losing concentration, interrupting them or asking questions. This does not come naturally, it has to be taught and practised. We all have emotional filters which enable us to block the things that we don't want to hear. The task is especially difficult for volunteers who are also the parents of abused children and who have had the same kinds of feelings and experiences. In these circumstances it is also a temptation to interrupt speakers with comments such as, 'Yes, I know. I felt that way too but don't worry, you'll get over it. I did!'. It can be very off-putting for clients to be interrupted and have their concerns and feelings 'put down' as normal and something that they will 'get over'. Questions should be asked only to clarify points and to keep the client's attention on track. Listening exercises provide useful practice (see below). There are some basic hints which should be given to new counsellors.

*Do not offer good advice* Support workers must *never* interrupt speakers to offer suggestions for action. They should avoid questions such as, 'Didn't you think about . . .?', 'Have you thought of . . .?', or 'Why didn't you . . .?', suggesting that the parents were remiss for not thinking these things for themselves. To be beneficial, answers to problems must be worked out *by the clients themselves* from a variety of options to be presented after their needs and priorities have been correctly identified. They are more committed to solutions if they have planned them. Also, by presenting instant solutions, supporters put themselves in the class of instant experts and this creates barriers to parents who need to work out their own solutions.

*Try not to react emotionally to the client's distress* The most appropriate attitude towards the parent seeking help is one of interest and concern. Any excessive response on the part of the support worker, whether it is indifference or sympathy, will prevent the parent from handling the situation appropriately. If the listener becomes distressed and weeps with the client, the latter senses that the support worker has problems. This can result in resentment and loss of confidence. The distressed parent stops the emotional flow, thinking, 'What is she crying about? She hasn't been hurt! I'm the one who is suffering. She has no business to burden me with her problems when I'm suffering so much'.

*Try not to interrupt the discharge of emotions* It can be distressing for a volunteer, especially one who is also a survivor of abuse, to witness the excessive release of emotion by another parent. When the listener becomes upset, there is a tendency to interrupt the flow of emotion with an offer of a cigarette, a cup of coffee or paper tissues (which should always be readily available). Volunteers should become very sensitive to their own feelings and reactions to distress. If someone stops crying or yelling or banging the table, support workers need to ask themselves what happened immediately prior to the reduction of anger. Was there a distraction or was it a natural step? What was said? Did someone come into the room? Did the telephone ring? What other distractions took place? Whatever the answer, those distractions should be avoided on another occasion.

Most adults will only cry in public when they feel comfortable about doing so. We cry in the cinema because it is dark. When lights are switched on, we blow our noses, gulp, hide our tears and pretend that we have all suddenly acquired a headcold. When people burst into tears in an uncomfortable environment, they dash out of the room and head for privacy. To be effective, support groups must facilitate the free expression of emotion; in other words, the clients should sense that they have permission to release their sadness, frustration and anger in safety. That does not mean that they have permission to break up the office furniture but there must be avenues for the safe release of aggression.

*Watch for clues as to which problems are the most serious* Parents of sexually abused children have many problems and find it difficult to prioritise them for attention. Sometimes, parents talk about the least important issues because these can be resolved with the least stress and they serve as a distraction from the more painful subjects. Some parents begin with minor problems to test the counsellor—if the support person helps, parents may develop sufficient trust to share other concerns; if the parent is dissatisfied, he or she is unlikely to return.

Sensitive listeners pick up clues to identify the most hurtful situations and gently return clients to these matters when they attempt to hide them away. They will ask parents whether these are painful and difficult to discuss. They stress that difficult problems become less difficult when they are shared.

Remember, concentration is essential and the listener must be deeply involved in the interaction for counselling to be successful.

*Sensitivity to body language*

New support workers are often unaware of the importance of body language in communications. A useful exercise is for trainees to be told to 'freeze' (remain absolutely still, albeit with arms in the air and mouths open) when they are engaged in conversation. Some trainees are then asked to translate the frozen 'message' that is being held in the body. The group leader then checks these assessments with the person concerned.

Volunteers also need to know that, in new situations, people spend at least the first five minutes of contact making assessments of each other. When clients and counsellors meet, they look at each others' dress, hairstyles and other characteristics to decide whether they like them or not. They try to think who the new person resembles. They attempt to place new people in categories based on previous experiences. A useful exercise is to invite an unfamiliar person into the room to talk to the group leader for a few seconds. When that person leaves the room, the trainees should be asked to write down a description of the visitor. Usually, they presume that someone who is well-dressed and who carries documents is a senior professional administrator. People who show signs of strength are often mistakenly described as wearing strong colours and severe hairstyles. Using role-play, trainees could work on developing the skills needed to genuinely welcome new clients and make them feel comfortable.

*Reflective listening reflects feelings*

The reflection of feelings means that the listener clarifies the feelings of the speaker with a few appropriate words. For example, the mother says, 'I'm not sure whether to leave him or not. He's got his good points. He's always been good to me. But I'll never forgive him for what he did to the kids. I'll never trust him again'. The listener may say, 'I can see that you are feeling very confused at the moment'. The listener realises that the mother is feeling a wide range of emotions such as fear, frustration, isolation, insecurity, love and hate. The listener watches the body language and listens to the tone of voice for further clues. Does the voice soften or harden when she talks about the man? Does it soften or harden when she talks about her children? The reflective statement briefly sums up the total picture.

In cases of child sexual abuse, listeners often latch on to the facts and miss the emotions. Some interrupt the flow of conversation with practical hints on how to leave the abuser and survive, cutting off the emotional discharge. Poor listeners demand that speakers stick to the facts.

When listening discourages the expression of emotion, we miss the relative importance of events to the speakers. We fail to pick up their main concerns and leave them feeling lonely and misunderstood.

*Sensing other people's feelings*

Most of us can sense how other people feel by their tone of voice, tears, appearance, manner and what they say or do not say. The problem is that we have been conditioned to take action to reduce the intensity of emotion when people are angry, sad or distressed. Counsellors who experienced the earlier abuse of their own children will understand the importance of controlling their urges to stop the emotional release. Having 'been there', they know its value. Other volunteers should concentrate on four things:

- the feelings behind the words;
- the content of the message;
- the nature of the body language;
- asking themselves 'How might I feel in these circumstances'.

Sometimes, the words and body language transmit conflicting messages. Sometimes, feelings are woven into the language as shown in the following exercises.

**Exercise 8.2 Reflective listening**

The leader should role-play a statement such as:

> 'That woman has wasted hours of my time. I spent five hours with her in the middle of the night and another five hours this morning. Now, she denies that there is a problem. It's all a mistake. She doesn't need any help. She reckons that her kids will forget about it if everyone just leaves them alone. The kids are completely screwed up but she's not even aware of it'.

Trainees should list the feelings that are incorporated in this statement. How do they know?

The art of good listening involves the ability to respond reflectively, that is the support worker restates the feelings or events that the speaker has communicated, using their own words in such a way that empathy and acceptance are transmitted. This is especially useful for improving child management methods as well as for listening to other parents.

**Exercise 8.3 Empathy for a child who falls**

A child falls and cuts his knee. The child cries in distress.

Response 1:
Mother says, 'Come along, we haven't got all day to waste. Stop that noise. It doesn't hurt'.
Response 2:
Mother stops to look at the knee and says, 'That must be sore. Would you like a Band-Aid when we get home?

Compare how these different responses will affect the child. How will he or she feel? How will the child respond and behave? Response 2 is a reflective response that empowers the child. Response 1 is not.

**Exercise 8.4 The child on the beach**

Dad takes the child across the pebbly beach to paddle in the sea. Both are barefoot. The child protests that he cannot walk because the pebbles are hurting his feet.

Response 1:
Dad says, 'Come along. Stop being a baby. Of course it doesn't hurt'.
Response 2:
'Yes, I'm sorry. Pebbles do hurt feet . . . mine hurt too'.

Compare how the child feels and behaves in each case. How will his or her responses affect his or her behaviour on return to the beach?

**Exercise 8.5 A bad day**

The alarm-clock fails to go off, the children are late for school, the telephone rings and the toast burns.

Response 1:
'I've been married to you for all these years and you still can't make toast without burning it'.
Response 2:
'What a bad start to the day! First the clock, then the 'phone, now the toast. What can I do to help?'.

**Compare:**

1 How would you feel if you received these two different responses?

2 What would you say in answer to them?

3 How would this affect you for the rest of the day and why?

In each case we find the essence of reflective listening in Response 2. It is:

- non-judgmental, even when wastage or carelessness has been involved;
- an accurate reflection of what each individual is experiencing and feeling;
- concise but reflects more than the words that were spoken.

Where the father denies that pebbles hurt bare feet, the child knows that he is either insensitive or lying and this causes frustration. The father's response tells the child that his judgment is unreliable and that will foster feelings of insecurity. On this and subsequent visits to the beach, the child is likely to nag about the soreness of his feet, feeling obliged to try to convince his father that there actually is a problem. All of this can be avoided by responding reflectively.

In the incident of the cut knee, the child's response will be similar. He is less likely to make a big fuss if the adult admits that the cut will hurt. The mother who burns the toast will probably respond in a very hostile way to the father who implies that she is stupid and inefficient. 'You can make your own bloody toast in future if you're so darned clever' is a typically angry response in such situations. The husband's response may even draw out other complaints about unresolved issues that occurred much earlier in the marriage. The mother is likely to have angry feelings throughout the day and possibly at breakfast the following day. The children will suffer because they are already late for school and, continuing the same line of attack, they will probably be blamed for her problems. In contrast, the reflective response gives a warm inner glow; someone understands and cares. Nothing else matters!

New counsellors feel very awkward when they begin to use reflective listening skills. They have to make a deliberate effort if they are not used in everyday life. Gradually, trainees begin to understand the many problems that are associated with communicating:

- We do not all share a common language.
- People often present their minor problems and hide the big ones. They then feel inadequate and stupid for not exposing their real problems.
- Listeners are often distracted.
- Listeners filter what is said according to their own biases and experiences.
- Speakers are often blind to their own emotions and blinded by them.

Reflective listening provides a quick check on accuracy and it disciplines the listener to really listen.

### *Reflective meanings*

When feelings and facts are joined together in one paraphrase, we have what is called a reflection of meaning. For example:

*Mother*: 'The case-worker keeps coming back to the house and asking more and more questions. I can't see the point of it. After all, it wasn't me who abused them. Next time she comes, I'll tell her to mind her own business'.

*Support worker*: 'I can see that you're annoyed because she's asking a lot of questions without explaining why they're necessary'.

Feelings may be triggered by specific events, such as the police refusing to take action, the removal of a child to a foster home or an unfavourable court decision. Trainee support workers should be given opportunities to practice reflecting meanings, working in pairs and sitting opposite each other but within arm touching distance. The speaker should describe a situation that caused strong feelings. The listener will respond reflectively using phrases such as: 'It seems that you're feeling anxious/ discouraged/ angry/ sad because . . . '. The speaker and the listener need these interjections at appropriate times to confirm understanding. Care must be taken not to add feelings that are not present.

*Summarising statements*

The summary is a brief statement which comes at the end of the conversation. The listener does not include suggestions or advice at this stage. The summary provides direction for future sessions and action. The secret of good paraphrasing is to be short and to-the-point, giving appropriate emphasis to the main facts in the listeners' own words. Paraphrasing focuses on the factual content of the message rather than the emotional content. At the same time, it should show an understanding of the feelings present in the conversation.

**Exercise 8.6 Exercise in practising paraphrasing**

Work in pairs, time needed, 20 minutes. The trainee listens carefully to the speaker without any interruption for a period of ten minutes. Suggested topics: a recent argument; a traumatic experience; a worrying experience; a negative experience, for example a court appearance.

The listener then paraphrases what has been said, first to ensure that the message has been heard correctly and, second, to provide clarity for the speaker. Five minutes should be allowed for this part of the exercise. Another five minutes should be given for discussion. Is the speaker satisfied with the paraphrasing? Were any major points missed? Did the listener emphasise the important issues?

**Exercise 8.7 Exercise in practising paraphrasing**

Again, work in pairs. One person from each pair receives a typed statement to read to the other. For example:

> I don't know whether I want to leave him or not. I can't get a job. I haven't been trained for anything. And, apart from that, there's the baby to look after. How can I work full-time with a baby? And if I left home, where would I go? The house is rented in his name, not mine. He isn't likely to leave. At the same time, I don't want to put the kids at risk again . . . and they would be at risk with him. I would have to watch them twenty-four hours a day and never let them out of my sight. That wouldn't be any good for any of us. I just don't know what to do.

The listener then paraphrases the statement for evaluation by the speaker. The pair should then change roles and use a different exercise.

Trainees' examples of paraphrasing may be discussed to demonstrate variety but not to show which is right or wrong or best or worst. Ideally, paraphrasing should sound something like this: 'I think you're saying that you really have to leave home to keep your children safe but you will need emergency housing and child care if you are to get a job. Is that right?'. If the paraphrasing is accurate, the speaker usually confirms, 'Yes, that's right'; if it is wrong, they will make the necessary correction.

The summary pulls together the main points: 'As I have been listening to you, it seems to me that your main concerns are . . .'.

*Interruptions*

One of the more important lessons in learning to listen to others effectively involves the identification of the many subtle and not-so-subtle methods that we use for stopping conversations. When and why do we interrupt others? Is it because we are bored and do not want to listen? Do we have a resistance to what is being said? Do we feel that we have something more important to say? Does the line of conversation seem to be interfering with our plans for what is going to happen next? Do we want to speak to another group member at this time? In other words, do we want to consciously or unconsciously gain control? Trainees should be encouraged to examine their own behaviour and to try to understand what they do, how and why they do it. They should be invited to describe their behaviour before discussing how it affects communications. It is useful to keep reminding trainees why they are there: they are there *for* the other person and not themselves.

Examples of different kinds of interruption:

1 Interrupting too soon: 'Yes, I understand what you mean'—this cuts the speaker short. The hidden message is, 'I am so clever, you

don't need to tell me, I know it all. I've heard it all before so don't bore me to death'.

2 Pretending to misunderstand: 'I'm sorry, I don't really understand what you mean' can imply that 'your communication skills are poor and I don't really want to hear about it anyway'.

3 Passing the buck: 'Well, that's really your problem'—this can imply that the client should be able to sort out his or her own problems without help and, if they are unable to do this they must be dumb.

4 Changing the subject abruptly: 'Excuse me just a moment, I must have a word with Jane before she leaves'. This can leave people feeling 'up in the air' as if what they said was not important.

5 Changing the subject by referring to the factual or intellectual content rather than the emotional issues: 'Yes, I've read that children do that. Why do you think that it happens?'. This implies that the problem is really quite trivial and the speaker should not take him or herself too seriously.

6 Showing boredom or absent-mindedness: 'Sorry, what was that? I'm sorry but I've just remembered that I should have telephoned someone half an hour ago'. In other words, keep it short, you're wasting my time because I have more important things to do.

7 Shock: 'He didn't really do that did he?', indicating that the listener cannot cope with what has been said.

8 Denial: 'I don't believe it! You must be exaggerating. It can't be true!' (usually with appropriate body-language).

9 Reassuring the speaker before he or she has finished, suggesting that, 'We don't need to hear any more because you are now in our capable hands. We'll fix everything'.

10 Condescending: 'Do tell me about it. I know that I can help you'.

11 Acting the role of lawyer: 'You should say the alleged abuser, he hasn't been convicted yet' or, 'I'd be careful who I say that to if I were you . . . it could be slanderous', or 'I'll pretend that I didn't hear that'.

12 Joking about what has just been said, showing that it is not worth worrying about and should not be taken seriously.

13 Making no response at all when a response would be appropriate.

14 Punishing the speaker: 'I don't think that you should have said that' . . . 'That's not fair' . . . 'You have no right to say that'.

15 Interrupting with your own irrelevant feelings: 'Yes, that happened to me too', implying 'Why don't you listen to me. My feelings and experiences are just as important'.

There are many other examples of how we interrupt and stop conversations and trainees should be encouraged to make their own lists.

**Exercise 8.8 Role-play**

Role-play can be used effectively to demonstrate how interruption methods are used and to what effect. Work in pairs and discuss a topic of mutual interest with one member of each pair being briefed in advance to attempt to try out different techniques for distracting and interrupting the flow of conversation. After, say, ten minutes, those who interrupted should be invited to describe and discuss their various attempts at interruption. Those whose conversations were disrupted should be asked to describe how they felt.

## Questioning

Questioning is a powerful teaching tool. It is used to determine and change the direction of thought and conversation. Questions encourage trainees and clients to think about matters which they had not previously considered. Open questioning can:

- Motivate and arouse interest in something that had not been considered before. Questions should be open-ended—they cannot be answered using 'Yes' or 'No'.
- Draw out existing knowledge to relate to different possibilities.
- Clarify knowledge and understanding—'What do you think might happen if . . .', 'What do you think is happening?'.
- Find out whether group members have learned what was required —'How?', 'Why do you think?', 'Suppose that . . .', 'What is . . .'.
- Help to apply knowledge—'Can you tell me what will happen if . . .?'.
- Develop relationships.
- Control—'Do you think you should have done that? How do you think you could have handled it differently?'.
- Help to recall facts—'Do you remember the first time when . . .? Can you recall what was said?'.
- Challenge and encourage creative thinking, such as 'What do you think might happen if . . .? What do you really want to happen?', 'What else could you do?'.

*Helpful hints on how to avoid misunderstandings*

- Start out with questions that new clients will be able to answer easily so that their self-confidence grows.
- Plan questions that are in short, clear sentences: avoid using either/or choices.

- Ask one question at a time and wait for the answer before asking another.
- Ask questions in a logical sequence.
- Use open-ended questions to avoid misunderstandings.
- Accept a part response and acknowledge that the question was hard; thank the client for making the effort.
- Repeat questions if necessary, changing or stressing key words until the meaning is clear: 'Let's see if we can put the question another way . . .'. Remember that we use jargon that new clients may not understand.
- Ensure that all clients are encouraged to answer questions.
- Avoid favouritism: when the same people are selected repeatedly, others stop attempting to answer.

When questions are put to a group of people, each contribution must be acknowledged courteously, irrespective of whether the answer is the one that is expected. Some group leaders ask questions but ignore the answers from people who do not say exactly what is required. The leaders' method of communication is to point at the group member, giving permission to speak. They do not call group members by name nor do they thank them for their responses. As soon as these leaders realise that the answer is not the one they need, their eye contact moves elsewhere and, without saying a word, they point to someone else. The process is repeated until the required response is heard. This method of questioning devalues group members to the extent that they soon stop responding. When the questioner fails to acknowledge their statements, they feel resentful.

Parents in groups are often nervous about how they will be judged by other people when they answer questions. Nervousness affects their answers, causing panic and hesitation when questions are directed to them. They worry that they will look foolish and that others will be rude and laugh at them. If anxiety is high, they will avoid answering rather than risk the possibility of being criticised.

People only enjoy questions when they have a reasonable chance of answering them well. They need encouragement and praise for effort, recognition that 'sorry but it was a hard one'. They need open-ended questions for which there is no right and wrong answer. They may need help, for example, 'That was a good try but can you think of something even safer?' . . . 'Can you think of someone who would be even more helpful?' rather than 'Don't be silly!'.

*Helping parent–clients to find direction*

There are often many difficult decisions to be made by the non-offending parents of child victims of sexual abuse. Parents should be helped to identify the problems and identify the variety of possible options that are available to them. The question and answer method is very useful for helping clients to think things through for themselves. Questions may refer to the children's safety for the future. For example: 'What will happen if you stay with him? How can you ensure that the children are safe? Do you have anywhere to go if you leave home? What will happen if you leave him? How do you see the future if you stay? What do you want for the future for yourself? What kind of future do you want for your children?'. Flow charts are useful teaching aids as some people learn more easily visually than verbally.

It is possible that recently enrolled clients will not know the answers to some questions. Counsellors can help by informing non-offending parents of their rights, other support services available and possible options for legal aid, accommodation, job-seeking, child care and safety. The counsellor also has the right to state his or her own position: 'I know that you could handle it with some support from other mothers here' . . . 'I suggest that . . . . would be a good place to start'.

## Handling manipulative people

Not all clients or volunteers are nice, kind, co-operative people who are easy-to-get-on-with. Some are manipulative and demand more of everything than anyone else. Such people prevent quiet members from making their contribution. Some talk constantly to familiarise themselves with what is happening but they never pause to listen to anything that is said. There are several dos and don'ts for group leaders for handling manipulative people effectively.

1 Be courteous at all times. Never use sarcasm or 'put downs' because these will have a ripple effect and damage the relationships in the group.
2 Fix time limits for group discussion so that dominant members can be reminded that they only have one minute left and, at the end of that minute, their time is up.
3 If an individual persists in talking continuously and dominating the group, the leader should take that person aside at a convenient moment and say, 'I can see that you are really anxious tonight. Will you come to talk to me after the group session? In the meantime, everyone has to be given the same amount of time to express their feelings and views'.

4 If the dominant person disregards polite requests, the leader should interrupt in a calm, quiet way and say that it is time that someone else had a turn to speak.
5 Always speak from the 'I' position—'I can't allow one group member to take control of the entire session' . . . 'I get very angry when . . .' (*not* 'You make me angry').
6 Describe the unacceptable behaviour in an unemotional, factual way without suggesting motives or personality defects.
7 Respect your own rights and the rights of other group members.
8 Never argue. Make your statement simply, clearly and, if necessary, repetitively. Arguing will weaken your position and enable the manipulator to side-track you. Ignore hostile remarks about your capabilities.
9 Ensure that responsibility for the problem is correctly allocated. Make your responsibility to the group quite clear.
10 When all else fails, walk away and say, 'I'm very angry about this. I shall have to give myself time to simmer down and think it over'. It is important to remain in control. However, in serious cases of breach of confidence and unacceptable behaviour, it is appropriate to show our anger in a controlled way. Remember that manipulative people gain control when we lose it.

Use the following exercise to provide students with the opportunity to work on a case study involving unacceptable client behaviour.

*Case study* Mrs R never stops talking. She uses every group meeting to talk about her problems. Other people's problems are disregarded. She is boring and repetitive and goes over the same things again and again. Members complain that 'No-one else can get a word in'. Whose responsibility is it to resolve this problem? How would you do it?
Try role-playing the conversation between yourself and Mrs R using different approaches until you find one that is satisfactory to both parties.

## Gender differences in communications

Research shows that power is reflected in the use of language. Sociologist Pamela Fishman (1975) found that women have to work harder to participate in conversations in mixed company, especially conversations involving their husbands. She analysed how many topics 'succeeded' and 'failed' when they were introduced by men and women in mixed groups. Even though the couples considered themselves to be liberated from traditional sex-role stereotypes, the topics introduced by men took up 96 per cent of the time while topics introduced by women were pursued only 36 per cent of the time. Women asked three times as many questions as men and said, 'You know', ten times more frequently than men to try to gain their interest. Men 'killed' women's attempts to express concerns by saying 'Um' or making no response at all and/or returning to a point made by another male speaker earlier in the conversation, devaluing the woman's contribution.

When conversations involved husbands and wives, women found it difficult to talk and be heard. In groups, women listened respectfully to men but groups of men did not show women the same courtesy. In mixed groups, men are likely to assume the right to talk, to choose the topic and to take control. Dale Spender (1979) found that, in a group of thirty-two females and five males, men dominated the conversation for thirty-two minutes out of fifty-eight. Simultaneously, a survey of the group showed that most people believed that the women talked much more than men.

If females want to talk in mixed company, they have to talk to each other and, even then, they may be interrupted by men. Researchers Zimmerman and West (1975) found that men interrupt women more than women interrupt men. When leaders are women, they accommodate politely to men. When men lead, they give priority to members of their own sex.

These findings are relevent to leaders of mixed groups. They suggest that it might be difficult for wives to express their views and feelings openly and without interruption in the presence of their husbands. On the other hand, some dominant women may answer questions addressed to their husbands using the royal 'We'. Leaders should discreetly tape and carefully observe what happens at mixed meetings.

## Communications checklist

| | |
|---|---|
| Non-verbal encouragement | A nod of the head with eye-to-eye contact<br>Smiles and eye-to-eye contact<br>A gentle touch on the hand or arm<br>A hug or pat on the shoulder |
| Verbal encouragement | 'Yes, I see'<br>'Yes, I understand'<br>'Mmmm' |
| Reflecting feelings | 'I can see that you're angry'<br>'I can see that you're upset'<br>'You're feeling very confused right now'<br>'It is very difficult for you' |
| Reflecting meanings | 'You are feeling angry/hurt/sad because . . .' |
| Open-ended questions | 'How do you feel about . . . Can you tell me about . . .?'<br>'What do you think about . . . What might happen if . . .?' |
| Closed questions | 'Did he . . .? When did . . .? Am I right in thinking that . . .?' |
| Paraphrasing | Repeating essential points in a succinct way, focusing on the main message. |
| Summarising statements | 'Let's go over what you've told me so far' 'Can I just see if I've understood you correctly' |

# 9 Some practical considerations for managing parent groups staffed by volunteers

## The skills needed by group leaders

Most groups appoint a salaried part-time or full-time coordinator. Curtis and Noble (1988) describe the term coordinator as a misnomer in this context: the job involves the recruitment, selection, training and deployment of volunteers, the development of a policy on volunteering, maintaining communications with professional bodies and media, attending community and management meetings, publishing newsletters, budgeting and fund-raising while maintaining a democratic policy within the group. The managers liaise with other community agencies and assist in setting up new groups. These tasks all require skills beyond those of a coordinator: they include the skills of a personnel manager, training officer, public relations officer, fund-raiser and service provider. In the early stages of the group's development, they may be undertaken by one person who, fortunately, does not pause to look at the breadth of the task. Most group organisers learn these skills on the job, out of sheer necessity.

The skills needed can be summarised as follows:

- interviewing and listening to volunteers and parents;
- decision-making on a day-to-day and long-term basis;
- managing conflict in a positive way;
- conducting meetings efficiently;
- writing reports and submissions;

- enthusing others;
- creating a positive, supportive environment for workers and clients;
- developing skills in others;
- utilising community and professional resources to the advantage of the group.

Personal attributes must include:

- empathy for parents and volunteers and sensitivity to their needs;
- patience and persistence;
- optimism and strength of commitment;
- energy;
- the ability to relate well to others, irrespective of race, social class or religion.

For personal growth and survival, leaders should:

- establish support networks for themselves with others in related fields;
- develop a sound knowledge of local resources and personnel involved;
- attend seminars, workshops and conferences relating to child sexual abuse (in the early stages, this necessitates publicising the existence of the group to ensure that it appears on professional mailing lists);
- acknowledging the advantages of working with volunteers and ensuring that their needs are nurtured and their wishes safeguarded;
- delegate.

Volunteer leaders, like all good managers, need to be concerned about people. Ultimately, the success of leaders is not judged by how much personal effort they put into the job, but by the size and efficiency of the workforce and the quality of the service provided. The future of the group depends on the leader's ability to motivate and delegate. Unless volunteers gain job satisfaction and can see their value to clients, they will take their energies elsewhere.

The greatest danger occurs when the group is run by a small number of workaholic long-serving devotees who view the service possessively as their own 'baby'. Because their lives centre around the agency, they become close friends and maintain contact in non-working hours. In tight cliques of this kind, volunteers are deprived of responsibilities of any worth and, feeling undervalued, they resign. This ensures that the group either becomes so small that it collapses or the leaders are constantly training volunteers whose services are wasted. In the long term, either of these situations will result in the destruction of the group because no organisation can operate successfully with a handful of workaholics, least of all when they are functioning in one of the most emotionally draining areas of work.

## The need for a volunteer recruitment policy

Good recruitment policies result in more satisfied and committed volunteers, less strain on management and better service delivery. Groups should be specific about how many new volunteers they expect to need in the forthcoming year so that there is no massive recruitment campaign that results in too many bodies, not enough trainers and not enough work.

Recruitment policy should target specific categories of people who are most likely to have the necessary skills to contribute to the agency. In child protection work, the people most likely to show interest are those parents whose children have been abused, survivors of childhood abuse and those who have had contact with abused children in other areas of work. It is worth noting however that Parentline-Hamilton (NZ) recruits twenty-five new trainees annually, 80 per cent of whom are 'caring people' in the community who do not fall into any of the above categories. This is regarded as an advantage because those who have experienced abuse need to resolve their own anger and hurt before they can help others. They may need a lot of time-consuming support and help before they can take on the counselling role. When hurting people take on the role prematurely, they tend to relate all that they hear to their own experiences and cannot listen attentitively to other people's distress.

It should be noted that all volunteers do not have to become counsellors—there are many roles in an organisation, including typists, book-keepers, telephonists and public relations officers. There are many different reasons why volunteers offer their services. Their four basic needs can be seen in the following table:

**Table 9.1 Volunteers**

| *Volunteers' needs* | *Volunteers' expectations* |
|---|---|
| To fill personal aspirations | • Satisfaction from doing good works and helping other people worse off than ourselves<br>• To tackle realistic challenges<br>• To improve the world |
| To meet social needs | • To make new friendships<br>• To have team involvement |
| Help to manage a personal problem | • To gain coping skills |
| To develop self-esteem, status and new skills | • To develop confidence and competence |

When developing a recruitment policy, these needs and expectations need to be taken into account.

Successful interviewing requires special skills that should be included in the group leader training programme. Interviewers should remember that interviewees are volunteers and they are doing the agency a favour. The service would not be able to function without them. Interviews should be conducted on time, in privacy and assurances must be given that personal disclosures will be confidential. This is especially important if recruits are survivors of child abuse. Disclosures of abuse require very careful, sensitive probing to see whether the applicant has recovered from the ordeal and is ready for training or whether counselling or further counselling is advisable. Interviewees should be helped to feel as comfortable as possible. A cup of tea is a good idea and remember that, if there are forms to complete, people who are either not accustomed to form-filling or those who use English as a second-language may prefer help. Applicants are often nervous, even though they are applying to give their free time to the organisation. They may worry about the possibility of being rejected or, alternatively, about the risk of 'biting off more than they can chew'.

When applicants are fully aware of the variety of tasks involved, they should be asked what kind of work they would like to do in the agency. A mutual decision then has to be made. Is the applicant a person who listened carefully or one who dominated the conversation with very rigid, black and white views? Although some people talk when they are nervous, there will be little scope for using interviewees as counsellors if they never stop talking. The success of the agency depends on listening skills and, however great the shortage of workers, clients' needs must be borne in mind. Other roles should be readily available for those who lack counselling skills.

If the answers to the questions were realistic and the volunteer is not expecting to change the universe single-handed, a trial period should be suggested, fixing a date for a review of progress. Some clients ask for time to consider the implications and this request should be respected. It often indicates that the applicant is not yet ready to make the necessary commitment.

**Leadership styles used with volunteers**

Four types of leadership are used with groups of volunteers:

- Direction Needed for volunteers who have a high level of commitment but lack relevant knowledge or experience.
- Tuition Direct teaching and support are needed for those who have some competence and not much commitment.

- Support Praising effort and improvement, listening, giving responsibilities to competent volunteers who have varying levels of commitment.
- Delegation Volunteers are given responsibilities for making decisions in areas where they are competent and show commitment.

One of the dangers for experienced leaders is that they often convince themselves that they are the only people who have the skills and experience needed to fulfil important tasks. That line of thinking results in leaders becoming overloaded while the volunteers make tea. Those leaders who attempt to hold all the reins and accept responsibility for everything invariably fail.

Leaders should bear in mind that they must not do jobs that others have the time to do and could probably do better. They should ensure that they do not saddle themselves with jobs that they dislike when others might enjoy them. They should forget that age-old saying, 'If you want a job done well, do it yourself'. Delegation involves job-sharing, ensuring that more work is accomplished and that others gain competence in a variety of skills. Delegation is essential for growth and survival. It increases democratic participation so that volunteers feel that they are valued partners in the provision of an important service. Leaders who do not delegate, lose their staff.

There are times when delegation is unwise, for example, when the job requires continuity or full-time commitment and the volunteers attend only infrequently, or if volunteers lack the necessary skills to undertake the task successfully. To develop their skills, it is usual for volunteers to accompany leaders engaged in complex tasks. There *must* be trust in delegation. Instead of checking up on the volunteer's performance, good leadership encourages self-evaluation, i.e. volunteers are given regular opportunities to consider their own performance and identify their own strengths and weaknesses and those skills in need of further development.

## Delegation

The volunteers' skills will have been assessed at the first interview and further assessment may be necessary to take account of recent experience and training. To ensure the efficient utilisation of staff:

- involve volunteers and co-workers in the decision-making process;
- identify all the tasks involved in the organisation;
- split the larger tasks into subsections, for example public relations will involve a variety of jobs including contact with the press,

professional agencies and community education which all require different expertise;
- assessment should then be made of what skills are needed for each job;
- job descriptions may be written, showing duties and skills needed;
- select the jobs to be delegated and seek volunteers for the tasks;
- identify how much support the volunteers will need;
- ensure that the volunteers know the limits of their responsibilities, know the arrangements for feedback and debriefing and how to get access to support.

## Decision making

Some people try to avoid making decisions. Mothers who have spent most of their adult lives at home with children may have had most major decisions made for them. They bring their procrastination to the group, hoping that if they delay decisions, problems will go away. The reverse tends to be true. Guidelines for decision making can be summed up as follows:

- Recognise when a decision is important or unimportant. Ask 'Could this decision have far-reaching consequences that require careful thought? What are those consequences?'.
- Consider the picture as a whole. How does the problem or the decision relate to the group's philosophy and goals? Who will be affected by the decision? Have they been consulted? It is much easier to make changes if the parties most affected recognise the need for change and are supportive. However, do not take that recognition and support for granted.
- What are the likely causes of the problem? Differentiate fact and opinion.
- Who is in the best position to provide an informed opinion based on knowledge of the total situation? Have they been consulted?
- Examine all aspects of the situation with factual information. Brainstorm the advantages and disadvantages with the people concerned and draw up a list consisting of arguments 'for' and 'against' so that differences can be seen clearly.
- Brainstorm other options for action in the short term and the long term.

Remember that most people are afraid of change and resist it because it makes them feel uncomfortable and out of control. In voluntary agencies, the introduction of new methods and new goals often results in the resignation of members. This possibility must be considered when change is debated.

*Checklist for decision makers*

| | Often | Sometimes | Never |
|---|---|---|---|
| I enjoy making decisions | | | |
| I make decisions when I have a gut feeling | | | |
| I consider who is the best person to talk to and rely on their opinion | | | |
| I involve anyone who happens to be around | | | |
| I only get involved in minor decisions | | | |
| I leave major decisions to the committee | | | |
| I don't want the responsibility of making decisions | | | |

**Exercise 9.1 Decision making**

1 Think of a decision that needs to be made in the parent support group and use the above guidelines for working out how the decision should be made.
2 Think of a decision that has already been made when results were unsatisfactory. Using the guidelines, work out what went wrong. How should it have been handled?

## Showing appreciation

Everyone needs positive feedback for their efforts. They need to be appreciated whether they are paid or unpaid. Volunteers do not have to put up with miserable working conditions and they will leave if they feel that they are being taken for granted. New volunteers are especially vulnerable when they lack confidence in themselves, are afraid of criticism and of 'doing (or saying) the wrong thing'. When people do not receive regular feedback, they quickly lose interest.

Recognition of effort can be shown by sending thankyou cards when an outstanding job has been done, by visiting volunteers when they are sick, by having social occasions such as barbecues, group birthday celebrations, group outings to shows or cinemas followed by supper. These events are important for building the social network of supporters and make all the difference between a paid job and a voluntary role. Responsibilities for organisation should be shared whenever possible.

Leaders should ensure that volunteers eat and have coffee breaks when they are on duty. Coffee and tea are usually provided free of charge to volunteer workers.

Another form of recognition is for leaders to take volunteers to meetings, workshops and conferences. Additional training and responsibility increases confidence, commitment and competence.

A personal interest should be shown in the volunteer who is suffering from stress, such as a sick child, a husband in hospital or a bereavement. Telephone calls, a bouquet of flowers and a card signed by other support workers can do much to boost morale in these circumstances.

## Confronting inappropriate behaviour

When a volunteer is not performing satisfactorily, it is best to approach the problem from the volunteer's perspective, enquiring whether he or she is enjoying the work and feeling confident and discussing what can be done to increase the volunteer's confidence and skill. It is better for volunteers to identify their weaknesses than for leaders to criticise.

When there are serious difficulties with a volunteer's performance however, the problem has to be confronted. When workers are troublesome within the group, it is often because they are not being sufficiently challenged and they are bored. When volunteers are aggressive, abrupt and rude, it is necessary to find out what is troubling them. 'I am concerned about you. I know that you're unhappy about something. You have been very sharp lately. Can we talk about it?'. If the behaviour persists, it will be necessary to discuss moving the volunteer to an area of work that is less stressful and where there is less contact with other people. Asking volunteers to resign is a last resort although, at that stage, workers usually recognise that they have problems. They are usually unhappy and are sometimes relieved that the decision has been taken for them.

## Conflict resolution

Conflict often arises in voluntary agencies. This can be attributed to the fact that volunteers realise that they do not have to be there and will only stay if the experience brings satisfaction. Most volunteers have high expectations of the benefits available from membership of the organisation and they will not be prepared to 'put up with' procedures and behaviour that make them feel uncomfortable.

There is also always a high level of emotional commitment to voluntary work. Long-established workers may resist change and feel threatened by the arrival of new workers who bring new perspectives and suggestions for change. The pioneer workers argue that they have been doing things in the same way for years and this is how they should continue. They imply, even if they do not say, that 'Everything was alright until you came. We don't need you'. This kind of situation has to be tackled quickly because it results in the fragmentation of the group; the old members stick together and make the new members feel unwelcome. This is a recipe for disaster because no organisation can continue without responding to changes in knowledge and clients' needs.

Different people have different goals within the same organisation. Successful organisations are those which manage to accommodate these differences, for example some people may think that the support group should operate on a one-to-one counselling basis while others prefer group work. Both types of service can be made available in one organisation. Some members may want to make maximum use of media publicity to increase support; others find publicity embarrassing. The matter can be resolved if the media enthusiasts ensure that the unenthusiastic members are not involved. Some members may have ethical reasons for wanting to decline funds from, say, breweries, lotteries or cigarette manufacturers. Others believe that sexual abuse is a community problem and that all sectors of the community should pay.

In addition, all groups find themselves dealing with internal problems that stem from malicious gossip, the group's failure to meet commitments, ignorance, prejudice, favouritism, poor management, lack of planning and personality problems. Some people want power for themselves and they try to dominate others. If they don't 'get their own way', they behave like children who threaten to 'take their bat home'. This is a form of emotional blackmail that can work very successfully. When the blackmailers were the early pioneers of the organisation, the long-serving members leap to their defence, making pleas for them to withdraw their resignation. Satisfied that they are loved and irreplaceable, they can ensure that change is delayed. New members feel that they are wasting their time and resign.

Different strategies are used for dealing with group problems:

- Avoidance Look the other way, pretend that you did not see or hear it. Tell yourself that if you do nothing, the problem will go away and 'they'll worrying about something else next week'.
- Defusion Cool the situation down, make a cup of tea, postpone confrontation, operate delay tactics—set up a meeting in a week's time with a sub-committee that does not have to report back, ask

someone to enquire into the problem, knowing that they move only slowly. If the problem is minor, the delay may work but, in most cases, members become dissatisfied with the quality of leadership.

- Confrontation Use power, authority and threats, resulting in resentment and withdrawal of support.
- Negotiation Analyse where the problem lies and seek a resolution that is acceptable to the main parties involved.

Negotiation can be conducted as follows:

- React to the complainant with: 'I am glad that you decided to come to talk to me about this. I've been concerned too. Let's take a look at how we can resolve this problem together'.
- Listen carefully to the complainant's point of view then summarise what has been said, calmly and unemotionally: 'What I hear you saying is this . . . Now, have I understood you correctly?'.
- If another party is involved, approach that person in a similar, calm way: 'I sense that there are difficulties relating to . . . Can we talk about it?'. The discussion should take place in a room where there is absolute privacy and no risk of disturbance.
- Jointly clarify the issues and where each person stands. Examine how the dispute relates to the agreed rules, philosophy and values of the organisation. Brainstorm possible solutions and record them. Examine each suggestion for advantages and disadvantages for the individuals concerned as well as clients and other workers. Decide which strategy to try, arrange a trial period and another meeting to discuss whether the strategy worked.

**Exercise 9.2 The resolution of conflict**

Think of a conflict that caused serious problems in the group. What was the cause? How was it handled? What was the result? Discuss how it might have been handled more effectively.

## Record-keeping

The maintenance of records requires time, space and organisation. When setting up a new group, pioneers tend to keep every piece of paper. The move to another venue changes that trend and group leaders need to ask themselves what should be recorded and stored, why, when, by whom and for what purpose.

Individual work records are useful for personal recognition. They also help groups to gain financial support if it can be shown how many hours

**Figure 9.1 Record of work experience**

| | |
|---|---|
| Name: | Dates: |
| Face-to-face counselling with parents: | |
| Telephone counselling: | |
| Report writing: | |
| Clerical work: | |
| Typing: | |
| Public relations: | |
| Press releases: | |
| Transporting/accompanying parents/children to court: | |
| Transporting/accompanying parents/children to medical examinations: | |
| Participation in community education: | |
| Participation with a parent group: | |
| Lobbying: | |
| Home visits: | |
| Other experiences with the parent support group: | |

of voluntary work were contributed in a year and how workers were deployed. Similarly, organisations should be able to present statistics relating to how many parents they have helped in a given period, how those parents learned about the service, who referred them and from which locality. It is also beneficial to quote how many telephone counselling sessions took place in the previous year when writing submissions for financial assistance towards the payment of telephone bills. When applying for help with accommodation, it is usual to show how many clients have joined parent support groups and how many called at the centre for informal support or formal counselling.

A decision has to be made about the format to be used for record-keeping (see Figures 9.1, 9.2, 9.3), how and where records will be filed, bearing in mind the need for accessibility and, on the other hand, the importance of confidentiality and security. Once that decision has been made, the appropriate forms have to be produced, files created and responsibility apportioned for filing, collating and reviewing records.

**Figure 9.2 Training record**

| Date | Training session attended |
|---|---|
| | |
| Conferences, seminars and workshops attended: | |
| | |

Please note that this record must be made available to the individual concerned. It should be updated regularly to ensure that support workers can see the record of their developing skills.

The question must then be asked, 'What training is needed to make record-keeping efficient?'.

*Recording telephone calls from clients*

Every telephone call should be recorded in a book. For convenience, the pages should be divided into columns to note the following information:

- Reference number.
- Date and time of the call received.
- Name and telephone number of caller (if provided).
- Name and age of the child referred to.
- Name of the accused person and his/her relationship to the child.
- The reason for the call.

**Figure 9.3 Sample of client record card**

| | | |
|---|---|---|
| Client No. . . . . . . . . . . . . . . . . . . . . . | First contact made: . . . . . . . . . . . . . . . . | |
| Name of client: . . . . . . . . . . . . . . . . . | Male/female | |
| Address: . . . . . . . . . . . . . . . . . . . . . | | |
| . . . . . . . . . . . . . . . . . . . . . . . . . . . | | |
| Home telephone No. . . . . . . . . . . . . . | Other contact No. . . . . . . . . . . . . . . . . . . . | |
| Marital status: . . . . . . . . . . . . . . . . . | No. of children . . . . . . . . . . . . . . . . . . . . | |
| Referred by: . . . . . . . . . . . . . . . . . . . . . . . . . . . . . . . . . . . . . . . . . . . . . . . . . . . . . . . . | | |
| Telephone counselling: | | |
| . . . . . . . . . . . . . . . . . . . . . . . . . . . . . . . . . . . . . . . . . . . . . . . . . . . . . . . . . . . . . | | |
| . . . . . . . . . . . . . . . . . . . . . . . . . . . . . . . . . . . . . . . . . . . . . . . . . . . . . . . . . . . . . | | |
| . . . . . . . . . . . . . . . . . . . . . . . . . . . . . . . . . . . . . . . . . . . . . . . . . . . . . . . . . . . . . | | |
| Attendance at group sessions: . . . . . . . . . . . . . . . . . . . . . . . . . . . . . . . . . . . . . . . . . | | |
| . . . . . . . . . . . . . . . . . . . . . . . . . . . . . . . . . . . . . . . . . . . . . . . . . . . . . . . . . . . . . | | |
| Informal attendance: . . . . . . . . . . . . . . . . . . . . . . . . . . . . . . . . . . . . . . . . . . . . . . . . . | | |
| Referred to: . . . . . . . . . . . . . . | on: . . . . . . . . . . . . . . | by: . . . . . . . . . . . . . . . . . |
| Help needed for: | | |
| Progress: | | |

Personal record cards should be made available to the clients on request. Confidential information should always be filed in a locked filing system.

- Name of person receiving the call.
- Action taken and/or name of agency to whom the caller was referred.

## To meet or not to meet?

Meetings can become habit-forming, time-consuming and irritatingly wasteful, especially when they are routine and have no specific purpose. Managers of voluntary groups often get carried away with meetings, especially if they enjoy power games. Many talented people are then lost because they are unwilling to waste their valuable time sitting at sessions which focus on matters that could be settled informally. When formal meetings are necessary, an agenda must be delivered to participants well in advance and a time limit must be set. There must be an efficient chairperson and a secretary. Minutes must be kept and copies forwarded to the relevant parties after the meeting.

The chairperson must be sufficiently confident to call the meeting to order and keep the discussion strictly on track. The chairperson has a duty to ensure that the meeting sticks to the time limit, that discussion focuses on agenda issues and permission to speak is obtained from the chair. There are many books available on how to run meetings efficiently. Leaders should remember that, if a meeting is worth the time involved, it is worth doing well.

## Group programme reviews and evaluations

Each group should compile its own list of aspects to be reviewed or evaluated annually. In parent support groups, the list may include:

- Discussion of the recruitment of volunteers:
  Does the system of recruitment attract people of the right calibre?
  If not, what changes can be made?
  A brainstorming session with members might throw up suggestions not previously considered.
- Community relations: are potential clients aware of the service?
  Where is the service currently publicised?
  Have there been staff changes in professional agencies?
  Should visits or telephone calls be made to those agencies?
  What other action could be taken to ensure that the service reaches people in need?
- Working conditions: are they comfortable?
  Do they provide privacy when necessary? What steps can be taken to improve the facilities? Are work materials always available when needed? (If not, identify the cause of the problem and how it can be remedied).
- Efficient deployment of volunteers: are their skills fully utilised? Provide evaluation forms to check the levels of satisfaction experienced by workers. Why are they satisfied or dissatisfied with what they do?
- Training: ask volunteers to complete evaluation sheets.
  Check whether their training prepared them adequately for their roles.
  What changes would they like to see implemented?

- Support: is this designed to build self-esteem and confidence?
  How many volunteers have developed new skills?
  How many have resigned and why did they resign?
- Staff relationships: do these demonstrate trust and a shared commitment to helping children and families or do staff back-bite, gossip and put each other down? If the latter, attention should be given to leaders setting a better example.
- Relationships with professional agencies: is the group receiving maximum support from related professional agencies? If not, why not?
  How are thanks expressed for help received?

Group programme evaluation sheets should be completed and reviewed.

## Summary

There is a huge potential workforce within the community. That workforce has political and social implications if it can be harnessed to help families whose children have been abused. For the volunteer worker, the parent support group offers the opportunity to benefit from personal development in a welfare and community education field and to lobby for a better justice and protection system for children. Volunteers enhance and extend existing services, ensuring that there is a direct line between the community need and government service providers. Those who help others, help themselves and there is much to be gained from volunteer involvement by clients and volunteers alike.

Group leaders are urged to read:

Curtis, M., Noble, J., (1988) *Volunteer Management: A Resource Manual*, published by the Volunteer Centre of South Australia which was of enormous assistance in writing the section of this book relating to the care and selection of volunteers. The manual has been widely used in the training of volunteers for parent support groups. There are many other useful publications on this subject:

Blanchard, K., Johnson, S., (1987) *The One Minute Manager*, Fontana/Collins Paperbacks.

Bolton, R., (1986) *People Skills*, Prentice-Hall Australia.

Brown, K.M. (1982) *Keys to Making a Volunteer Program Work*, Ardemn Publications, Richmond, Calif.

Schindler-Rainman, E. and Lippitt, R. (1984) *The Volunteer Community*, International Authors, BV USA.

Sheard, J. (1986) *The Politics of Volunteering*, Advice and Development for Volunteering and Neighbourhood Care, London.

# 10 The grief process for parents of sexually abused children

When a child we love has been sexually abused, we grieve for the loss of the child's innocence. We grieve for the loss of the life that we knew, realising that nothing will ever be quite the same again. If the abuser was someone we know, there will be grief for the loss of trust. If the abuser is a spouse or partner, there will be devastating changes to the relationship and to family life, possibly resulting in separation, the loss of the family home and financial security. The world becomes a very hostile and lonely place and it is easy to slip into thinking that there is nothing left to live for.

Grief is the difficult process that we must go through if we are to reach an understanding of the extent of our loss and to make the necessary adaptations for survival. Although no two people grieve in exactly the same way, several distinct stages can be identified, each of which has a specific purpose. These include shock, denial, emotional release, anger, blame, shame and guilt, an inability to return to normal life and, finally, healing and adjustment. Some people pass through these stages sequentially while others experience several stages simultaneously. The situation varies from day to day and changes according to circumstances. It is useful if support counsellors can draw parents' attention to this normal sequence.

## Shock

It seems that human beings are capable of suffering great pain, sorrow and tragedy and not only survive but emerge to create a new but different life. The first emotional and physical defence mechanism is shock. A state of shock produces chemical reactions in the brain which have two functions: first, to provide the energy that we need to attend to the business aspects of the tragedy; second, to cushion us from the succession of blows that follow any major loss. Shock produces a sense of light-heartedness and disconnection. This may give such an appearance of calm and detachment that support-workers say, 'She's taking it very well', or even, 'She doesn't seem to care. She just carried on ironing. Her husband was watching the cricket on TV. He doesn't want to know anything about it. We had to talk in the kitchen. He kept telling his wife to shut up'.

Some shocked parents appear to function on 'automatic pilot'. Like zombies, they go through the motions of living but cannot remember anything of importance. Afterwards, they can recall their feelings at the time of the disclosure but they forget most of what was said. For that reason, it is often useful for support workers to help parents to recollect what happened.

### Denial

When we learn that something terrible has happened to someone who plays a significant part in our lives, one of our first responses is likely to be that of denial: 'Oh no! It can't be! You must be mistaken!'. What we are really saying is, 'Please don't tell me this. I can't bear it. The implications are too awful'. Denial is one way of protecting us from the full impact and long-term implications of what has happened and how this event will affect us and our future lives.

To counteract the awfulness of sexual offences, most affected people go through the denial phase. They struggle to find innocent explanations for what has been reported. They refuse to believe that their trusted partners, siblings, parents, other relatives or friends would do that to them or their children: 'He wouldn't do that to *my* kids! How could he hurt them . . . he loves them. You are mistaken'.

The mother's denial is likely to be greatest when the offender is her husband or sexual partner. For the mother to accept that there is a problem, she has to accept that she has been deceived by the offender. The abuse devalues every aspect of her past relationship and makes a future relationship seem impossible. To protect her children from harm, she has to make substantial changes to all their lives at a time when she is in a state of shock. She may have to separate, accept sole responsibility for the care of her children, find somewhere else to live, set up a home from 'scratch' with little or no money and little or no support from embarrassed relatives. In the chaos which follows the disclosure of abuse by fathers and father-figures, the offence itself is often trivialised to avoid these daunting responsibilities. Mothers who are also survivors are especially likely to see themselves as helpless and unable to provide protection. Denial of the abuse becomes the most convenient option. To avoid confronting reality, the mother finds it easier to say, 'My child is lying' or, 'It's her fault. She must have led him on. He's weak but he's not a bad man'. The problem is, of course, that denial deprives victims of essential emotional support and protection. This deprivation may result in long-term psychological damage and a high risk of re-abuse.

Fathers also have difficulty in accepting disclosures of sexual abuse when they involve male friends, relatives or men they know and trust. Few dads have any understanding of the risks. They only hear the myths which tell them that the incidence of sexual abuse is greatly exaggerated and children make false and malicious claims. If males commit offences, it must be because they were seduced by young, promiscuous victims. These myths ensure that fathers are completely unprepared for sexual abuse occurring in their own social environments.

Both mothers and fathers are slow to accept that they have mistakenly trusted someone who was untrustworthy. Acceptance implies that they cannot rely on their own judgment. If they made such an enormous error, how many others have they made? Who else has 'pulled the wool over their eyes?'. With their own security and self-confidence in tatters, parents, and fathers in particular, are likely to confront the abuser. They demand an explanation. The offender obliges, assuring them that their fears are groundless, '. . . after all, I'm your brother [say]. Would I hurt your kids? You know how much I care about them'.

The offender recognises the parents' unwillingness to believe the allegation. He knows that the police have not been called and denial will make them happy. The parents, in turn, have to accept the denial. Few adults have the courage to tell other adults, 'I don't believe you. I believe my child'. Offenders are then free to continue the offences and victims are devastated by the fact that their major protectors failed to believe and protect them.

When the offender has been trusted, denial is often so great that fathers refuse to allow their children to be interviewed by child protection workers. The fathers extol the virtues of the offender, pointing to the number of occasions on which he acted as babysitter or took their children on outings. It does not occur to these naive and loyal fathers that there might be devious reasons for the pleasure that their friends or relatives derived from the company of children. In their confusion, fathers are likely to accuse the child protection workers of being dirty-minded trouble-makers who have nothing better to do than concoct allegations about innocent citizens.

After the disclosure of abuse, parents want to forget all about it and pretend that it never happened. They also try to impose this wish on their abused and unhappy children. They convince themselves that they do not need help from counsellors or anyone else. 'If only people would go away, leave us alone and let us forget about it, everything would be alright'. These parents ignore their children's emotionally disturbed behaviours and tell themselves that the real problem lies with the professionals or someone outside their immediate social circle.

The denial and suppression of abuse is particularly powerful in incestuous families. When the offender is a family member, relatives feel obliged to protect each other from humiliation and blame. This enables offenders to put strong pressures on victims to withdraw their statements. Their relatives are also likely to 'gang up' on anyone who shows support for the victims. If father–daughter incest occurred, the mother is often blamed—she either imagined it or she 'didn't look after him properly'.

The 'cover-up' persists even when perpetrators are related only by marriage. Women's refuges insist on clients maintaining absolute secrecy about their whereabouts because women tend to telephone their mothers to inform them of what has happened. Their mothers then inform their husbands who, in turn, inform the offenders. This was well demonstrated by a client: 'When I came to the refuge, staff warned me not to give anyone my new address. I thought I could trust my mother. I phoned her to tell her where we were and why. She promised to keep it secret but she didn't. She told dad. He immediately contacted my husband at work, gave him the address of the refuge and said, "Start behaving like a real man. Get round there and take your wife and kids back home where they belong. And in future, make sure that she behaves like a proper wife. We want no more of this nonsense about abusing your kids"'.

Men have undergone a lengthy conditioning in mateship and, when male sexuality is involved, some men will support members of their own sex rather than their daughters and grandchildren.

Family denial varies from a slight distortion of the truth to serious delusion when adults flatly refuse to listen to the evidence. Most of us deny when our lives are in a state of turmoil. We select what we deny very carefully. It is normal to use denial as a temporary coping mechanism providing that we do not remain in that stage for long. For the grieving process to be effective, we have to move on.

If a victim's parent remains in a state of denial indefinitely, the victim is deprived of essential protection and support. If the offender is the parent-figure, the child is psychologically orphaned with no natural protector to provide the necessary care. The lack of a protective model may then have long-term detrimental effects on the development of the child.

## Anger

Anger is probably the strongest and least acceptable emotion associated with the normal grief process. It usually takes us by surprise because it is wide-sweeping and often involves everyone who has had anything to do with the events which caused the distress: child victims, social workers and all those involved in the justice system as well as abusers and their supporters.

The problem for women is that, although they have society's permission to release some sad feelings, they have not been taught how to handle angry feelings in a healthy way. These are often internalised, damaging their physical and mental health.

Anger is neither nice nor Christian. In grief, those who have been discouraged from expressing angry feelings become sullen and bad tempered with whoever is nearest. Supporters become bewildered and mistake the behaviour for selfishness, hardness and self-pity when it is often an expression of unbearable emotional pain. Anger focuses on the circumstances surrounding the abuse and is likely to be strongest if someone in the family contributed to the events. Feelings of hostility also arise from the frustration of being unable to prevent the abuse from happening and the fact that life now seems to be out of control.

In anger, parents become very critical of everyone and everything associated with the problem, sparing no-one in their systematic scrutiny of events. They are angry with their children who were abused because, however young they might be, they should have known that their parents could not cope with the consequences. They are angry because the police are 'useless, they still haven't arrested him', the social workers ask 'silly questions', the hospital kept them waiting, the interviewers would not allow the parents to be present. The potential for complaint is endless.

Religious people are even angry with their God. They ask, 'Why me? Why my child? What terrible thing have we done to deserve this?'. The abuse is then perceived as a form of punishment and their religious faith can be severely challenged, especially in cases of incest or abuse involving a church member or priest. The church does not encourage anger.

Christians are expected to forgive. Forgiveness may be appropriate in the long-term but it is not appropriate at this stage.

Fathers are especially angry when offenders are known but not loved. With no sense of loyalty to confuse them, they threaten to 'kill the bastard' but not before they have inflicted slow and painful torture involving primitive genital surgery. Angry fathers fantasise about revenge. They sense that, if they were 'real men' they would take matters into their own hands. Some may attempt to form a vigilante group. Most do nothing. They are deterred by the fact that their wives and children depend on them. Police would guess who was responsible if an offender had an unfortunate 'accident'. And police assure angry fathers that the matter is best left to the justice system, 'That's what we're here for'.

If these perpetrators are not convicted and jailed, fathers are left with a deep sense of disillusionment and a smouldering desire for revenge. When parents are angry and threaten to kill the abuser, child victims may become fearful. On the other hand, it can be beneficial for children to know that their fathers believe them and care so much that they will take extreme action to support them. Much depends on the nature of the child's relationship to the offender and the parent prior to the offences.

Anger is another survival mechanism which helps us to tolerate the intolerable. Anger produces a great deal of energy which can be used constructively. Parents are rightly angry with a society which tolerates and even ignores the sexual abuse of children. When groups of fathers get together they can channel their anger for productive purposes. Because of the power structure in politics and society, male lobby groups are likely to have a much greater impact than those led by women.

## Guilt and self-recrimination

Guilt and self-blame are inevitable when parents realise that they saw the signs of abuse but failed to respond protectively. The common reaction of adults receiving disclosures is to search for innocent explanations for what they see and hear. Taught only to suspect dangerous strangers, they cannot conceive that people in their own community might want to harm their children. Some parents accuse victims of misinterpreting the normal affectionate actions of a loving and trusted relative. Few delve deeply to establish the truth. As a result, parents of abuse victims often have to face the realisation that they unwittingly placed their children in positions of danger and ignored their cries for help. They feel guilty and inadequate because of their negligence.

When there is a family crisis, mothers and children traditionally lean on fathers. In cases of child sexual abuse, caring fathers rarely know what to do. They feel useless, helpless, guilty and they panic. For mothers who learn that their partner is the abuser, the emotional impact is enormous. Reared to nurture and protect their children, be good wives, homemakers and lovers, mothers of victims of child sexual abuse perceive that they have failed in every aspect of their lives. Those who also suffered physical or emotional abuse at the hands of their children's abuser, blame themselves for maintaining the relationship. They question their own sanity and their feelings of powerlessness are reinforced.

Parents who face the violation of their children analyse every aspect of their relationships with victims and offenders. They ask themselves, 'Why did this happen? Why didn't I suspect? Why did I trust him/her? Why was I so easily deceived?'. The answers are almost invariably self-deprecating: 'I must have been blind or stupid to have been fooled so easily. I must be a useless parent to have been taken in like that.'

It needs to be impressed upon parents that they are also victims of society's denial of child sexual abuse. Most parents trust other adults and think that their families are safe. Parents of victims need to be aware that offenders go to a great deal of trouble to gain the parents' trust and the most intelligent and caring of parents can be duped into making their children available for abuse.

Parents of children abused in American and Australian kindergartens suffered enormous self-blame because they had assumed that their children were safe in establishments staffed mainly by women. They also assumed that there was 'safety in numbers'. They assumed that women are maternal, nurturant and protective of children. And when teachers asked them not to spend time in the classroom because it 'unsettled the children', they assumed that the teachers knew best. And they were wrong! As a result, they dismissed their children's cries for help. With the benefit of hindsight, parents can always recall children's attempts to gain help. These recollections merely add to their pain and feelings of inadequacy.

Self-blame is inevitable because few parents have the comfort of knowing that they did all that was possible to keep their children safe. In counselling sessions, some parents admit that the possibility of abuse had crossed their minds but they dismissed the thoughts as 'dirty minded' and they felt ashamed. It is important for leaders of mothers' groups to discuss issues of power when abusers are the children's fathers, father-figures or grandfathers. Mothers need to be helped to examine the power struggles within their families, to recognise how the offender controlled and manipulated them (as well as the children) to ensure that the abuse remained hidden.

At appropriate times, it may also be useful to examine the role of women in society and the effects of sex-role conditioning and socialisation on the power relationships between men and women. Given permission to talk in confidence, some mothers reveal the emotional abuse, powerlessness and dependency they experienced in an incestuous home. The advantage of sharing this information in a group is that women from a variety of situations recognise the commonality of their powerlessness and dependency. They can help one another to discard their guilt and self-blame and develop the resolve to protect their children from further abuse.

Eventually, with help, parents swing from feelings of responsibility to a realistic acknowledgment that they did their best given their experience, upbringing and the knowledge that was available at the time. Only when that conclusion is reached can they move on to the next stage of grieving.

## Shame and anxiety

Fathers suffer deep feelings of shame when their children are abused by members of their own sex. They are ashamed to belong to the masculine world and, being male, feel personally responsible for what happened. There is an additional anxiety of a different kind if the molestation involves the homosexual abuse of a son. Dads need to give their sons assurance that they were not selected because they were 'weird' or feminine, they were selected because they were young. Fathers also need assurance that homosexual abuse does not necessarily affect later sexual preference nor does it necessarily cause their sons to become the next generation of abusers. The most significant factor in maintaining normality in their children's sexual development is their own affection, approval and support.

Mothers suffer a profound sense of shame when their children have been abused by their fathers or father-figures. Mothers feel ashamed that they chose and lived with men who behaved in this way. They view their gullibility as a reflection of their personal deficiencies. There is a sense of 'guilt by association'.

Parents are also ashamed when they see themselves as having contributed to the abuse. Shame is reinforced by the attitudes of other people. Former friends withdraw in embarrassment. They forbid their children to play with victims for fear of contamination. Parents want to hide away to avoid the stares and the questions. They find themselves crossing the road to avoid contact with neighbours. Their social lives are discontinued and they become more and more isolated.

## Inappropriate blame

When we feel badly about ourselves, another defence mechanism is to find a scapegoat. When the abuser is the child's father or father-figure, the mother invariably finds a dozen reasons for blaming the child. In sibling abuse, parents are torn between their love for the victim and their love for the perpetrator. Both are their children. They are distressed by what happened but, in their confusion, they make excuses, trivialise the behaviour and blame the victim. Parents need regular reminders that there is only one blameworthy person and that is the perpetrator.

Stresses occur in the marriage when one parent stops saying, 'Why didn't I know?' and says instead, 'Why didn't *you* know? You should have known that they were at risk. I was at work. How was I to know what was going on!'. When we need scapegoats we usually choose victims who will not challenge us and they are very often the ones who are already suffering great emotional pain.

Parents need to know that blame is futile. The important thing is to help each other to be strong, for the sake of the children. The last thing that abuse victims need is to see their parents arguing and their families falling apart because they told someone about what had been happening to them.

## Depression and sadness

Depression and sadness are associated with any major loss and are a part of the normal grief process. The disclosure of child sexual abuse changes the lives, outlooks and attitudes of all family members. Both mothers and fathers experience a deep sense of loss. One of the difficulties for both parents is, of course, that the expression of sadness is gender related: men and women have been taught to handle their sad feelings differently.

Most of the present generation of fathers were taught that it is unacceptable for men to express their feelings of sadness. Dads are supposed to be able to look after themselves and their families. Many men hate to reveal that they, too, find it difficult to cope. They cannot cry openly when they feel distress. They sense that they have to support everyone else and to weep is to let everyone down. For men who have been conditioned to be protectors, this brings further feelings of guilt and inadequacy. Fathers often try to internalise their sadness to protect everyone else and pretend that the problem doesn't exist. In this frame of mind, they are likely to withdraw their co-operation and announce that they do not wish to proceed with a prosecution.

Unfortunately, this does not restore family harmony. There is no going back, no forgetting, least of all for victims. The sad feelings have to be dealt with. When parents try to pretend that all is well, the problem merely goes underground and waits for an opportunity to explode. This often occurs when victims reach adolescence. Fathers who suppress their sad feelings are also likely to suffer major health problems in later years.

Depression is a common experience of mothers whose children have been abused. It is likely to be increased if mothers are also survivors of sexual abuse. They sense that they are trapped in abuse and that there is no way out. The depth of depression suffered by women varies with the amount of support they have and is likely to be greater in women who have to leave the family home and move to a different locality. When parents are depressed, children become fretful, unhappy and difficult to manage, exacerbating the problem. Mothers tend to smoke heavily, abuse alcohol, neglect their health and their distressed children, their homes and, most of all, themselves. They lack energy and drive but cannot sleep. Some shoplift in an attempt to steal back from an uncaring society what has been stolen from them and to draw attention to their sense of helplessness. Convinced that they are totally responsible for the family chaos, they embark on a range of self-destructive behaviours. Mothers who are also survivors of abuse may have made several suicide attempts by the time they reach a support group. For them, a state of deep depression has probably continued for many years. These parents need continuous, time-consuming, slow-handed and long-term intensive support which, from the practical viewpoint, can only be provided by groups staffed by volunteers. It might also be necessary for such women to be referred to competent therapists.

## Issues for step-parents and parent figures

A not uncommon situation is for stepfathers and father-figures to find that their step-children were sexually abused by their natural fathers either before the separation and divorce or on access visits. The first marriage may have broken down as a result of the abuse. Sometimes, children only gain sufficient confidence to disclose abuse after the divorce when the offender loses his power over them.

An extremely difficult situation for step-parents is when their young children or step-children have been abused by step-siblings living in the same house. This is not uncommon when teenage youths share homes with young adolescent girls in reorganised families. Sometimes older girls also abuse their younger stepbrothers. Step-siblings live in very close proximity with no incest taboos to inhibit them. These situations require very careful handling, often with professional counselling for all the parties involved. They are very stressful situations for parents, placing the marriage in jeopardy if both parents are not supported and helped to understand their feelings. Parents are likely to rush to the defence of their own offspring. This prevents them from making a rational analysis of the situation. Arguments arise with references to 'your kid' and 'my kid' rather than 'our children'.

The seriousness of the abuse must be assessed realistically: who did what with whom, why it happened, what is the age and power difference between the participants, how much force or coercion was used and who needs help. When the parents find the situation too difficult to handle, they often tell themselves that there is no problem, dismissing all step-sibling sexual behaviour as normal curiosity (or blaming the victim). Others overreact in relatively harmless situations. When step-brother/sister abuse has occurred, counselling should be obtained for both the abusers and their victims. In addition, the parents should obtain counselling for themselves. Parents should remember that children who abuse others were often abused by someone else. If that is the case, they will need treatment to help to curb these impulses.

## The effects of child sexual abuse on parents' employment

One of the problems for working parents is the time involved in attending to matters associated with the abuse of their children. During criminal investigations there may be several appointments with police, social workers, child psychologists, therapists, and the Crown lawyer. There may be visits to the sexual assault assessment unit. Several days may be taken up by attendance at preliminary and subsequent court hearings. If the offender pleads 'Not guilty' or is found guilty and appeals, the parents can expect even greater demands on their time. This causes a tremendous strain, irrespective of whether they are salaried or self-employed (and time away means lost income).

For mothers involved in contested access or custody cases, the procedures can involve additional monthly court attendance for up to two years. Employers and work colleagues are unlikely to show empathy, least of all if they are being inconvenienced by the parent's absence. They may be mildly sympathetic if the offender was a stranger but there is a stigma attached to abuse by friends or relatives. Time off may be refused if employers cannot cope with the problem of child sexual abuse per se. They neither want to hear about it nor be inconvenienced by it. The presence of the parent may make them feel uncomfortable. A common reaction is for employers to actually increase the parent's workloads to hasten their resignation.

Not surprisingly, some parents find it impossible to continue their employment *and* support their children throughout the trauma of court appearances. With the risk of a substantial loss of income, they may refuse to co-operate with prosecuting authorities. Professional employers are no more supportive than shop proprietors or factory managers. Even the Deputy Superintendent of a hospital found it necessary to resign when she was refused permission to take time off work to deal with the legal aspects of her child's abuse.

**Separate groups are needed for mothers and fathers of abuse victims**

Because of gender differences in handling the grief process and because most mothers are seeking help in relation to abuse by men, support groups find it necessary to create separate subgroups for fathers. Some issues are of specific concern to males who tend to feel more relaxed in all-male company. Some mothers feel uncomfortable discussing their personal feelings about their children's male abusers in the presence of other males. It is particularly unwise to place mothers who are also survivors of abuse in mixed groups. There are many reports of survivors inappropriately using fathers as targets for their anger. Men who seek help from parent support groups are at high risk of being used as scapegoats because they are representatives of the male gender, happen to be available (and usually constitute a minority) in a safe environment at a time when group members are being encouraged to express their feelings. Given that fathers of abused children are also suffering, leaders have to ensure that they are not exposed to the risk of verbal attacks based on gender.

An additional reason for creating separate groups is the fact that there are sometimes power games involved in communications in mixed groups. Men take longer than women to reach the stage where they can express their feelings openly. In the meantime, they may try to stop the women from speaking if they are discussing something which makes them feel uncomfortable. There is a tendency for men to interrupt women or ignore them when they wish to speak. Furthermore, fathers' priorities are seldom the same as mothers' priorities. If men take control of sessions, this reinforces the mothers' sense of powerlessness. This is particularly undesirable for mothers in incestuous families.

When mixed sessions are held, leaders should record some sessions to analyse input, who contributes most and least and who controls what aspects of the discussion.

Decisions about when to hold mixed and separate groups will depend on the circumstances surrounding the abuse. If a large number of children have been molested by trusted authority figures in schools, preschools or other social groups, it may be helpful for all parents to meet and discuss some aspects together and some aspects separately, according to the needs of the members. Personal feelings about the abuse are best tackled in single-sex groups. Information relating to child sexual abuse and how to support children should be available to both parents simultaneously to ensure that they are both receiving the same messages and are given equal responsibilities for protecting their children.

As with mothers' groups, some fathers will reveal, possibly for the first time, that they were abused in childhood. The abuse of their own children then brings back painful memories of what happened to them and this is likely to increase their anger, frustration and feelings of helplessness. Where there are sufficient numbers of father-survivors, they should be given the opportunity to form separate survivor groups to deal with those issues. When it is not feasible to provide such support, father-survivors should be encouraged to seek professional counselling from a known and respected professional in this field. Both mothers and fathers should recognise that they are unlikely to be able to support and protect their own children satisfactorily if they have not dealt with the issues surrounding their own earlier abusive experiences.

# *11* Planning therapeutic programmes for the parents of sexually abused children

## The three support phases

The needs of families for therapeutic support and intervention after the disclosure of child sexual abuse can be divided into three distinct phases:

1 Disclosure. This is the panic period, lasting from eight to twelve weeks. A therapeutic model is needed to provide:
   - individual crisis therapy for each of the (non-offending) family members;
   - informal and planned support from other parents who are experiencing similar situations, i.e. group support.

2 Assessment period. This is the time when family members develop awareness of the wider implications of what has happened. The assessment period continues from six to eighteen months. What is needed at this time is:
   - individual counselling and, if necessary, therapy for each member of the family to help with the confrontation of feelings about the abuse and related issues;
   - group therapy to assist in the above;
   - informal group support;
   - parent–child therapy to set and achieve goals.

3 Restructuring the family and the power structures within that family. This is essential when the offender is a member of the victim's family (as parent/parent figure, sibling). It is imperative that therapists work separately with individuals until they are ready for family group sessions. The duration of this period is from one-and-a half to two years. Therapists work towards the readjustment of relationships, changes of attitude and changes to the power structure within the family until members reach the stage where they can help others in the support group and benefit from giving that help.

Parent support groups are able to help non-offending parents in all three phases.

## The aims of group programmes for non-offending parents

Parent support groups have many different aims and structures. Some provide formal groups with therapeutic and learning programmes; others are simply meeting places where parents can talk informally about their problems with other parents and trained staff. No two groups are alike but all groups have some features in common:

- Groups provide information about sexual abuse, family services and the assessment and justice systems and provide practical help as necessary.
- They provide support in a safe environment where people can express their feelings and raise concerns about the impact of the abuse on the family and themselves.
- Groups help parents to regain control over their own lives so that they can provide their children with the stability and reassurance that they so desperately need.

Another major aim of groups is to raise the self-esteem and self-confidence of previously powerless mothers so that they can deal more effectively with the trauma associated with abuse and provide better care and protection for their children. To achieve this, a wide variety of approaches are used. There is a need for flexibility in programming so that free-flowing discussion can take place.

See Figure 11.1 to show how support groups operate.

## The organisation of parent support groups

When parent support groups are planned, decisions have to be made relating to their organisation. New clients are likely to be referred by

**Figure 11.1 How parent support groups operate**

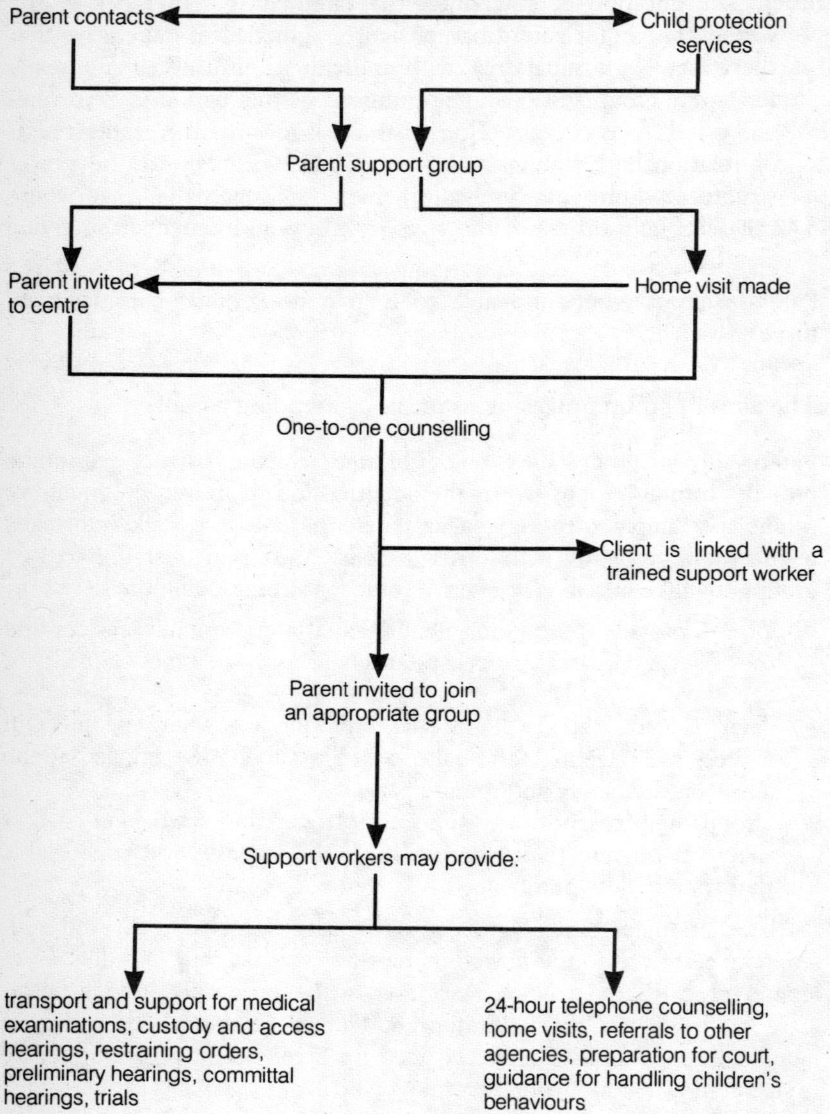

child protection services intermittently, either singly or in twos and threes. The question is, should they be allowed to join an ongoing, established group or remain separate until numbers are sufficient for a new group to be formed? Should the group be continuous, allowing parents to join and leave whenever they wish? Or should there be groups running for a fixed period of time? There are advantages and disadvantages of both systems.

### *Open groups*

The open group structure is continuous with no fixed number of sessions. The structure has several advantages. First, parents can join a group immediately and they may remain in the same group for as long as necessary. Second, new arrivals join parents who are already comfortable and can make them feel welcome.

There are also disadvantages to open groups. For example, it can be embarrassing for parents to join an established group in which members speak freely about what, until now, may have been a taboo subject. In the early stages, new arrivals are likely to feel uncomfortable with the level of frankness in the expression of feelings. There is also a risk that the established members may attempt to dominate sessions, forgetting that they, too, were experiencing the same problems and feelings only a few months earlier.

Open groups are always changing: new members arrive and old members move on. It is difficult for group leaders to plan programmes for group members when they are all at different stages in the grief and recovery process and have substantially different needs.

### *Closed groups*

Within a closed group structure, the programme runs for a fixed period of time, usually for not less than twelve weeks. New members are not usually allowed to join a group after the second week. This enables participants to get to know one another and their leaders. The regular membership makes it easier to create a comfortable, safe and trusting environment. The group develops a strong sense of cohesion which is valuable for creating supportive relationships. Members feel more comfortable about disclosing sensitive information when they are with the same people for several weeks.

If closed groups are selected, leaders must decide what to do with new arrivals who seek help after the formal group has begun its activities. Should they provide one-to-one counselling until there is a sufficiently large number of people to form a new group? Should they admit new clients to a separate orientation group until a larger group can be formed?

Closed groups are often preferred when there is a shortage of trained and experienced leaders. It is much easier to plan sessions to meet clients' needs over a twelve week period than to cater for a continuous programme. At times, it may be necessary to create separate groups to meet specific needs. When members feel the need for a longer period of support after completing the twelve week programme, an additional group may be formed.

Parents of children who have been abused in groups in satanic rituals or, at school camps, for example, will have quite different needs to mother-survivors facing the decision of whether to support or leave a husband who has committed incest with their children. Parents of children abused by community figures may also require less time to handle their feelings and more time to discuss matters relating to the justice system, the need for reform and lobbying.

*Orientation groups*

If the organisers decide to offer closed groups, it may be necessary to create separate orientation programmes. New clients are then placed automatically in these introductory settings before they 'graduate' to the larger, longer-term group. The focus of the orientation group is to help new arrivals to deal with the immediate crisis of disclosure, to deal with the practicalities of assessment and court procedures and provide appropriate support for their children. The first few weeks after disclosure are often the most crucial in working with non-offending parents. In the initial stages, there are powerful feelings of shock and guilt but some parents quickly realign themselves with offenders, especially if they are close members of the family.

Orientation groups are relatively small, friendly, kind, supportive and safe. They provide information. They deal with parents' initial anger and the everyday family problems which arise relating to the abuse. Parents in such groups are not encouraged to examine their feelings in any depth. They develop supportive friendships and meetings often take the form of comfortable get-togethers. Group cohesion develops and members often socialise and make contact at other times. Towards the end of the orientation programme, some members begin to worry about leaving the group to move into a more challenging environment. Contact with members of the long-term group usually confirms that the next stage will involve the hard work of confronting their feelings about the abuse. Some parents try to avoid their personal issues and may leave the group at this stage.

Parents who were also victims of sexual abuse in childhood are the ones most afraid of confronting their deep-seated sadness, anger, insecurity and inability to trust their own judgment in forming new relationships. They demand constant reassurance that they are 'OK'.

Parents who are referred by police or child protection services (i.e. they are not self-referred) are the ones most likely to support their children's abusers and continue to deny that sexual abuse is damaging to victims. They can be a disruptive influence in the group and, if their denial continues beyond six or eight weeks, there is little value in transferring them to the next programme. The case worker should always be informed when parents remain in the stage of denial.

### For how long do parents need help?

Three months of attendance would appear to be the minimum amount of time needed by most parents attending one two-hour group session per week. Some parents feel the need to be involved in group programmes for up to eighteen months while others leave after a few attendances. Many reappear later. The length of time that parents are involved in groups depends on various sets of circumstances, many of which are beyond their control. For example, whether the:

- abuser had a close relationship with the client;
- parent and children have to leave the family home for safety reasons and, if so, whether the offender continues to provide financial support;
- offender seeks treatment and treatment is available;
- offender wants to be reunited with the family;
- offender seeks access to or custody of victims;
- offender is prosecuted or not;
- accused admits or denies the offences;
- child and/or parent are required to give evidence in court;
- offender is found guilty or not guilty;
- offender appeals or there is a retrial.

All of the above are critical issues for (non-offending) parents and will have different impacts on the continued need for support from understanding people.

### Limitations to group membership

Parents who are suspected or accused of being actively involved in the sexual abuse of children are not appropriate clients for support groups for non-offending parents. Groups should not attempt to provide counselling for abusers but should persuade them to obtain treatment from experienced therapists. While it is recognised that there is an urgent need for offender treatment programmes, their needs are very different to those of other parents and their therapy groups should be quite separate.

This ruling may place a group in a difficult situation. For example, a supporting father joined a group as a non-offending parent when his children claimed to have been abused by their stepfather on access visits to their (non-custodial) mother. Several months later, his ex-wife lodged a counterclaim that the group member was the offender. Police investigated the complaint and, although he was not charged, the father experienced a long and difficult custody battle in court. He then needed a great deal of support but did not feel that he could turn to the group for help. At the same time, he had nothing in common with the support group formed specifically to help offenders. He felt that he was in limbo and had nowhere to turn for help.

The majority of parent programmes cater for mothers. It is recognised that dads need help too and it is recommended that separate group programmes be set up for the non-offending fathers of sexually abused children.

## The establishment of group expectations

When a new group is created, whether it is for parents or for training counsellors, it is important that group expectations be established at the first meeting. The rules should be determined by group members and not by their leaders. Decisions will be necessary on domestic and housekeeping matters, such as bans on smoking, obscene language, drugs and alcohol. No violence should be allowed and group members usually agree to replace breakages. The issue of confidentiality should be discussed thoroughly at the first session. Members usually agree that they do not want people outside the room to know about their problems and feelings. This gives every person an obligation to maintain confidentiality. Group participants must agree to the rules which should be recorded and exhibited where they are clearly visible. Rules of this kind are essential for the development of order, trust and safety.

Members need to be made aware that, if there are disclosures of further offences against children, the information will be reported by group leaders to child protection authorities. Apart from the leaders' professional or legal responsibilities, the emphasis in the group must be on the protection of children. Neither the group nor its members can be seen to collude with abusers by not disclosing offences.

In some circumstances, it is useful to ask new members to sign forms giving leaders permission to discuss their cases with therapists and/or case workers where and when appropriate.

All group sessions must be evaluated regularly by members and leaders.

## Group leadership

One of the strengths of a parent support group is the self-help, mutual help component which enables those who have experienced the trauma associated with the abuse of a child to give and receive support from others who have been in the same situation. Nevertheless, structured group leadership is essential to the success of group programmes.

In analysing the needs of the mothers of abused children, frequent concerns involve their poor self-concepts, lack of confidence, depression and their 'victim' stance to life in general. Strong positive female leadership can provide a sound role model, enabling these mothers to adopt a more positive approach to themselves and their lives. Leaders who are experienced in group work and who understand the dynamics of sexual abuse can help women to weave slowly through their maze of confused feelings. Effective leaders use a style of leadership which allows mothers to become empowered at an individual level. An autocratic style merely reinforces their dependency and does more harm than good.

Ideally, each group should have two co-leaders who provide support for each other during group activities and at later debriefing sessions. It is important that leaders give themselves sufficient free time to express their own feelings, privately and confidentially. Although groups tend to cater mainly for women, this does not negate the possibility of male–female leadership teams with males providing counselling and leading special groups for fathers.

A number of important issues must be addressed if male leaders work with groups of women. First, new arrivals are likely to distrust men if their children have been abused by men. Second, the presence of men may inhibit the mothers' capacity to express their feelings. At the other extreme, they may choose to focus years of pent-up angry feelings on the only available representative of the male gender. None of these situations benefit the mothers or their leader. An additional consideration is that mothers of incest victims have often spent their entire lives under male domination. One of the beneficial aspects of groups with female leadership is that members learn to think and act for themselves and make progress without dependence on males.

It should be noted however that the Salvation Army has successfully used males as managers of womens' refuges. The NSPCC has also used male counsellors for 'Walk-in Centres' used predominantly by mothers with problems relating to child maltreatment. They have provided therapeutic programmes which covered most of the issues referred to in this book. The men were chosen for their gentleness, sensitivity to male–female power issues and their ability to present caring male models to women who may never have encountered gentle and caring males.

Whatever the gender of group leaders, they must ensure that mothers are encouraged to feel in control of their involvement in group programmes.

## Introductory exercises for new members

The use of introductory exercises can help new group members to get to know one another and to overcome their initial shyness. When mothers are also survivors, their low self-esteem and their learned distrust of others makes it imperative that leaders develop a trusting environment in which self-disclosure can occur.

One useful exercise is to divide the group into pairs and ask each person to spend five minutes talking about themselves to their partner. At the end of the stipulated time, each person then introduces their partner to the remainder of the group. It is also helpful to begin group meetings with a ritual that involves the sharing of information. For example, each member introduces him or herself with the words, 'I am . . . and I am here because my son/daughter was abused by . . .'. This focuses on the commonality of experience of child sexual abuse and invites some initial disclosure from new members. Without this kind of encouragement, some parents avoid facing up to the reasons for their presence.

It is also important to give new members the opportunity to declare what they would like to achieve in the group. This begins the process of allowing the group to take responsibility for itself. A review of each member's goals should take place on a regular basis.

**Exercise 11.1 Expectations worksheet**

1 Hand a copy of the worksheet to each new member.
2 When completed, create small groups of no more than five new members.
3 Use a blackboard or large sheet of paper to record a composite list of the new group's expectations.
4 Prioritise the expectations by numbering them in order of importance in terms of urgency and whether or not they are realistic.
5 If there are several groups, bring them together and combine the lists.
6 Leaders will use these priorities as a basis for planning individual and group sessions and evaluating progress.

**Exercise 11.2 My reasons for joining this group**

I am here because ..........................................................

..........................................................

..........................................................

What I want most from being here is ..........................................................

..........................................................

..........................................................

I need to talk about ..........................................................

..........................................................

..........................................................

I want to learn about ..........................................................

..........................................................

..........................................................

I need help to. ..........................................................

..........................................................

..........................................................

## Planning and evaluating group sessions

Group leaders should plan one or two realistic objectives for each session to meet the needs of parent participants. The objectives must be carefully considered so that group members can see and understand the value of what they are doing. Within this planning, there must be an element of flexibility because no two people have identical problems and needs and successful groups are those which manage to cater for individual differences. Some parents make good progress while others remain at one stage for a very long time. Most regress when there are major difficulties in their lives. Individual problems must be tackled in one-to-one counselling rather than in the larger group.

At each session, group leaders should introduce and explain the objectives of the session to members. It is important that participants understand what is happening, what leaders hope to achieve and why the session is necessary. Misunderstandings may leave members feeling that they are wasting their valuable time. Objectives may be worded as follows. This session will:

- help group members to . . .;
- introduce new members to . . .;
- reinforce what members have already learned about . . .;
- help to develop the members' understanding of . . .

At the end of individual sessions, and at the end of each week and month, members should sit down together to give their opinion of how far the leaders have achieved their stated objectives. See samples of evaluation sheets below.

**Exercise 11.3 Evaluation of a session by group members**

I would like to know more about. . . . . . . . . . . . . . . . . . . . . . . . . . . . . . . . . . . . . .

. . . . . . . . . . . . . . . . . . . . . . . . . . . . . . . . . . . . . . . . . . . . . . . . . . . . . . . . . . . . .

. . . . . . . . . . . . . . . . . . . . . . . . . . . . . . . . . . . . . . . . . . . . . . . . . . . . . . . . . . . . .

I was pleased that . . . . . . . . . . . . . . . . . . . . . . . . . . . . . . . . . . . . . . . . . . . . . . . . .

. . . . . . . . . . . . . . . . . . . . . . . . . . . . . . . . . . . . . . . . . . . . . . . . . . . . . . . . . . . . .

. . . . . . . . . . . . . . . . . . . . . . . . . . . . . . . . . . . . . . . . . . . . . . . . . . . . . . . . . . . . .

I was disappointed that . . . . . . . . . . . . . . . . . . . . . . . . . . . . . . . . . . . . . . . . . . . . .

. . . . . . . . . . . . . . . . . . . . . . . . . . . . . . . . . . . . . . . . . . . . . . . . . . . . . . . . . . . . .

. . . . . . . . . . . . . . . . . . . . . . . . . . . . . . . . . . . . . . . . . . . . . . . . . . . . . . . . . . . . .

One thing that I did not like was . . . . . . . . . . . . . . . . . . . . . . . . . . . . . . . . . . . . . . .

. . . . . . . . . . . . . . . . . . . . . . . . . . . . . . . . . . . . . . . . . . . . . . . . . . . . . . . . . . . . .

. . . . . . . . . . . . . . . . . . . . . . . . . . . . . . . . . . . . . . . . . . . . . . . . . . . . . . . . . . . . .

What I enjoyed most was . . . . . . . . . . . . . . . . . . . . . . . . . . . . . . . . . . . . . . . . . . . .

. . . . . . . . . . . . . . . . . . . . . . . . . . . . . . . . . . . . . . . . . . . . . . . . . . . . . . . . . . . . .

. . . . . . . . . . . . . . . . . . . . . . . . . . . . . . . . . . . . . . . . . . . . . . . . . . . . . . . . . . . . .

I gained most from. . . . . . . . . . . . . . . . . . . . . . . . . . . . . . . . . . . . . . . . . . . . . . . . .

. . . . . . . . . . . . . . . . . . . . . . . . . . . . . . . . . . . . . . . . . . . . . . . . . . . . . . . . . . . . .

. . . . . . . . . . . . . . . . . . . . . . . . . . . . . . . . . . . . . . . . . . . . . . . . . . . . . . . . . . . . .

I wish I could . . . . . . . . . . . . . . . . . . . . . . . . . . . . . . . . . . . . . . . . . . . . . . . . . . .

. . . . . . . . . . . . . . . . . . . . . . . . . . . . . . . . . . . . . . . . . . . . . . . . . . . . . . . . . . . . .

. . . . . . . . . . . . . . . . . . . . . . . . . . . . . . . . . . . . . . . . . . . . . . . . . . . . . . . . . . . . .

Right now, I feel that . . . . . . . . . . . . . . . . . . . . . . . . . . . . . . . . . . . . . . . . . . . . . .

. . . . . . . . . . . . . . . . . . . . . . . . . . . . . . . . . . . . . . . . . . . . . . . . . . . . . . . . . . . . .

Next week, I hope to . . . . . . . . . . . . . . . . . . . . . . . . . . . . . . . . . . . . . . . . . . . . . .

. . . . . . . . . . . . . . . . . . . . . . . . . . . . . . . . . . . . . . . . . . . . . . . . . . . . . . . . . . . . .

**Exercise 11.4 Evaluation of sessions by group members (for the benefit of group organisers)**

| Objectives of the sessions | Level of success achieved (Please indicate with a tick in the column) Successful most of the time | Unsuccessful | Don't know |
|---|---|---|---|
| To create a comfortable atmosphere in which you felt welcome | | | |
| To encourage you to talk freely about things that trouble you | | | |
| To help you to understand your situation better | | | |
| To provide friendship and support | | | |

Leaders should ask questions which relate to specific aspects of the programme. For example, on sessions relating to handling children's unacceptable behaviours, questions should specifically seek information to reveal whether members have understood practical hints for handling problems, whether they feel comfortable about trying them out and, later, how well they worked. Checks should also be made after sessions to assess parents' understanding of children's reactions to sexual abuse.

Future sessions should be planned to meet group members' needs, bearing their criticisms and future hopes and expectations in mind. Although every group meeting must allow some free time for informal contact, there should always be some part of the session which is carefully planned with long-term progress in mind.

Opportunities should be provided for parents to complete their evaluation sheets anonymously when the leader is out of the room. Because anonymity is so very important, leaders must never refer to individual evaluations if they recognise the identity of the writer. Members will not be honest if they think that their comments might be recognised and publicised. At the end of each session, group leaders should get together to discuss what went well, what went badly and why. The questions to ask are:

- How far did I achieve my stated objectives?
- Who learned what (and how do I know)?
- Who needs more help (what and why)?
- What would I change if I repeated the session again next week?

It is useful for leaders to keep records of sessions and to make notes on how to avoid the pitfalls previously experienced. These observations should be shared with fellow group leaders during feedback sessions.

## Samples of exercises used in parent groups

**Introductory exercise** **To encourage discussion about society's attitudes towards sexual harassment and sexual abuse. Teaching method used: brainstorm and record, summarise then discuss findings.**

Ask both male and female group members to contribute one sentence responses to the following questions:

1 How do men view sexual harassment and abuse?
2 How do women view sexual harassment and abuse? Compare findings.
3 How do mothers contribute to the attitudes of their sons?
4 How do fathers contribute to the attitudes of their sons?
5 Discuss different male–female sex roles in the family.
6 How does the media contribute to these attitudes?
7 What changes are necessary to generate changes of attitude?

**Exercise 11.5 'I have a right to be angry about . . .'**
**'What I could do about it is . . .'**

Some parents will express anger about child protection services and the justice system. Most will be angry with the abuser. When parents have had the opportunity to express their angry feelings, group leaders should encourage them to consider how they can use the energy generated by anger to create change. Answering the question, 'What can we do about it?' reduces the sense of helplessness and empowers members to seek better responses from central and local government services.

Some parents will need help to draft and type letters of complaint. Some will need assistance to make and keep appointments with service administrators. It should be noted that, for some parents, it is easier to focus anger on an impersonal bureaucracy than to tackle more important and more difficult personal issues.

Parents need to know that their children also need help to express their angry feelings.

Focus on the following statements: 'I have a right to be angry about . . . ', and 'what I could do about this is . . . '.

**Exercise 11.6 'I am angry with my child because . . .'**

Although it is hard to admit, most parents are angry with their abused children. In cases of father–daughter incest, mothers sometimes admit that they hate their daughters. Negative feelings related to delays in disclosure, disclosure to other people, jealousy and the sense of deception must be verbalised. Parents who concentrate entirely on their own hurt feelings are unlikely to realise that blaming victims is unreasonable. Parents seldom realise that their children are angry with them.

Focus on the statement: 'I am angry with my child because . . . '.

**Exercise 11.7 'How I feel about my child's abuse'**
**'How I feel about the abuser'**

New group members experience many conflicting emotions depending on the circumstances of the abuse. They swing from feelings of sadness to hostility and the desire to commit violence against the abuser. These complex feelings are difficult to express and they can be easily internalised or misdirected unless leaders encourage their free expression in a safe and controlled environment.

Anger must always focus on the deed rather than the person. This enables parents to maintain their self-esteem if they cared (or still care) for the offender. Different techniques may be used for the expression of anger—beanbags, punchbags or pillows may be used to release aggression. The parent may address an empty chair, imagining that the abuser is sitting on it. Alternatively, a confident and experienced leader may represent the person who has caused the anger.

**Exercise 11.8 Focus discussion on these issues:**
**'I am anxious because . . .', 'What worries me most is . . .', 'One thing I could do to reduce my anxiety is . . .'.**

**Exercise 11.9 Informing others about abuse**

Informing others about abuse is a very stressful experience. Former friends may shun the family because they fear the contamination (by association) of their own children's innocence. In their distress, maternal grandparents may blame their daughters for choosing the wrong partner or for failing to protect their grandchildren. Other people take sides and distribute blame.

Centre discussion around these issues 'What my relatives said when they heard about the abuse', 'What his relatives said. What he said/did', 'How I feel about it. What I can do about it'.

# 12 Planning therapeutic programmes for parents who are survivors of sexual abuse

## Group structure

When parents seek help for their abused children, they often reveal that they still feel very guilty and angry about their own abusive experiences. When parents' own emotional needs have not been met, it is extremely difficult for them to identify and attend to their children's needs. Support groups are well situated for helping adult survivors to overcome the traumas of the past. In these caring environments, survivors are free to express their emotions about their childhood experiences. Mutual support is encouraged and it is common practice for members to exchange telephone numbers and make contact between sessions.

In setting up a new group programme for parent-survivors, two of the most important elements involve leadership style and matters of trust. A major factor in the dynamics of all child abuse is the powerlessness of victims. The lack of control over their bodies and emotions can affect their whole lives. A fundamental aim of group programmes must be to empower members to initiate a process where they can regain control. Whether or not this is allowed to occur will depend on the methods used by the group leader. If members sense that they have some control over what happens in the group and can influence its directions, they have taken an important step towards gaining control over other aspects of their lives.

There are many ways in which this can be achieved. The first task for the new group must be the establishment of rules and guidelines to ensure confidentiality and personal safety for individuals. The second task is to identify the issues that members wish to tackle during the ten or twelve sessions. Individual members should also be asked to identify one or two achievable, personal goals.

Any form of decision-making is difficult for parents who are trying to cope with the shock of their children's abuse and, simultaneously, suffer the reminders of their own earlier abuse. Most groups adopt the catch-phrase, 'One step at a time and one day at a time'. Members are reminded of it whenever they feel overwhelmed by the complexity of their problems. In planning the programme, there should be a balance of structured activities and opportunities for members to raise their own issues for discussion. If a crisis has arisen during the week, a member will wish to talk about the problem as a matter of urgency. This necessitates the facility to withdraw for private counselling.

Although group leaders promote the self-help concept, they must provide the initial group structure. Group members, through lack of experience or fear of autonomy need to feel that they are in a non-threatening and secure environment with a competent and reliable leader. Structure and leadership are necessary to provide the security and the control necessary for the safe exploration of emotional issues.

## Trust and confidentiality

The trust issue is extremely important to survivors. Most group members will be victims of incest or abuse by stepfathers or father-figures. In childhood, our parents are our primary objects of trust. When child victims find that their main caregivers cannot be trusted, they lose their trust in everyone, including themselves. Unable to rely on their own judgment, they find it difficult to make decisions. As a result, they suppress their own needs and allow stronger individuals to make decisions for them. When the decision is not in their best interests, they feel frustrated and despise themselves for being weak.

To develop the trust of individuals, there has to be a group emphasis on confidentiality. At the first meeting, the leader seeks the assurance of every member that 'everything that is said in the group must remain within these four walls'. The only exception to this rule is when someone reveals that a child or a group member is in danger. There is usually complete agreement that current abuse must be reported to child protection authorities. There should also be discussion about procedures for when a group member expresses suicidal thoughts or intentions.

When group members reveal suicidal thoughts, leaders should first approach them for permission to contact their personal therapists. If they do not have one, they should be persuaded that professional help is needed. In life-threatening situations, leaders retain the right to seek outside help. It should be noted, however, that depressed and suicidal people become very angry when leaders contact their therapists without permission.

When individuals are dissatisfied with rules and procedures, it is important to be able to show that those procedures were agreed by a consensus of group members. It is the leader's responsibility to ensure that each member understands and accepts the importance of confidentiality in the context of group membership.

## Making a start

There are many different ways of helping new group members to feel welcome and comfortable. It is useful to begin sessions with refreshments so that members can talk informally before the serious work begins. At the first meeting, individuals can either introduce each other (see Chapter 11) or each person can introduce him or herself—'My name is . . . I was abused by . . . when I was . . . years old. I am here to . . .'. Survivors who have never discussed their abuse with anyone else find it difficult to say, 'I was abused'. The aim of the ritual is to emphasise the common bond of experience, decrease the sense of shame and stress a positive goal.

No-one wants to be the first to talk about abusive experiences, least of all if they have remained hidden for many years. Group members need to know that they can share their personal experiences when they feel sufficiently comfortable to do so. Group members should be taught how to provide appropriate support. Group leaders must model supportive behaviour whenever they are working with survivors.

It is helpful when someone breaks the ice and refers to his or her abusive childhood experience. It provides permission for others to tell their stories. Some mothers choose to remain silent for a long period of time because they believe that what happened to them is more embarrassing and more degrading than anything that happened to anyone else. When they hear what happened to others, some will find the confidence to say, 'I'm sorry that it happened to you. It happened to me, too. I thought that no-one else could possibly have been humiliated in that way'.

Sometimes, group members minimise the importance of their abusive experiences by using the word 'only', 'he only touched me . . . it only happened a few times'. They often apologise for their presence in the group. When individuals persist in discounting the damaging effects of abuse, they should be encouraged, in private, to examine the abuser–victim relationship, how they felt about the behaviour and how the abuse has affected their lives.

## Planning the formal part of the programme

Programmes for survivors concentrate on the development of self-confidence and self-esteem so that group members can gain some measure of control over their lives and provide better care and protection for their children.

To develop assertiveness and control, survivors must perceive themselves as positive, worthwhile people. Because their feelings of worthlessness are deeply entrenched, progress is slow and frustrating. As one group member explained, 'I'm afraid of trying to view myself as a worthwhile person because, when I think I'm beginning to succeed, something or someone always comes along and destroys whatever I've achieved. In the end, I stop trying. It's easier to accept that I'm a mess than suffer the highs and lows of thinking that I'm making it then finding that I'm back in square one'.

Positive reinforcement is constantly needed to encourage individual progress. And while leaders must listen empathetically, they must also resist the urge to rush in, take over and resolve other people's problems. When survivors have always been told what to do, they may resist learning how to resolve problems for themselves. Eager helpers merely reinforce their helplessness.

Survivors' groups can be frustrating workplaces for group leaders because, when parents have viewed themselves negatively throughout most of their lives, they are unlikely to change overnight. Growth is particularly slow because most members are, for the first time, dealing with their own abuse and, simultaneously, their children's abuse.

The first efforts towards the development of a positive self-image must be directed towards the reduction of the survivor's sense of guilt about their own abuse. Guilt seldom disappears completely but it diminishes when survivors begin to understand the powerlessness of children and how their own guilty feelings were created by their abusers.

For a healthy outcome, survivors also need the opportunity and encouragement to express their feelings about the abuse, the abuser and other relevant persons. When they eventually accept that their feelings of guilt and low self-worth are inappropriate, survivors can begin to view themselves in a more positive light. At that stage, group leaders encourage them to reconsider the abuse of their children and to work out how they can be helped.

The therapeutic programme can be planned in four stages:

*Stage 1* Understanding the power of the offender in relation to the powerlessness of children.
*Stage 2* The release of feelings about the abuse.
*Stage 3* The development of a positive self-image.
*Stage 4* How group members can provide better support for their children.

Exercises are useful for the structured part of group sessions. Brainstorming techniques are commonly used, encouraging each group member to contribute a one sentence response to the topics under consideration. All responses are listed. Findings are discussed, compared and summarised. The leader then relates findings to the dynamics of sexual abuse and the conditioning process used by abusers and/or society.

*Stage 1 exercises*

1 Group members list (separately) and compare the characteristics of the average adult male and the average child. Use the lists to demonstrate that children have no influence over adults' behaviours and are never to blame for what adults do to them.

For this exercise, it is useful for leaders to display pictures of male adults and young children.

2 Offenders use messages deliberately designed to coerce victims into co-operating with them and keeping the abuse secret. Using brainstorming methods and recording responses, invite group members to share the messages they received from their abusers. These messages are usually deeply ingrained in their memories. Findings usually demonstrate that abusers use similar messages to manipulate victims.

When survivors become more aware of how children are manipulated, their guilt decreases and their anger towards their offender increases. Opportunities are then needed to deal with the anger.

3 Abusers use 'brainwashing' techniques to gain total control over their victims. These techniques are similar to the ones used with political prisoners. Group members are asked to identify which techniques were used by their abusers and how they were used. They analyse how *their abusers*:

(a) ensured that the focus of attention was always on themselves;
(b) demonstrated that they had absolute power over their victims;
(c) isolated victims from other potentially helpful people;
(d) made their victims feel incompetent and dependent;
(e) used threats to maintain their silence;
(f) maintained control by enforcing trivial demands and granting occasional indulgences;
(g) exhausted the resistance of victims.

Group leaders list responses. They then encourage group members to consider the effects of the 'brainwashing' methods used by offenders. Finally, they summarise findings to show the power of offenders and the powerlessness of child victims. This exercise is likely to involve more than one session.

Incest victims reveal that they were expected to serve their abusers and other family members in highly personal and demeaning ways. Most incest victims are also given inappropriate domestic tasks. Most survivors report that there were some emotional 'positives' in their relationships with abusers. They were granted some emotional or material indulgences which were not available to other members of the family. It is useful to discuss how these indulgences alienated victims from their siblings and assisted in the process of social isolation and dependency on the abuser. Power is increased further by the destruction of children's self-esteem. Victims are taught (by actions and words), that they are incapable of functioning independently. Lacking the opportunity to gain social skills, they become totally reliant on the offender for their social and emotional interaction. As adults, survivors find it difficult to relate effectively to others. Often, the parent-survivor group becomes their first social network. (See Chapter 1 for a more detailed discussion of the victim–abuser relationship.)

*Stage 2 exercises*

The effects of abuse clearly influence the survivor's ability to develop strong, positive, emotional and sexual relationships. Deep-seated distrust ensures that they are never fully able to trust their partners. Some unconsciously choose partners who resemble their abusers. The dependence continues, exposing them to further abuse. In addition, their emotional needs have been suppressed so that they can no longer express them.

Survivors often have problems in accepting the physical proximity of others. They have an aversion to touching and being touched. Signs of affection may cause discomfort. Sexual activity brings painful reminders of their abuse. One well-established group ritual is for members to have the opportunity to hug one another at the end of each session. Members have a choice whether to participate or not. For many, this is the first step in receiving physical touching in a safe, non-sexual context. Body awareness exercises may also be introduced to help members to feel more positive about their bodies.

Exercises are used to encourage members to analyse and express their negative feelings about the abuse, their abuser, their mothers and themselves. The first formal exercises are likely to revolve around the issue of guilt. Group members are encouraged to:

- analyse their feelings of guilt and identify what makes them feel guilty about their own abuse;
- recall how children are taught to feel guilty about all rude behaviour;
- discuss the implications of guilt for survivors of sexual abuse;
- explore how the guilty feelings were created—how did the offenders transfer the guilt for their own behaviour onto their victims?;
- write a letter, 'Dear guilt . . .';
- disclose how they feel about themselves in relation to the abuse and their abusers, what would they like to do to them (no holds barred)?;
- finish a sentence relating to sad feelings, for example 'I feel sad about . . . I want to cry when. . . . It's alright to cry when. . . .';
- identify how they were taught that they were helpless. Who benefited?

These exercises are helpful because most survivors admit that they despise themselves as much as their abusers. The different responses can be used for discussion. At every available opportunity, group leaders should help members to realise that their guilt is inappropriate. It is the direct result of the offender's manipulations and society's conditioning.

Survivors come into the group with deeply repressed feelings of rage. Most survivors are afraid to acknowledge this anger because of its intensity. It must be emphasised that, to release angry feelings, survivors need to feel that they are in safe and capable hands and that group leaders will protect them from losing control.

From the modelling provided by leaders, members learn how to accept tears and give permission for others to cry without embarrassment. When distressing issues are raised, leaders refer back, as necessary, to the dynamics of sexual abuse to help members to regain a realistic perspective of where the responsibility lies for the tragic train of events.

It is helpful if survivors can identify how their feelings of low esteem relate to their childhood experiences of learned helplessness. Who taught them that they were helpless? How were they taught? How did the offender contribute to those feelings? How did the offender benefit? Did it make victims more dependent upon the offender?

It is useful to brainstorm the things that survivors would like to do to their abusers. Survivors are then encouraged to draft letters addressed to them explaining why they are angry. Writers are invited to read their letters to the group. The letters are not posted. For that reason, members should participate even if their abusers are dead.

## Confronting the offender

When survivors feel strong, they often express a desire to confront the offender. This must be discussed thoroughly to ensure that all the possible risks of confrontation are understood. First, there may be no rewarding impact. Typical responses include outright denial and allegations of lunacy such as, 'I can't remember. You must be mistaken' or 'You must be crazy making up stories like that'. Then, there is self-justification and blame, 'It wasn't all that bad. You could have said "No". You liked it really' or, 'I was only teaching you the facts of life . . . It was better doing it with me than with a stranger'.

These are just a few of the excuses commonly used by offenders to justify their behaviour, albeit twenty or thirty years later. Without therapy, their attitudes are not likely to have changed. Additional evidence of their lack of empathy and their continued denial of the child's needs can be devastating for survivors. Furthermore, adult survivors who disclose their abuse to other family members often meet the same lack of understanding, even when those members were also victims.

When an incest survivor found the strength to travel from New Zealand to England to confront her father, she was greeted by her sisters with, 'Who do you think you are coming here to cause trouble . . . upsetting everyone about something that happened years ago. Go back to New Zealand where you belong and leave us in peace'.

The names of the locations may change but the messages remain the same wherever there are incestuous families. Relatives protect the offender to protect themselves from having to confront the awful reality. They protest that the offender (or their mother) is too weak, too sick or too old to be distressed by events from the past.

Ideally, the survivor needs the offender to accept responsibility for the behaviour and apologise to remove the sense of guilt. This is sometimes achieved when the survivor is accompanied by an experienced support worker whose presence adds a sense of importance to the visit. When survivors have maintained a shallow relationship with the offender, they are often still afraid of losing that relationship as well as their relationship with their ineffective and unsupportive mothers. For some survivors, any form of family relationship is better than none . . . even if it necessitates the continued suppression of their own needs. Suppression has, after all, become a lifelong habit. When abusers ignored victims' rights and feelings, they grew up believing that they had no rights.

After years of suppressing their own needs and feelings, survivors need permission and encouragement to assert themselves. This demands a positive feeling of self-worth. Irrespective of whether they are given the opportunity to direct their anger towards the offender in person, they need to be able to say, 'I have suffered great pain. I can accept that it was not my fault and I did not deserve to be treated in that way. It is alright for me to be angry with the person who caused this'.

## Confronting survivors' unsupportive mothers

Survivors need help to tackle their negative feelings about their mothers. Again, it is useful to brainstorm how members feel about them. Whether their perceptions are accurate or not, most survivors think that their mothers failed to protect them, or, worse, that they contributed to the abuse. These notions result in long-term feelings of abandonment, rejection, confusion and anger. 'Why didn't she stop it?', is the common question. For those who were rejected by their mothers, the message received from both parents was, 'Our feelings and needs are more important than yours. Your needs don't count. You don't count'.

Some group members feel the need to deny the rejection by making excuses for their mothers: 'My mother was wonderful. She loved me. She was just powerless to help'. Denial is a survival mechanism which helps survivors to cope with life, it can also be destructive if it masks deep-seated resentment. Again, it is useful for members to write letters to express their feelings about their mothers, sharing them with others in the group so that they can see the similarities of feeling. Group members will only post their letters after considerable discussion with leaders about the possible results of confrontation. Without guidance, the recipients of such letters are unlikely to be sympathetic about incidents from the past.

## The development of a positive self-image

### *Stage 3*

Throughout the programme, emphasis is placed on the identification of survivors' feelings relating to their abuse and where those feelings come from. It is equally important to stress the individual's ability to create change. One way of achieving this is to invite each group member to identify one unwanted feeling. What triggers this feeling? What kind of behaviours result? How can this be changed? Group members may not be able to identify their own strengths but they can provide positive feedback to other people. It is important to encourage mutual support. Everyone needs approval. When survivors have been 'put down' throughout their lives, it takes a great deal of patience and effort to convince them that they are worthwhile people.

It is useful to ask group members to identify the negative things said about them by their abusers, parents and teachers to destroy their self-esteem in childhood. They can then identify and compare what their needs were in childhood and what they actually received.

There are many adults' and children's books available for the development of self-esteem. These can be found in educational, health and feminist bookshops.

## How group members can provide better support for their children

### *Stage 4*

When there are clear indications that parents understand the powerlessness of children and are prepared to accept that offenders are wholly to blame for sexual abuse, it is time to move on to tackle the issues relating to the more recent abuse of their own children. When they are ready, group members should leave the survivors' group and join or rejoin the parent support group.

For the planning and content of survivors' programmes, it is recommended that group leaders use Ellen Bass and Laura Davis' book, *Courage to Heal* Harper and Row (New York), Mandarin (London) and Octopus (Australia), 1990. Laura Davis' Workbook bearing the same title is also strongly recommended.

# Appendix 1

## Resources for parents of children who have suffered child sexual abuse

Please note that the telephone numbers given here were correct in 1992. If they are no longer available, please consult your telephone directory and/or your local department for health, social/family and community welfare services. New groups are often formed to meet local needs. Contact your local Rape Crisis Centre, Crisis lines or the above statutory services for current information.

**AUSTRALIA**

**Australian Capital Territory—Canberra**

- Parent Support Service (06) 247 0519
- St John's Care
  PO Box 219
  Canberra ACT 2601
  Telephone: (06) 248 7771
  Parent support, survivor and offender therapy programmes. Personal counselling.
- Partners of Sexual Abuse Survivors
  PO Box 593
  Dickson ACT 2602
  Telephone: John (06) 249 7911, Geoff (06) 247 6876 or Russell (06) 288 7335.
  The group caters specifically for men and women whose partners are survivors of childhood abuse and still suffer from negative effects.

Other useful contacts:

- Rape Crisis Centre:
  PO Box 31
  Lyneham ACT 2602
  Telephone: (06) 247 2525
  Provides 24 hour counselling for all types of abuse, group therapy for survivors, practical and court support.

- ACT Government Child Protection services can be contacted at:
  PO Box 158
  Canberra ACT 2601
  Telephone: (06) 207 1069

- Incest Centre
  Telephone: (06) 249 6070
  Provides counselling for boys up to the age of 12 years and will refer to expert male counsellors as necessary.

**New South Wales**

For enquiries relating to current support services in New South Wales contact Dympna House, Sydney, telephone (02) 797 6733.

- Parents Support Network (PSN)
  PO Box 40
  Rooty Hill NSW 2770
  Support line: (02) 832 1242
  Hours of operation: Monday–Friday 9.30 am–2.30 pm
  Monday–Sunday 8.00 pm–7.00 am
  Office hours: (02) 625 0335 Monday 9.30 am–2.30 pm
  Thursday–Friday 9.00 am–4.30 pm
  This organisation provides 'total support' for parents of abused children and caters for individual needs. It is the only long-term group in New South Wales which focuses entirely on parents. Services include home visits, group therapy, peer support and companions through the assessment and legal process. Twenty five volunteers provide 24 hour telephone counselling on five hour shifts. Training consists of an eight week package plus regular in-service education supervised by a social worker. The Family and Community Service Department funds two part-time paid workers for a total of 30 hours a week and accommodation is provided by the Health Commission.

- Other services will assist parents but parents are not their prime focus.

- All Health Department health centres have counsellors who will help non-offending parents.

- Men's Support Groups and Counselling
  For information, telephone Tony Phiskie or Mark Griffiths
  Newtown Community Health Centre
  Telephone: (02) 516 2066

- The Pretrial Therapy Diversion Programme
  Telephone: (02) 891 6199
  Offers counselling to a limited number of victims and non-offending parents when the offender is participating in the Diversion Programme.

Sexual Assault Services

The following provide support and information for victims, partners, friends and families, including support groups and court support.

The service is confidential.

- Child Protection Units are available at the Royal Alexandra Hospital for children, Pyrmont Bridge Road, Camperdown, telephone (02) 629 6434, (02) 519 0466 (AH) and Prince of Wales Children's Hospital, High Street, Randwick, telephone (02) 399 4412/4413 and 339 0111 (AH).
- Sexual Assault Centre
  Westmead Hospital
  Hawkesbury Road
  Westmead NSW 2145
  Telephone: (02) 633 7940 or 633 6333 (AH)
- Prospect Sexual Assault Service
  Blacktown Community Health Centre
  Main Street
  Blacktown NSW 2148
  Telephone: (02) 622 8111
- Wentworth Sexual Assault Service
  Nepean Hospital
  Somerset Street
  Kingswood NSW 1747
  Telephone: (047) 32 0512 AH (047) 32 2577

**South Western Sydney**

- Liverpool Sexual Assault Service
  Liverpool Health Centre
  Floor 2
  203–209 Northumberland Street
  Liverpool NSW 2170
  Telephone: (049) 601 2333 or (049) 600 0555 (AH)
- Bankstown Sexual Assault Service
  Bankstown Community Health Centre
  47 Stanley Street
  Bankstown NSW 2200
  Telephone: (049) 790 0055
- Macarthur Sexual Assault Service
  Campbelltown Community Health Centre
  Cnr Moore/Cordeaux Street
  Campbelltown NSW 2560
  Telephone: (046) 29 2111
  (after hours use the Liverpool service)

**Other services**

| | |
|---|---|
| Aboriginal Medical Service | (02) 699 5823 |
| Auburn, Barnado's Australia (CSA counsellors) | (02) 646 2770 |
| CAPS (Child Abuse Prevention Service) (24 hrs) | (02) 344 7646 |
| Child Protection and Family Crisis (24 hrs) | (02) 818 5555 |
| Croydon—Centacare | (02) 745 3133 |
| Dulwich Hill, Rosemount Good Shepherd Service to Youth | (02) 560 4588 |
| Leichhardt Women's Community Health Centre | (02) 560 3011 |
| Liverpool, Rosebank Cottage (CSA counsellors) | (02) 601 3790 |
| (answer machine) | (02) 601 3676 |
| Liverpool Women's Health Centre | (02) 601 3555 |
| Penrith Women's Health Centre | (047) 21 8749 |
| Petersham, Centacare (CSA counsellors) | (02) 550 9988 |
| Riverwood Counselling Services | (02) 534 3953 |
| | (02) 534 4586 |
| Rooty Hill, Rosie's Place (CSA counsellors) | (02) 625 2878 |
| Sydney Rape Crisis Centre | (02) 819 6565 |
| (after hours) | (02) 633 6333 |
| Young Women's Resource Centre, Ashcroft | (02) 607 7536 |
| Sydney Women's Refuge and Resource Centre | (02) 4563/4415 |

**Country**
**Illawarra**

- Wollongong Women's Centre (counsellors available)
  (042) 29 6240

- Wollongong Sexual Assault Service
  Wollongong Hospital
  Crown Street
  Wollongong NSW 2500
  Telephone: (042) 20 1408, 29 8233 (AH)

- Nowra Sexual Assault Service
  Shoalhaven Hospital
  Scenic Drive
  Nowra NSW 2541
  Telephone: (044) 21 3322 and (044) 21 3111 (AH)

- Nowra—Shoalhaven Women's Centre (044) 21 0730

- Nowra—Waminda Aboriginal Women's Centre (044) 21 7745

- Illawarra Women's Health Centre
  Warilla NSW 2528
  Telephone: (042) 96 7077

- Muruya, Cathy's Place (CSA counsellors)
  Telephone: (044) 74 3699

- Muruya Women's Resource Centre
  Telephone: (044) 74 2747

**Central Coast**

- Sexual Assault Centre
  Gosford Hospital
  Gosford NSW 2250
  Telephone: (043) 20 3175 or (043) 20 2111 (AH)

- Sexual Assault Service
  Wyong Hospital
  Pacific Highway
  Kanwal NSW 2259
  Telephone: (043) 93 8270 (telephone Gosford after hours)

**Hunter**

- Newcastle Women's Centre
  Telephone: (049) 68 2511

- Newcastle Sexual Assault Service
  Cnr Stewart Avenue and Parry Streets
  Hamilton NSW 2303
  Telephone: (049) 69 4022

- Lower Hunter Sexual Assault Service
  Lower Hunter Community Health Centre
  58 Stronach Avenue
  East Maitland NSW 2323
  Telephone: (049) 33 4422

- Upper Hunter Sexual Assault Service
  Muswellbrook Community Health Centre
  District Hospital
  Brentwood Street
  Muswellbrook NSW 2333
  Telephone: (065) 43 1777
  After hours: all areas (049) 26 6234

**South West**

- Albury-Wodonga Women's Health Centre
  Telephone: (060) 41 1977

- Albury Sexual Assault Centre
  Albury Base Hospital
  Wodonga Place
  Albury NSW 2640
  Telephone: (060) 23 0340, (060) 23 0370 and (060) 23 0310 (AH)

- Sexual Assault Service
  Wagga Community Health Centre
  Docker Street
  Wagga Wagga NSW 2650
  Telephone: (069) 23 4811, 21 5755 (AH)

- Wagga Wagga
  Lindan Place (CSA counsellors)
  Telephone: (069) 21 4441

- Griffith Sexual Assault Service
  Griffith Community Health Centre
  39 Yambil Street
  Griffith NSW 2680
  Telephone: (069) 62 3900 or 62 1266 (AH)

**New England**

- Richmond—Hawkesbury Area Women's Cottage
  Telephone: (067) 66 2555

- Sexual Assault Service
  Tamworth Base Hospital and Community Centre
  180 Peel Street
  Tamworth NSW 2340
  Telepone: (067) 66 2555 or (067) 66 1722 (AH)

- Quirindi Hospital
  Nowland Street
  Quirindi NSW 2343
  Telephone: (067) 46 1466 (24 hours)

- Gunnedah Hospital
  Marquis Street
  Gunnedah NSW 2380
  Telephone: (067) 420 666 (24 hours)

- Glen Innes Hospital
  Taylor Street
  Glen Innes NSW 2370
  Telephone: (067) 32 1366, (067) 32 1166 (AH)

- Armidale Community Health Centre
  Rusden Street
  Armidale NSW 2350
  Telephone: (067) 73 4738 and (067) 73 4622 (AH)

- Armidale Women's Centre
  CSA counsellors
  Telephone: (060) 72 9977

- Narrabri Community Health Centre
  100 Maitland Street
  Narrabri NSW 2390
  Telephone: (067) 92 1522 or (067) 92 1666 (AH)

- Moree Hospital
  Alice Street
  Moree NSW 2400
  Telephone: (067) 52 9222 (24 hours)

**South Eastern**

- Goulburn—St Saviours Neighbourhood Centre
  Telephone: (048) 21 3077

- Goulburn Sexual Assault Service
  Goulburn Community Health Centre
  Cnr Goldsmith and Faithful Streets
  Goulburn NSW 2580
  Telephone: (048) 21 9009, (048) 27 3111 (AH)

- Bowral Sexual Assault service
  Bowral Community Health Centre
  399–405 Bong Bong Street
  Bowral NSW 2576
  Telephone: (048) 61 2744

- Mudgee Community Health Centre
  Telephone: (063) 72 1577

- Young District Sexual Assault Service
  Young Community Health Centre
  Allanan Street
  Young NSW 2594
  Telephone: (063) 82 1522, (063) 82 4368, (063) 82 1222 (AH)

- Far South Coast Sexual Assault Service
  Bega Community Health Centre
  McKee Drive
  Bega NSW 2550
  Telephone: (064) 92 9120 ( office hours)

- Cooma Sexual Assault Service
  Cooma Community Health Centre
  Cnr Bombala and Victoria Streets
  Cooma NSW 2630
  Telephone: (064) 52 1324 or (064) 52 1333 (AH)

- Bega Resource Centre
  Telephone: (064) 92 9120

- Queanbeyan Sexual Assault Service
  Queanbeyan and Area Community Health Centre
  Antill Street
  Queanbeyan NSW 2620
  Telephone: (06) 298 9233, (06) 298 9211 (AH)

**Orana and Far West**

- Orana Health Centre
  Cnr Palmer and Cobra Streets
  Dubbo NSW 2830
  Telephone: (068) 85 8999 or (068) 85 8666 (AH)

- Broken Hill Community Health Centre, Eyre Street, Broken Hill
  Telephone: (080) 88 5800, (080) 88 0333 (AH)

- Dunedoo War Memorial Hospital
  Sullivan Street
  Dunedoo NSW 2844
  Telephone: (065) 75 1408 (24 hours)
- Coonabarabran District Hospital
  Edwards Street
  Coonabarabran NSW 2357
  Telephone: (068) 42 2211 (24 hours)
- Nyngan District Hospital
  Telephone: (068) 32 1707 (24 hours)
- Walgett District Hospital
  141 Fox Street
  Walgett NSW 2832
  Telephone: (068) 28 1066 (24 hours)

**North Coast**

- Taree: Manning Valley CSA Counselling Service
  Telephone: (065) 52 4854
- Taree Sexual Assault Service
  Community Heath Centre
  22 York Street
  Taree NSW 2430
  Telephone: (065) 52 2799, (065) 52 1077 (AH)
- Hastings Valley Sexual Assault Service
  Community Health Centre
  Morton Street
  Port Macquarie NSW 2444
  Telephone: (065) 83 9344, (065) 82 1066 (AH)
- Coffs Harbour
  Child and Parent Support (CSA counsellors)
  Telephone: (066) 52 6266
- Coffs Harbour Sexual Assault Service
  Community Health Centre
  38 Gordon Street
  Coffs Harbour NSW 2450
  Telephone: (066) 52 2000, (066) 52 2866 (AH)
- Coffs Harbour Women's Health Centre
  Telephone: (066) 52 8111
- Grafton Sexual Assault Service
  Grafton Community Health Centre
  Arthur Street
  Grafton NSW 2460
  Telephone: (066) 42 3933
- Lismore Women's Health Centre
  Telephone: (066) 21 9627

- Lismore Neighbourhood Centre
  Telephone: (066) 21 9861

- Lismore Sexual Assault Service
  Lismore Base Hospital
  Lismore NSW 2480
  Telephone: (066) 23 1380, (066) 21 8000 (AH)

- Tweed Valley Sexual Assault Service
  Tweed Heads Community Health Centre
  Keith Compton Drive
  Tweed Heads NSW 2485
  Telephone: (075) 36 0540, (075) 36 1133 (AH)

**Central West**

- Community Health Centre
  Bathurst NSW 2795
  Telephone: (063) 31 5533

- Women's Health Centre
  Bathurst NSW 2795
  Telephone: (063) 31 4133

- Central West Sexual Assault Service
  Bathurst Base Hospital
  Howick Street
  Bathurst NSW 1795
  Telephone: (063) 33 1311 (24 hours)

- Forbes District Hospital
  Elgin Street
  Forbes NSW 2871
  Telephone: (068) 52 1000 (24 hours)

- Orange Base Hospital
  Dalton Street
  Orange NSW 2800
  Telephone: (063) 62 1411 (24 hours)

- Condobolin District Hospital
  Madline Street
  Condobolin NSW 2877
  Telephone: (068) 95 2600 (24 hours)

**Blue Mountains Region**

- Blue Mountains and Lithgow Women Against Incest (CSA counsellors)
  Telephone: (047) 82 5397

- Blue Mountains Women's Health Centre
  Telephone: (047) 82 5113

**Northern Territory**
**Darwin**

- Ruby Gaea House
  Telephone: (089) 45 0155
  Free counselling for women and children; medical, legal and resource information; emotional and practical support during police or court proceedings; emergency accommodation; survivors' and relatives' support groups; library and community education.

- Sexual Assault Referral Centre (SARC)
  Casuarina Plaza
  Darwin NT 0800
  Telephone: (089) 22 7156
  24 hour service for confidential counselling and support by female counsellors for crises and long-term needs, including help for adult survivors and family members. 24 hour emergency medical care by female doctors. Peer support group. Library. Funded by DHCS.

- Darwin Aboriginal Women's Shelter
  Provides counselling for Aboriginal mothers
  Telephone: (089) 45 2284

**Country**

- Alice Springs

  Sexual Assault Referral Centre
  Telephone: (089) 52 6006

  Women's Information Centre—Monday–Friday 8 am–5 pm
  Telephone: (089) 50 3644

- Gove District Hospital
  Matthew Flinders Way
  Nhulunbuy NT 0880
  Telephone: (089) 87 0211

- Katherine Hospital
  Gorge Road
  Katherine NT 0850
  Telephone: (089) 72 1555

- Tennant Creek Hospital
  Schmidt Street
  Tennant Creek NT 0860
  Telephone: (089) 62 2202

**Queensland**

- PACT (Protect All Children Today)
  PO Box 1313
  Fortitude Valley
  Queensland 4006
  Telephone: (07) 852 2500

Support, counselling and practical help for survivors of sexual abuse and non-offending family members. Services include face to face and telephone counselling, group therapy, peer support, child witness support, court companions. Coordinated by social workers with fifty trained volunteers. Partially funded by the Health Department.

- Sexual Abuse Counselling Support Service
  15 Elliott Street
  Woolloongabba Qld 4102
  Telephone: (07) 391 6066
  Assistance for families affected by child sexual abuse and for male and female survivors aged 13–17. Referrals through Department of Family Services and Aboriginal and Islander Affairs. Training for community agencies.

**Other relevant agencies**

- Crisis Care (24 hours)
  Telephone: (07) 22 7599 or (008) 17 7135 (no cost)

- Women's Health Centre
  165 Gregory Terrace
  Spring Hill
  Brisbane Qld 4000
  Telephone: (07) 839 9988 or (08) 01 7676 (no cost)
  Occasional group support for adult survivors. Library of resources.

- Women's House
  14 Brook Street
  Highgate Hill
  Brisbane Qld 4000
  Telephone: (07) 844 4008
  24 hour telephone counselling for survivors and concerned relatives. Women's Refuge (07) 844 4009

- Women's Legal Service
  81 Russell Street
  West End Qld 4000
  Telephone: (07) 846 2066
  Information and consultations on legal matters concerning women.

- Youth and Family Support Services Inc
  2 Rowan Street
  Kingston Qld 4400
  Telephone: (07) 208 8199
  Provides counselling and support for domestic violence and sexual abuse.

- Department of Family Services and Aboriginal and Islander Affairs
  Queensland Centre for the Prevention of Child Abuse
  Family Services Building
  George/Elizabeth Street
  City Centre Qld 4000
  Telephone: (07) 224 7588
  Lends resources at no cost.

**Country**
**Gold Coast**

- Sexual Assault Service
  Queen Street
  Southport Qld 4215
  Telephone: (075) 911 164
  Provides free counselling and assistance to parents and survivors.

**Sunshine Coast**

- Women's Emergency Service
  PO Box 74
  Cotton Tree Qld 4558
  Telephone: Business (074) 43 4711 Crisis (074) 434 334
  Free (008) 012 023
  24 hour counselling relating to child sexual abuse and domestic violence. Provides access to women's refuge.

For men

- Men's Awareness Support Group (MASG)
  PO Box 353
  Woodridge Qld 4144
  Telephone: (07) 200 5300 (H and W) Gerald Lodge
  (07) 847 1433 (W) Steve Cambridge

**South Australia**

**Adelaide**

There are three partially funded support groups providing community based parent/family support; telephone, face-to-face and group counselling; home visits; survivors' groups; drop-in facilities; parent and community education; advocacy and lobbying for reforms in laws and procedures; companions through the legal process. Part-time paid coordinators and voluntary (trained) support workers with access to professional services as necessary.

- Friends of Abused Children Taskforce (FACT)
  PO Box 77
  Smithfield SA 5114
  Telephone: (08) 254 6588
  24 hour service with divert night 'phone.
- Parents Against Child Sexual Abuse (PACSA)
  PO Box 231
  Woodville SA 5011
  Telephone: (08) 347 3445 Monday–Friday 9.30 am–4.30 pm
- SSAFE
  Floor 4
  Noarlunga House
  Noarlunga Centre SA 5168
  Telephone: (08) 384 2924 Tuesday, Wednesday, Friday 9.30 am–4.30 pm
  Child care facility available.

**Country**

- South East Sexual Abuse Centre (SESAC)
  144 Lake Terrace East
  Mt Gambier SA 5290
  Telephone: (087) 23 0448 AH 68 6211
  Staff present Tuesday–Thursday plus answering machine at other times.
  Offers the same services as the Adelaide groups plus a befriender scheme whereby former clients support new ones. Direct supervision is given by the Department for Family and Community Services.

**Other services**

- Parent Support Group
  Flinders Medical Centre
  Bedford Park SA 5042
  Telephone: (08) 347 1809—5.00–11.00 pm
  Telephone counselling is provided by twenty trained volunteers using a divert system from their homes. Parent aides are assigned as a back-up for mothers at home. The group handles problems relating to all kinds of child maltreatment. Voluntary staff are trained and supervised by Dr David Lines, Flinders Medical Centre.

- Crisis Care Unit
  Telephone: (08) 232 3300 (free country calls)
  Telephone counselling and out-of-hours mobile service for all types of crisis.

- Adelaide Rape Crisis Centre
  Telephone: (08) 293 8666

- Adelaide Medical Centre for Women and Children
  72 King William Street
  North Adelaide SA 5006
  Telephone: (08) 204 7000
  Assessment of child sexual abuse, medical help for all forms of child maltreatment, parent counselling.

- Queen Elizabeth Hospital SARC
  Woodville SA 5011
  Telephone: (08) 243 6836
  Assessment, counselling and medical assistance for adolescents and adults.

- Child and Adolescent Mental Health Services (CAMHS)
  Adelaide Children's Hospital
  Telephone: (08) 204 7389

- Flinders Medical Centre
  Oaklands Centre
  Telephone: (08) 298 7744
  Provides therapeutic services for child victims and counselling for parents throughout the State.

- Women's shelters: see local telephone directories.

- Men's support groups and counselling
  For information, contact The Men's Contact and Resource Centre (08) 410 2552 or Ian Johnson, Breaking Free, (08) 384 6848
- Sexual Offender Treatment Programme (SOTAP)
  64 Fullarton Road
  Norwood SA 5067
  Telephone: (08) 362 3022

**Tasmania**

The Department of Community Services is only aware of the following services:

- Hobart: Clare House
  Telephone: (002) 71 8612
- Hobart: Sexual Assault Support
  Telephone: (002) 31 1811
- Launceston: Laurel House
  Telephone: (003) 34 2740
- Burnie: North West Sexual Assault Support
  (a new service: no telephone number available at the time of publication — see telephone directory).
- Child Protection Assessment Board
  Telephone: (002) 302 921

**Victoria**

- People Against Child Exploitation (PACE)
  Parent Support
  Telephone: (03) 802 9343 Joan Gill
  Offers legal advice and telephone counselling. Membership, newsletters, lobbying. An unfunded group staffed by volunteers to provide parent support when children have suffered sexual abuse. The group operates from founder's home at Glen Waverley.

Centres against Sexual Assault

Metropolitan CASAs

- Monash Medical Centre
  246 Clayton Road
  Clayton
  Telephone: (03) 550 2289 (24 hours)
- Centre Against Sexual Assault
  Royal Women's Hospital
  270 Cardigan Street
  Carlton
  Telephone: (03) 344 2210
- North East Centre Against Sexual Assault
  9 Martin Street
  Heidelberg
  Telephone: (03) 450 570 and 459 3190

- Western Region Centre Against Sexual Assault
  21 Ballarat Road
  Footscray
  Telephone: (03) 687 8637

Rural CASAs

- Loddon Campaspe Sexual Assault Centre
  Bendigo Base Hospital
  Bendigo
  Telephone: (054) 43 0411

- Ballarat Sexual Assault Centre
  Ballarat Base Hospital
  Ballarat
  Telephone: (053) 32 1771

- Geelong Rape Crisis Centre
  224 Malop Street
  Geelong
  Telephone: (052) 22 4802

- Alvestone Clinic Sexual Assault Centre
  Banyon Street
  Warrnambool
  Telephone: (055) 61 2821

- Goulburn Valley Centre Against Sexual Assault
  63 Edward Street
  Shepparton
  Telephone: (058) 31 2343

- Mildura Sexual Assault Centre
  1 Jenner Court
  Mildura
  Telephone: (050) 22 3444

- Kalparrin Centre against Sexual Assault
  PO Box 1127
  Morwell
  Telephone: (051) 34 3922

**Other resources**

- Domestic Violence and Incest Resource Centre
  Telephone: (03) 387 9155

- Incest Support Group
  c/- Westgate Community Health Centre
  101 Hudson Road
  Spotswood Vic 3015
  Telephone: (03) 391 0444
  AH (03) 369 6281

- Dr Elizabeth McMahon
  PO Box 262
  Balwyn 3103
  Telephone: (03) 836 2544
- Women's Information Exchange
  Telephone: (03) 654 6844
- Women's Refuge referrals
  Telephone: (03) 329 8433
- Fran Quigley
  Ballarat
  Telephone: (03) 32 3256
- West Gippsland Parents United
  PO Box 321
  Warragul 3820
  Telephone: (056) 23 4488
  Contact: Phyllis Kruk
- Davey House Family Resource Centre
  Wonthaggi and District Hospital
  Wonthaggi 3995
  Telephone: (056) 72 1422
  Contact: Sue Armstrong, Family Counsellor
- North West Sexual Abuse Program
  253 Reynard Street
  Coburg 3058
  Contact: Cathie O'Shea Telephone: 383 5188
  Jeannie McIntyre Telephone: 389 2751
- Bethany Family Support
  1 Gibb Street
  North Geelong 3215
  Telephone: (052) 78 8122
  Contact: Intake worker
- Sebastopol Community Health Centre
  260 Vickers Street
  Sebastopol 3356
  Telephone: (053) 35 7801
- Delacombe Community Health Centre
  6 Warrina Drive
  Delacombe 3356
  Telephone: (053) 35 5322
- Ballarat East Community Health Centre
  109 Humffray Street South
  Ballarat 3350
  Telephone: (053) 33 1635
- Fran Sutherland
  Counsellor
  Wodonga
  Telephone: (060) 24 1849

- Bairnsdale Community Resource Centre
  115 Main Street
  Bairnsdale 3875
  Telephone: (051) 53 1444

Victoria has approximately 50 Community Health Centres in metropolitan and rural areas. Many have counsellors who have expertise in the area of sexual abuse. Some Community Health centres run groups for non-offending parents. Telephone numbers are listed in the telephone book.

Each regional Community Services Victoria office will be able to refer people to local services for parents of children who have been sexually abused.

**Western Australia**

- People Against Child Sexual Abuse (PACSA-WA)
  PO Box 172
  Mirrabooka WA 6061
  Telephone: (09) 343 1866
  An unfunded community service offering parent counselling, support, referral and lobbying.

- Sexual Abuse Self Help Association WA Inc (SASHA)
  154 Morrison Road
  Medland WA 6056
  Telephone: (09) 250 2185
  Not officially operating mid 1992 due to funding cuts but some telephone counselling continued. A new group is expected: check with your local community services.

- Incest Survivors' Association
  88 Edward Street
  East Perth WA 6004
  Telephone: (09) 227 845
  A senior counsellor and four salaried workers provide support and counselling for all those affected by incest. Government funded. Office hours. Groups for parent-survivors. Witness preparation and court support. Lobbying and community education.

- Princess Margaret Hospital
  Telephone: (09) 382 8222
  Medical assessment, therapy for children and counselling for family members.

- Sexual Assault Referral Centre
  King Edward Hospital
  411 Barker Road
  Subiaco WA 6008
  Telephone: (09) 382 3323

- Women's Health Care House
  North Bridge WA 6003
  Telephone: (09) 227 8122

- Motiv Parents Support Group
  11 Bournan Heights
  Parmelia WA 6167
  Telephone: (09) 439 2286
  24 hour telephone counselling, one weekly meeting on Tuesday 9.30 am–12.30 pm. Voluntary.

- Waratah Support Centre
  c/- PO Box 644
  Bunbury WA 6230
  Telephone: (097) 91 2884

- Incest Survivors Group
  Albany WA 6330
  Telephone: (098) 41 4807

- Sexual Assault Referral Centre
  Telephone: Geraldton (099) 64 1833
  Toll free (008) 19 9888

## NEW ZEALAND

### Help Foundation Centres

HELP centres are independent organisations providing the full range of services for child, adolescent and adult victims of sexual abuse, adult survivors and non-offending family members.

HELP centres provide an emergency, gender and culturally appropriate help, medical and counselling service for survivors of sexual assault. Services include:

24 hour crisis service, telephone counselling and attendance by a counsellor and woman doctor;
follow-up counselling and support through the investigatory and criminal justice process as needed;
long-term counselling for survivors of past abuse;
support groups for children, teenagers and adult survivors;
community education and counsellor training.

- Auckland Help Foundation/Te Whanau Kai Tiaki
  Whakamarie 0 Nga Ngakau Pouri
  PO 10345, Dominion Rd./2 Conway Rd., Mt Eden
  Auckland
  Telephone: (09) 623 1316, 623 1296, and 622 1700 (24 hours)
  This Foundation is committed to the payment of staff who are selected on the basis of their previous experience. In-service training is provided.

- South Auckland Help Foundation
  22 Alexander Avenue
  Papatoetoe
  PO Box 22–859
  Otahuhu
  Telephone: (09) 277 9324

Provides services for women and children. The Foundation employs Maori, Niuean, Samoan and European New Zealanders to provide an appropriate multi-cultural perspective. 24 hour medical services.

- Tauranga Help
  PO Box 2213
  Tauranga
  Telephone: (07) 578 8227—24 hours
  An unfunded community service with accredited, trained volunteer counsellors and supervisors. Medical facilities for emergencies. Counselling for both men and women.

- Wellington Sexual Abuse Help Foundation: HELP Centre—24 hours
  PO Box 16-129
  Wellington
  Telephone: (04) 389 2472
  The HELP Centre was established as a charitable trust in 1985 to fill gaps in existing services. It provides the same services as the Auckland groups with a 24 hour roster of trained voluntary counsellors and education workers. Available at the Women's Hospital, Outpatients' Department, Riddiford Street, Newton.

**Pacific Island Women's Project Aotearoa Inc**
A national organisation created in 1986 to provide information services and see to appropriate levels of funding to support Pacific Island Programs dealing with sexual and family abuse. Assistance is given to families and individuals for dealing with problems relating to sexual abuse.

- Wellington Pacific Island Women's Project
  21 Kensington Street
  Te Aro
  PO Box 6181
  Wellington
  Telephone: (04) 801 6901

- Tongan Women's Association
  c/- 16 Dryden Street
  Grey Lynn
  Auckland

- South Auckland Ina'i Lau O Tama'i ta'i
  18 Christmas Road
  Manurewa

**NZ Child Abuse Prevention Society**
Parentline/Parent Help/Child Help Line

- NZCAPS
  PO Box 12-139
  Wellington
  Telephone: (04) 499–9994

- Parent Help—Auckland
  PO Box 39-217
  Telephone: (09) 276 3311
  24 hour telephone counselling, face-to-face counselling and drop-in centre. Services provided by paid staff and volunteers.

- Child Help Line
  53 Somerset Court
  Christchurch
  Telephone: (03) 665 590

- Parentline
  PO Box 11 077
  48 Palmerston Street
  Hamilton
  Telephone: (07) 8394 536
  Fax (07) 8394 515
  Personal counselling, drop-in-centre, therapy for child victims, parent groups. Paediatrician available.

- Parentline—Hauraki
  PO Box 395
  Hauraki
  736 Pollen Street
  Thames
  Telephone: (0843) 88644 (number to be changed in 1993/4)
  Services available for the prevention and stopping of abuse, family support, education and advocacy services. Staffed by six volunteers and six paid workers, funded by the McKenzie Foundation, Lotteries Commission and Department of Social Welfare.

  24 hour telephone counselling service on five days of the week, counselling at the centre and clients' homes. Groups operate to meet mothers', fathers' and survivors' needs. Therapy for child victims. Preparation for court and support in the legal process. Support for other groups with similar resources, resource sharing and networking.

- Parentline—Hastings
  Telephone: (06) 876 3658

- Parentline Manawatu
  PO Box 2014
  Palmerston North
  Telephone: (06) 356 2679 office (06) 358 1144—24 hours
  Fifteen volunteers and five paid workers provide 24 hour telephone counselling at the centre and clients' homes. Groups for mothers and parent-survivors of sexual abuse. Community education. Government funding, grants and fund-raising.

- Parentline—Wanganui
  85 Bell Street
  Wanganui
  PO Box 4347
  Telephone: (06) 3455331 (24 hours collect) (06) 345 8396 office
  Five part-time paid workers and fourteen volunteers are employed with funds from government, NGOs and foundations. 24 hour telephone counselling, home counselling, counselling and group sessions for parents at the centre. Individual counselling for parent-survivors. Support in the legal process. Caters for all parents under stress.

- Parentline
  162 Molesworth Street
  Wellington
  PO Box 12-139
  Telephone: (04) 499 9994, 499 8406
  Three paid and eleven voluntary workers are employed with government and trust funds to provide 24 hour telephone, face-to-face counselling, parents' and parent-survivors' group and community education.

- Northland Child Abuse Prevention Society Inc (NORCAPS)
  PO Box 5012
  Regent
  Whangarei
  Telephone: (09) 43 88852
  Employs six paid workers with 80 per cent government funds and 20 per cent fund-raising. 24 hour telephone counselling, counselling at clients' homes and the centre, groups for parents and therapy for child and adolescent victims.

- Barnardo's Family Support Services

  Provide free, home-based support to family under stress.
  Auckland: (09) 698 609 (to be changed in 1993)
  Auckland (Henderson): (09) 836 1910
  Auckland: Mangere (09) 275 4481
  New Plymouth: (06) 758 2721
  Palmerston North: (06) 358 9448
  Wainoni (Christchurch): (03) 653 923
  Porirua and Lower Hutt—see telephone directory or contact
  Wellington Office: (04) 385 7560

- *SUPPORT: Presbyterian Support Services*

  SUPPORT provides a wide range of social services for people needing help regardless of religious beliefs or ability to pay. Specific counselling and family support services are available at the following centres.

  Head Office:
  PO Box 9079
  Wellington
  Telephone: (04) 801 6055
  SUPPORT (Northern) Newmarket: (09) 520 2621
  SUPPORT (Central) Wellington: (04) 3850 309
  SUPPORT (South Canterbury) Timaru: (03) 688 1748
  SUPPORT (Southland) Invercargill: (03) 214 4202
  SUPPORT (East Coast) Havelock North: (06) 877 8193
  SUPPORT (Christchurch) Christchurch: (03) 665 472 (changes August 1993)
  SUPPORT (Otago) Dunedin: (03) 4777 115

- *Te Kakano O Te Whanau*

  A national Maori women's organisation which provides support in relation to sexual abuse and family violence. There are twenty-five branches, at Auckland (3), Blenheim, Christchurch, Dunedin, Hamilton, Hastings, Hawera, Kaikohe, Napier, New Plymouth, Opotiki, Rotorua, Taihape, Taumarunui, Taupo, Tauranga (2), Thames, Waitara, Wellington, Westport, Whangarei.

- *Runanga Tane*

  A collective of Maori men working to stop all forms of abuse. Has links with *National Men for Non-Violence Network* which also provides help for men who wish to change their behaviour. There are groups at Auckland (2), Christchurch, Dunedin, Hamilton, Invercargill, Kaikohe, Nelson, Palmerston North, Porirua, Rotorua.

- *Te Puna Oranga* (Maori Sexual Abuse Centre)
  56 Cathedral St
  Christchurch
  Telephone (03) 365 5715

- Alai Mai (for Pacific Island families)
  c/- The Health Alternatives for Women (THAW)
  Cranmer Square
  Christchurch
  Telephone (03) 379 6970

**Other New Zealand support groups**

- New Plymouth: Sexual Abuse Families Education and Rehabilitation Trust (SAFER)
  51 Barrett Street,
  PO Box 5087,
  New Plymouth
  Telephone: 758 4178
  Twelve volunteers (including male) and one paid worker provide services for male and female adults, children and other family members. Government, local authority, NGO, foundation funding and fund raising. Face to face counselling and in the client's home, mothers' groups, therapy for children, preparation and support for movement through the justice system. This group also counsels young and adult sexual offenders.

- Whangarei—Genesis Centre
  PO Box 4355,
  Kamo
  Whangarei

  Whangarei—Miriam Centre
  22 Mill Road
  Whangarei
  Counselling primarily relating to victims of sexual abuse.

- *Rape Crisis Centres* are available nationwide. Contact the national office for details
  PO Box 6181
  Te Aro
  Wellington
  Telephone (04) 3847 028

- *Women's Refuges* provide support and information with a 24 hour service. There are 51 refuges throughout New Zealand with parallel Maori services. See your telephone directory for details.

## UNITED KINGDOM

### National Organisations: England, Wales and Northern Ireland

- NSPCC—National Society for the Prevention of Cruelty to Children

  The NSPCC and its Scottish (RSPCC) and Irish (ISPCC) counterparts provide nation-wide counselling services, therapy and support services for abused children and their families. The NSPCC offers free 24 hour Child Protection Helpline counselling and referral services on *0800 800 500* taking 120,000 calls a year.

- NSPCC Head Office
  67 Saffron Hill
  London ECI N8RS
  Telephone: (071) 242 1626
  Fax: (071) 831 9562

  There are sixty NSPCC Child Protection Teams in England, most of which would provide counselling and support for parents. Parent groups are made available when there is a demand and there is a suitably experienced worker available.

  Telephone your nearest NSPCC Centre for up to date information.

- NSPCC Child Sexual Abuse Consultancy Service
  175 Station Road
  Swinton
  Manchester M27 2BU
  Telephone: (061) 794 4252
  Fax: (061) 727 7078

  Two social workers/psychotherapists, Anne Bannister and Eileen Craig, provide on-going support and therapy for non-offending parents, survivors and play therapy for children aged 2 years and upwards. They assess and treat sexually aggressive children and child victims.

  Charges are fixed by mutual agreement.

- NSPCC
  Grosvenor House
  41 High Street
  Wivenhoe
  Essex CO 79BE
  Telephone: (0206) 325 442
  Fax: (0206) 825 243

  Groups for non-offending parents and caregivers have been run jointly with local services.

  Individual counselling is offered by workers involved in providing therapeutic help to carers' children.

- NSPCC (Janet Chipping)
  Swinton Welcome Centre
  Grounds of Brible Hill School
  Lyndhurst Crescent
  Park North

Swinton SN3 2RW
Telephone: (0793) 486 806

Specialises in the support of parents and children who have been sexually abused.

- Barnardo's Family Services
  Head Office:
  Barnardo's
  Tanners Lane
  Barkingside
  Ilford
  Essex 1G6 1QG
  Telephone: (081) 550 8822
  Fax: (081) 551 6870

The following Barnardo's projects provide support for families in which children have been sexually abused:

Elizabeth Bishop Centre
52 Aston Church Road
Nechells
Birmingham B7 5QD
Telephone: (021) 328 3856

114 Centre
114 Whitehall Road
Bristol B55 9BH
Telephone: (0272) 55 1703

Fulford Family Centre
Fulford Road
Hartcliffe
Bristol BS13 9PD
Telephone: (0272) 78241

Lawrence Weston Family Centre
Home Farm
Kings Weston Lane
Lawrence Weston
Bristol BS11 0JE
Telephone: (0272) 824578

Hull 348
348 Holderness Road
Hull
North Humberside HU9 3DQ
Telephone: (0428) 23671

Family Therapy Service
Mornington Terrace
29 Upper Duke Street
Liverpool L1 9DY
Telephone: (051) 709 0540

Livingston Families Project
6/8 Hazel Grove
Craigshill
Livingston EH54 5JW
Telephone: (0506) 38666

St John's Day Care Centre
2–4 St John's Crescent
London SW9 7LZ
Telephone: (071) 733 2141

Windermere Families
72 Westow Street
Upper Norwood
London SE19 3AB
Telephone: (081) 653 2825

Redditch Family Centre
26 Salop Road
Redditch
Worcestershire
Telephone: (0527) 550 577

Elms Family Centre
70/72 Elmsleigh Drive
Midway
Swadlincote
South Derbyshire DE11 8JA
Telephone: (0283) 551 251

Churchill Street Family Centre
Howdon
Wallsend
Tyne & Wear NE28 7TE
Telephone: (091) 234 5026

- Barnardo's Family Services in Wales

Family Institute
105 Cathedral Road
Cardiff CF1 9PH
Telephone: (0222) 226 532

Ely Family Centre
87 Grand Avenue
Ely
Cardiff
Telephone: (022) 578918

Rhondda Family Centre
Grange Terrace
Llwynypia
Mid Glamorgan CF40 2HT
Telephone: (0443) 440856

- Barnardo's Family Services in Northern Ireland:

Windsor Avenue Family Support Unit
23 Windsor Avenue
Belfast BT9 6EE
Telephone: (0232) 667 586

Newry Family Resource Centre
61 Dominic Street
Newry
Co Down BT35 9RL

PACT Project
25 Windsor Avenue
Belfast BT9 6EE
Telephone: (9232) 682 286

Family Service Units (FSU)

A national social work charity, funded mainly by local authority grants, specialising in helping families at times of severe stress, especially in cases of intra-familial sexual abuse. Clients are seen either at home or at the unit and there are often parent and survivor groups sharing their experiences. Each unit covers a specific geographic area. FSU has received Department of Health assistance to develop work with adolescent offenders.

Head Office: FSU

207 Old Marylebone Road
London NW1 5Q P
Telephone: (071) 402 5175/6

Northern Regional Office
4 Claremont Street
Bradford BD7 1B Q
Telephone: (0274) 721 549
Fax: (0274) 721 887

Parent Services are available from the following units:

FSU London and South East

- Brent
60 Nicholl Road
London NW109AS
Telephone: (081) 453 0969/1226
- Camden
5 Bayham Street
London NW1 OEY
Telephone: (071) 387 5972/0401
- East London
The Highway Club
Lowood Street
London E1 OBP
Telephone: (071) 790 7122
- Queens Park
604 Harrow Boad
London W10 4NJ
Telephone: (081) 960 3266

- South London
  5 Baldwin Crescent
  London SE15 9LQ
  Telephone: (071) 733 6291/2

- Thamesmead
  Maran Way
  Thamesmead
  Erith
  Kent DA18 4BP
  Telephone: (081) 310 6570

- Thurrock
  154 Centurion Way
  Purfleet
  Essex RM16 IPF
  Telephone: (0708) 868 291

- Waltham Forest
  344 Hoe Street
  London E17 9PX
  Telephone: (081) 509 0119

- Wandsworth
  144 Bedford Hill
  London SW12 9HW
  Telephone: (081) 673 2281

- West London
  289 Westbourne Park Rd
  London W11 IEE
  Telephone: (071) 229 9941

FSU Midlands

- East Birmingham
  723 Coventry Road
  Small Heath
  Birmingham B10 0JL
  Telephone: (021) 772 4217

- South Birmingham
  45 Barratts Road
  Pool Farm
  Birmingham B38 9HU
  Telephone: (021) 459 4232

- Leicester
  26 Severn Street
  Leicester LE2 ONN
  Telephone: (0533) 543 352

*FSU North East*

- Bradford
  207 Cutler Heights Lane
  Bradford BD4 9JB
  Telephone: (0274) 651 652

- East Leeds
  15 Lavender Walk
  Leeds LS9 8TX
  Telephone: (0532) 484 847

- West Leeds
  3 Chiswick Street
  Leeds LS6 IQE
  Telephone: (0532) 757 600

- Newcastle
  Grindon Lodge
  Beech Grove Road
  Newcastle upon Tyne NE4 6RS
  Telephone: (091) 273 5642

- Sheffield
  88 Upper Hanover St
  Sheffield S3 7RQ
  Telephone: (0742) 750 981

FSU North West

- Liverpool
  197 Edge Lane
  Liverpool L7 2PQ
  Telephone: (051) 263 7268

- Rochdale
  37 St Albans Street
  Rochdale OL16 IUT
  Telephone: (0706) 48997

- Manchester and Salford
  St Luke's
  Sawley Road
  Miles Platting
  Manchester M10 8DB
  Telephone: (061) 205 7402

National Children's Home (NCH)

NCH has allocated 4 million pounds to the provision of new services for sexually abused children and their families. Sixteen such centres will be available by 1993. Future developments depend on NCH's ability to attract 1:1 funding from local authorities. In addition NCH 'Carelines' offer telephone and face-to-face counselling. 'Touchline' in Leeds and 'Careline' in Preston have specialists for handling these calls.

For further information contact NCH Child Sexual Abuse Service, Stelling Hall, nr. Newton, Stocksfield, Northumerland, NE 43 7UT Telephone (0661) 842 907.

- NCH Head Office:
  85 Highbury Park
  London N5 1UD
  Telephone: (071) 226 2033

Child sexual abuse projects available in 1992/93

London:

Enfield NCH CSA Service
117 The Chine, Winchmore Hill
Enfield, N21 2EG
Telephone: (081) 360 5104

NCH Newcomen Research Project
Guy's Hospital, St Thomas Street
London SE1 9RT
Telephone: (071) 955 5000 ext 3880

The Hospitals for Sick Children,
Great Ormond Street, London WC1.
Telephone (071) 405 9200
Assessment and treatment of
child victims, parent counselling and
offender treatment programmes.

Cumbria:

NCH Cumbria CSA
The Wedgewood Centre
14 Hollins Close
Whitehaven CA28 8EX
Telephone: (0946) 69 3359

| | |
|---|---|
| Essex: | NCH Careline<br>The Cardinal Heenan Centre<br>326–328 High Road<br>Ilford<br>IG1 1QP<br>Telephone: (081) 514 5444 |
| Kent: | NCH Careline<br>12 Romney Place<br>Maidstone<br>Kent<br>ME15 6LE<br>Telephone: (0622) 67 7943 |
| Nottinghamshire: | NCH CSA Service<br>'Southbank'<br>28 Magdala Road<br>Nottingham<br>Telephone: Home (0602) 226 828 |
| Oxfordshire: | NCH Oxfordshire CSA<br>The Ark<br>19 Banbury Road<br>Kidlington<br>Oxfordshire<br>OX5 1AQ<br>Telephone: (0865) 84 2777 |
| Staffordshire/<br>Warwickshire areas: | NCH Careline<br>2/4 Guild Close<br>Ledham Street<br>Birmingham<br>B16 8EL<br>Telephone: (021) 456 4560 |
| Suffolk: | NCH Suffolk CSA Treatment Service<br>23 Henley Boad<br>Ipswich<br>Suffolk<br>IP1 3TF<br>Telephone: (0473) 28 1239<br>Fax: (0473) 28 0809 |
| Surrey: | Anne Bousfield c/-NCH<br>Ashwood Road<br>Woking<br>Surrey<br>GU22 7JR<br>Telephone: (Home) (0227) 45 8841 |
| Tyne & Wear: | NCH Sunderland CSA Service<br>25 Kayll Road<br>Sunderland<br>SR4 7TW<br>Telephone: (091) 567 4801/2 |

Yorkshire: NCH Family Care Centre
Oxford Chambers
Oxford Place
Leeds LS1 3AU
Helpline: (0532) 45 7777 9am–9.30pm Weekdays
Office: (0532) 45 3550
Telephone and face-to-face counselling and therapy for children, parents and family members.

Wales: NCH CSA Project Officer
Tan-y-Groes Corner
38 Tan-y-Groes Street
Port Talbot
West Glamorgan
SA13 1EE
Telephone: (0639) 88 8678

Parentline OPUS (Organisations for parents under stress)

There are more than 20 Parentline groups in Britain and Eire employing 8 paid workers and volunteers who have been trained to take calls from parents with problems. The organisation aims to prevent all forms of child maltreatment. 24 hour telephone counselling. Some groups offer face-to-face counselling. Dependent on corporate, charitable and government funding.

National Office
Westbury House
57 Hart Road
Thundersley
Essex, SS73PD
Telephone: (O268) 75 7077
FAX (O268) 757 039

Parentline Helpline Numbers

Altrincham
(061) 941 4011/4012
Belfast
(0232) 238800
Canvey Island
(0268) 511151
Croydon
(081) 668 4805
Doncaster
(0302) 328668
Dublin
(01) 733500
Havant
(0705) 452444
Leicester
(0533) 880898
Lichfield
(0543) 256399
Malvern
(0684) 568228
Milton Keynes
(0908) 317868
Newbury
(0635) 46217
Newcastle
091 281 4881
Nottingham
(0602) 624499
Nuneaton
(0203) 374120
Oxford
(0865) 726600
Peterborough
(0733) 312457
Redditch
(0527) 60266
Sheffield
(0742) 726575
Shrewsbury
(0952) 641370
Southend
(0702) 433222
Stowmarket
(0449) 677500
Uttlesford
(0799) 520000
Welwyn Garden City
(0707) 327541
Winchester
(0703) 694013

Avon—Bristol

- Amercrombie Walk Child and Family Support Centre
  1 (B) Amercrombie Walk
  Stockwood
  Bristol
  Telephone: (0275) 835832
  An Avon County Council service employing seven salaried workers to provide services for children and their families. Face-to-face counselling at the client's home or centre, group sessions for mothers (and fathers when there is a demand). Therapy for child victims and support while in the justice system. Training, family therapy, supportive education packages, groups for sex offenders, child protection packages for schools. Supportive education packages and alternatives to care.
- Avon Sexual Abuse Centre
  c/- Bristol RCL
  39 Jamaica Street
  Stokes Croft
  Bristol BS28JP
  Telephone: (0272) 428331 Monday–Friday 10.30 am–2.30 pm
  Parent support groups made available when needed.

Bedfordshire

- Mothers of Sexually Abused Children
  4 Aydon Road
  Runfold Estate
  Luton, LU32HB.
  Telephone: (0582) 581 039.
  Sheila Allen provides telephone and face-to-face counselling for parents. Self-help groups are made available when there is a demand. Home visits as necessary.

Birmingham

- Annie Mullins Child Protection Project, 73 Trinity Road,
  Birmingham, B6 6LS. Telephone (021) 523 3136
  (Birmingham City Council Social Services Department). The project offers therapy groups and counselling for mothers of children who have been sexually abused.

Cumbria

- Support Group for Mothers of Abused Children
  Chris Strickland, 25 Wampool Street, Silloth
  Telephone: (06973) 1432

Essex: SAMS Group (Sexual Abuse—Mum's Support)

SAMS is a voluntary agency which aims to provide drop-in and telephone counselling facilities for mothers throughout Essex and neighbouring counties.

There are currently two centres: Head Office is at 58, Queens Road, Southend-on-Sea, SS1 1PZ. There is also a drop-in centre at 95, Luncie's Road, Basildon (with creche). There are three telephone help lines: Basildon (0268) 559670 and Southend (0702) 435181 and 339673. Calls are received from clients throughout the United Kingdom. Support lines are manned by mothers, most of whom have experienced child sexual abuse. All are trained for their counselling role. Mutual support groups are available.

SAMS helps parents to overcome the emotional trauma related to the disclosure of abuse, to improve child-parent relationships and secure well adjusted children, to improve the self-confidence and personal development of parents and improve liaison with other, statutory and related agencies. Support is extended, when necessary, to partners and other family members. SAMS provides immediate referral for victims and offenders who need therapy. Staff work closely with NSPCC, Social Services, Police, schools and other relevant agencies and have professional back-up from professional consultants.

Kent

- Bexley, Dartford, Gravesend, Gravesham, Swanley.
  Family Matters, 5 Manor Road, Gravesend, Kent, DA12 IAA.
  Open 7 days 10 am–noon, 2–4 pm, 8–8.30 pm.
  Help-line (0474) 537392. Office (0474) 536661.
  Provides 1 : 1 personal counselling, 24 hour telephone counselling, survivors' groups, a family support group and a male survivors' group (Swanley). Survivors' groups are divided into 14–20 years and over 20 years. Service is provided by 43 volunteers many of whom are professionals in health and welfare services. They undertake an intensive 12 week training programme which uses Open University as well as other teaching materials.

- Medway, Maidstone and Gillingham
  *Sanctuary*, PO 23, Gillingham, Kent ME71AA.
  Midway (0634) 378300, Maidstone (0622) 691 430.
  Monday–Saturday 9.30 am–10 pm.
  Crisis telephone lines. Face-to-face counselling. Self-help parent and survivors' groups. Assistance for siblings, grandparents and non-offending extended family members. Volunteers undergo 33 hours of training and work on telephone counselling before proceeding to face to face counselling. Monthly in-service education is provided and staff are closely supervised and supported. *Sanctuary* is a charity dependent upon grants and donations.

London

- ISO-SAC—Support of Sexually Abused Children
  PO 526
  London NW6 ISU
  Coordinator: Angela Rivera
  This charity provides counselling for non-offending parents of children who have been sexually abused. There is a small charge, determined by the client and counsellor. Counselling is also available for male and female adult survivors and partners of survivors.
  Weekdays only 10.00 am–4.00 pm.
  Telephone: (081) 202 3024

Lancashire

- Mothers' Support After Child Sexual Abuse, Longsight Probation and After-Care Service, Longsight District Centre, Stockport Road Manchester M12 4LL
  Telephone: (061) 256 2610.

Somerset

- Pamela Crook, Key Cottage, Allerton, Axbridge, Somerset. Undertakes counselling with individual parents and is willing to assist in the running of self-help parent support groups.
  Telephone: (0934) 713 362

West Yorkshire

Catering for families in Bradford, Brighouse, Dewsbury, Halifax, Huddersfield, Mirfield and Wakefield areas.

- Northorpe Hall Trust Child and Family Project, Northorpe Lane, Mirfield, West Yorkshire, WF 140 QL
  Telephone: (0924) 492183/498242
  Fax: (0924) 492034.
  The centre aims to provide a welcoming and friendly environment and therapeutic help for sexually abused children and their families. Play and family therapists are employed to work with clients. The trust also provides training on child protection in cooperation with Bradford University. It is anticipated that parent/support groups will be available to meet demand.

Other Services for Parents of Sexually Abused Children

- The Children's Legal Centre
  20 Compton Terrace
  London N12UN
  Advice service 2.00–5.00 pm weekdays, telephone (071) 359 6251.
  General and sales enquiries (071) 359 9392, Fax (071) 354 9963.
  An independent national organisation offering free legal advice by telephone and letter on matters of law and policy affecting children in England and Wales.

- Exploring Parenthood: Latimer Education Centre
  194 Freston Road
  London W10 6TT
  Telephone: (081) 960 1678
  Offers a professionally based parent advice line. Two team members have expertise specifically in parent support for child sexual abuse. Exploring Parenthood is a registered charity funded by the Joseph Rowntree Foundation, London Boroughs Grants and other charities. The Director is assisted by professional consultants and 28 professional staff. The service includes parent education and publications. Help is given by correspondence if telephone counselling is inappropriate.

- Family Rights Group
  The Print House
  18 Ashwin Street
  London E8 3DL
  Advice line (071) 249 0008 Monday–Friday 9.30–12 noon. Wednesdays 1.30–4.00 pm. General information (071) 923 2628. A solicitor and social worker advise and help families.

- Incest Survivors—Women's Therapy Centre
  6 Manor Gardens
  London N7 6LA
  Personal counselling and group meetings.
  Telephone: (081) 263 6200

- Parents Against INjustice (PAIN)
  3 Riverside Business Park, Stansted
  Essex CM 24 8PL
  Telephone: (0279) 647171
  Fax: (0279) 812612
  Telephone Advice 10.00 am–4.00 pm.
  Five paid workers and a volunteer (with government, charitable and corporate funds) provide counselling to parents and others when they believe that a child has mistakenly been assessed as a victim of abuse of any kind.

- Parents Anonymous
  6 Manor Gardens
  London N1
  Telephone: (071) 263 8919
  Volunteers offer confidential help to parents who feel that they have 'reached the end of their tether'.

- Re-Unite—National Council for Abducted Children
  PO 158
  London N41AU
  Telephone: (071) 404 8356
  Provides assistance for parents and guardians of abducted children.

- Kingston Women's Centre
  66 London Road
  Kingston upon Thames
  Telephone: 541 1964
  Groups for women and girls.

- Lambeth Incest Survivors, South London Women's Centre
  55 Acre Lane
  Brixton
  London SW2
  Telephone: 274 7215
  Tuesday 11 am–12.30 pm.

- SCOSAC
  73 St Charles Square
  London W106EJ
  Telephone: (081) 960 6376
  (081) 969 4808
  Fax: (081) 960 1464
  Provides advice and consulation services for professionals working in the field of child sexual abuse. SCOSAC provides a wide range of in-service education programmes to suit all those who work with child sexual abuse cases.

- Tavistock Clinic
  120 Belsize Lane
  London NW 35BA
  Telephone: (071) 435 7111
  Offers a service to children and families under the National Health Service —including psychotherapy. The Monroe Centre, jointly funded with NCH was set up specifically to work with families where child abuse has contributed to or been the result of family dysfunctioning.

- Women's Advice and Counselling Service
  The Albany
  Douglas Way, Deptford
  London SE8
  Telephone: 692 6268
  Women's Centres, Rape Crisis Centres, Rape Crisis Lines and Incest Crisis Lines are widely available and they provide information relating to parents' and survivors' groups as well as individual counselling. See your telephone directory.

**Scotland**

- Women's Support Project
  Newlands Centre
  871 Springfield Road
  Parkhead, Glasgow G 314HZ
  Telephone: (041) 554 5669 9.30 am–5 pm
  Querty phone service for deaf clients. Appointments necessary. Resources for survivors, parents, trainers and counsellors in English, Urdu, Punjabi and Chinese languages. Provides groups and courses for mothers of sexually abused children and parent-survivors. Will assist those interested in setting up self help groups. A list of Scottish services is available.

National organisations

- Royal Scottish Society for the Prevention of Cruelty to Children (RSSPC)
  52 Lumsden Street
  Yorkhill, Glasgow
  Telephone: (041) 334 4801

- National Children's Home
  Glasgow Child Sexual Abuse Unit
  17 Newton Place
  Glasgow G3 7PY
  Telephone: (041) 332 6366

- Family Service Units
  18 West Pilton Park
  Edinburgh, EH4 4EJ
  Telephone: (031) 552 0305/6

**Argyll**

- Chisal Counselling Line
  1 Kilmartin
  via Lochgilphead
  Telephone: 05465-241 or 05465-305 (evenings)
  Counselling by trained counsellors, most of whom have suffered childhood abuse.
- RSSPC
  Telephone: (0324) 612256 (see Falkirk)

**Ayrshire**

- Ayr Rape Crisis Centre
  Telephone: (0292) 611301
- Kilmarnock Rape Crisis Centre
  Telephone: (0563) 41769

**Aberdeen**

- Incest Survivor's Group
  Telephone: (0224) 211079—24 hour line
- Grampian Action Against Sexual Abuse (GAASA)
  Telephone: (0224) 593381
  Advice, support and counselling for parents of sexually abused children and counselling for mothers who are also survivors.
  Monday–Friday 9 am–4 pm
  Other times by arrangement

**Clydebank**

- Women's Aid
  Telephone: (041) 952 8118
  Refuge, information and support for mothers and abused children.

**Dumbarton**

- Dumbarton District Women's aid
  Telephone: (0389) 51036
  Refuge and support for women and children who have suffered abuse.

**Dundee**

- Sexual Abuse Team, Royal Infirmary
  Telephone: (0382) 23125 Extension 2360
  Assessment, therapy for parents, victims, siblings and juvenile offenders.
  Monday–Friday 9 am–5 pm

**Edinburgh**

- Incest Survivor's Group and Crisis Line
  Telephone: (031) 556 9437
  Self help group for female adult survivors.
  Tuesday and Wednesday 6–8pm

- Edinburgh and Lothian Women's Aid
  Telephone: (031) 229 1419
  Individual counselling, refuge, legal and other advice.
  Monday 10 am–1 pm, Tuesday, Thursday, Friday 10 am–4 pm 24 hour answer phone.

- Shakti Women's Aid
  Telephone: (031) 557 4010
  Specialises in help for abused black children.
  Monday–Fridy 9 am–4 pm and 24 hour ansaphone.

**Falkirk/Stirling**

- Women's Aid
  Telephone: (0324) 35661 or 32802
  Monday–Friday 10 am–2 pm, (Drop-in)
  Telephone from 5pm and all day at weekends.

- RSSPCC
  30 Newmarket Street
  Falkirk
  and
  RSSPCC
  78 Commercial Road
  Strathaven
  Telephone: (0324) 612256
  Individual work with children and adults. Group work with teenagers and adults. Falkirk Self Help Group. Non-offending parent's group. Helpline Friday 7 pm–10 pm. Male and female counsellors

**Fife**

- Incest Survivors
  Woodlands Family Unit
  Methil
  Fife KY8 3LE
  Telephone: (0333) 28878
  Helpline Tuesday 9.30 am–12 noon.
  Self-help groups for female survivors of sexual abuse. Resources.

- Dunfermline Incest Survivors Group
  Telephone: (0383) 739084
  Self-help group for male and female survivors of sexual abuse. Family and individual counselling. Befriending. Help line.
  Monday–Thursday 9 am–11 am. Friday noon–2 pm
  Answering machine at other times.

**Glasgow**

- Asian Women's Counselling Service
  Telephone: (041) 227 6006
  Counselling by Asian women in Urdu, Hindi, Punjabi and English.
- CASA (Counselling Adults on Child Sexual Abuse)
  Drumchapel
  Telephone: (041) 944 1392
  Counselling for women survivors and mothers of sexually abused children.
  Monday 7 pm–9.30 am
  Wednesday 9.30 am–1.30 pm
  Thursday 7 pm–9 pm
  Friday 1.30 pm–3.30 pm
- Child Sexual Abuse Team
  Royal Hospital for Sick Children
  Telephone: (041) 339 8888 Extension 4229
  Direct work with victims, siblings, non-offending parents.
  Weekdays from 8.45 am–4.30 pm.
- Drumchapel Sexual Abuse Interest Group
  Telephone: (041) 944 4025
  Information on local resources and groups.
- Gryffe Asian Women's Aid
  39 Hope Street (Suite 3/3)
  Glasgow G26AE
  Telephone: (041) 204 4771
  Advice, refuge and support for Asian women and their children.
  Monday–Friday 10 am–4 pm and ansaphone at other times.
- NCH Child Sexual Abuse Counselling Unit
  17B Newton Place
  Glasgow G3 7PY
  Telephone: (041) 332 6366
  Counselling for children, adolescents and families in which sexual abuse has occurred. Monday–Thursday 9 am–5 pm. Friday 9 am–4 pm. *Male counsellor available*. No survivors' groups.
- North East Women's Support Services (N.E.W.S.S.)
  Room 215
  Possilpark Secondary School
  32 Carbeth Street
  Glasgow G 225PT
  Telephone: (041) 336 8810
  Individual counselling for women survivors and mothers of victims.
  Drop-in centre. Resources. Community education.
  Monday–Friday 9 am–4 pm.
- Notre Dame Child Guidance Clinic
  20 Athols Gardens
  Glasgow G12
  Telephone: (041) 339 2366
  Help for children, non-offending parents and significant others.
  Monday–Friday 9 am–5 pm.

- RSSPC—Sexual Abuse Unit
  15 Annfield Place
  Dennistoun
  Glasgow G31 2XE
  Telephone: (041) 556 1156.
  Individual counselling for parents, male and female adult survivors and children in the greater Glasgow region.
  Monday–Friday 9 am–4 pm.
- RSSPCC Overnewton Centre
  52 Lumsden Street
  Yorkhill
  Glasgow G3 8RH
  Telephone: (041) 334 4801
  Male and female counsellors available for referred children and families. Help available for related agencies including consultations and training.
- Strathclyde Rape Crisis Centre
  Telephone: (041) 221 8448
  Telephone, mail and face-to-face counselling for women and girl survivors.
- Women's Support Project
  871 Springfield Road
  Parkhead
  Glasgow G31 4hz
  Telephone: (041) 554 5669, (041) 556 5205
  (Qwertyphone for deaf callers)
  Office hours plus ansaphone. Occasional groups for mothers of abused children and women survivors. Advice, support, information, training, resources.

**Highlands**: Invernesshire

- 'Becomers'
  Seafield
  Kinlocheil
  by Fort William PH 337NP
  Telephone: (0397) 83208
  Twenty-four hours face-to-face counselling. Survivor's groups based on the book 'Becomers' using a Christian approach.
- Rape and Abuse Line for women and girls
  Dingwall
  Telephone: (0349) 65316
  Individual, phone or mail counselling. 7 pm–10 pm evenings.
  24 hour ansaphone.

**Paisley**

- Paisley and District Women's Aid
  57 Kilnside Road
  Paisley
  Telephone: (041) 8871643
  Refuge and support for women and children and support for female adult survivors. Monday–Wednesday and Friday 10 am–4 pm. Not weekends.

**Perth**

- Perth Association for Mental Health
  6 Milne Street
  Perth PH15QL
  Telephone: (0738) 39657—9 am–5 pm daily
  Survivor's groups and individual counselling.

- Tayside Education Psychology Service
  6–8 Methven Street
  Perth PH15PF
  Telephone: (0738) 38101
  Multi-disciplinary work to support children and their families, play therapy with child victims at school.
  Monday–Friday 9 am–5 pm.

**Western Isles**

- Western Isles Women's Aid, The Caravan, Bayhead
  Stornoway
  Isle of Lewis
  Telephone: (0851) 704750
  Individual counselling by telephone, face-to-face or by mail for women and children. Monday–Friday 10 am–4 pm.

# Appendix 2

## The interaction of the problems experienced by the parent/s, other adults and child/ren during and after an investigation of child sexual abuse

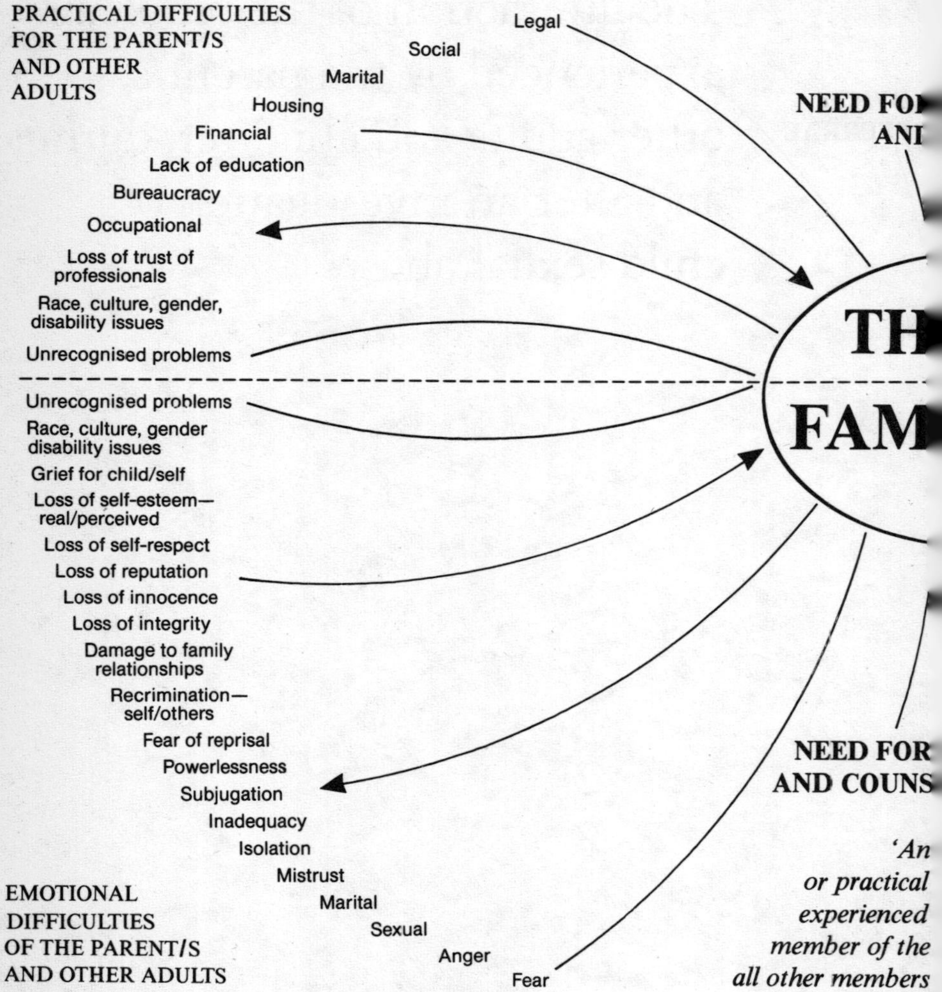


*Source:* PAIN — Parents Against INjustice, 1991

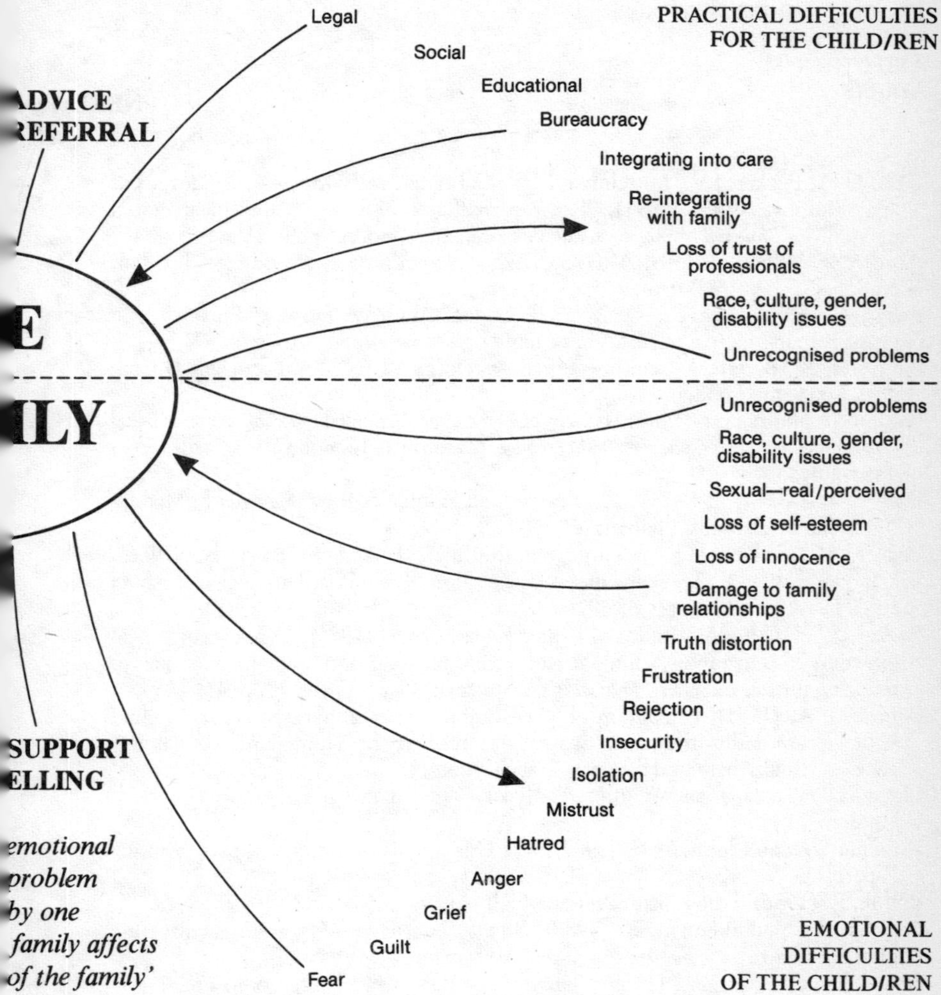

PRACTICAL DIFFICULTIES FOR THE CHILD/REN
Legal
Social
Educational
Bureaucracy
Integrating into care
Re-integrating with family
Loss of trust of professionals
Race, culture, gender, disability issues
Unrecognised problems
ADVICE
REFERRAL
E
ILY
Unrecognised problems
Race, culture, gender, disability issues
Sexual—real/perceived
Loss of self-esteem
Loss of innocence
Damage to family relationships
Truth distortion
Frustration
Rejection
Insecurity
Isolation
Mistrust
Hatred
Anger
Grief
Guilt
Fear
SUPPORT
ELLING
emotional
problem
by one
family affects
of the family'
EMOTIONAL DIFFICULTIES OF THE CHILD/REN

# Bibliography


Abel, G.G., Becker, J.V., Mittelman, M.S., Cunningham-Rathner, J., Rouleau, J.L. and Murphy, W.D. (1991), 'Self-reported sex crimes of non incarcerated paraphiliacs', *Journal of Interpersonal Violence*, vol. 2, no. 6, pp. 3–25

Armstrong, H. and Hollows, A. (1989), *Working with sexually abused boys*, London, National Children's Bureau

Baker, A. and Duncan, S. (1985), 'Child Sexual Abuse. A Study of Prevalence in Great Britain', *Journal of Child Abuse and Neglect*, vol. 9, pp. 457–67

Bannister, A., Barrett, K. and Shearer, E. (eds) (1990) *(NSPCC) Listening to Children*, Longman, London

Barnardo's North East (1987), *Family placement project: Child sexual abuse training programme for foster parents with teenage placements*, Jesmond, Newcastle upon Tyne, July

Bass, E. and Davis, L. (1990), *Courage to heal*, Harper & Row, New York; Mandarin, London; Octopus, Melbourne

Becker, J., Kaplan, M.S., Cunningham-Rathner, J. and Karoussi, R. (1986), 'Characteristics of adolescent incest perpetrators: Preliminary findings', *Journal of Family Violence*, vol. 1, pp. 85–97

Backer, J., Cunningham-Rathner, J. and Kaplan, M.S. (1986), 'Adolescent sexual offenders: Demographic, criminal and sexual histories and recommendations for reducing further offences', *Journal of Interpersonal Violence*, vol. 1, pp. 431–45

Bentovim, A. (1991), Evaluation of a comprehensive treatment approach to child sexual abuse within the family', paper presented at the Third European Conference on Child Abuse and Neglect, Prague, June

Blagg, H., Hughes, J. and Wattam, C. (eds) (1989), *Child sexual abuse*, Longman, London

Blanchard, K. and Johnson, S. (1987), *The One Minute Manager*, London, Fontana Paperbacks

Bolton, R. (1986), *People Skills*, Prentice-Hall, Australia

Brennan, M. and Brennan, R. (1988), *Strange Language*, Wagga Wagga Riverina Literacy Centre

Briere, J. and Runtz, M. (1989), 'University males' sexual interest in children—Predicting potential indices of 'pedophilia' in a non-forensic sample', *Child Abuse and Neglect*, vol. 13, no. 1, pp. 65–76

Briggs, F. (1986), *Child sexual abuse: Confronting the problem*, Longman Cheshire, Melbourne

Briggs, F. (1987), 'South Australian parents want child protection programs to be offered in schools and pre-schools', *Early Child Development and Care*, vol. 34, pp. 167–78, reproduced from *Australian Journal of Early Childhood*, vol. 12, no. 1, February

Briggs, F. and Lehmann, K. (1989), 'Significance of children's drawings in cases of sexual abuse', *Early Child Development and Care*, vol. 47, pp. 131–47

Briggs, F. (1990), First Report: Evaluation of the Protective Behaviours Program in eight Education Department Junior Primary Schools in South Australia, University of South Australia, Adelaide

Briggs, F. (1990), Second Report: Evaluation of the Protective Behaviours Program in eight Education Department Primary Schools, Stage 2: Checking children's retention rates after nine months, University of South Australia, Adelaide

Briggs, F. (1991), Evaluation of 'Keeping Ourselves Safe' Curriculum used with children of 5–8 years in New Zealand Schools, First report to New Zealand Police, University of South Australia, Adelaide

Briggs, F. (1991), 'Problems inherent in teaching personal safety skills to young children', papers presented to the *European Conference on Child Abuse and Neglect*, Prague, and the Fifth Early Childhood Education Convention, Dunedin, New Zealand

Briggs, F. (1991), 'Child protection programmes: Can they protect young children?', *Early Child Development and Care*, vol. 67, pp. 61–72

Briggs, F. (1991), 'Keeping Ourselves Safe: A personal safety curriculum examined', *SET*, no. 2, item 7, New Zealand Council for Educational Research, Wellington

Brown, K.M. (1982), *Keys to making a volunteer program work*, Ardemn Publications, Richmond, California

Budin, L.E. and Johnson, C.F. (1989), 'Sex abuse prevention programs: Offenders' attitudes about their efficacy', *Child Abuse and Neglect*, vol. 13, no. 1, pp. 877–88

*Bulletin*, 12 December, 1989, pp. 140–2

Canadian Government Publication Centre (1984), 'Sexual offenders in Canada', Summary of the report of the Committee on Sexual Offences Against Children and Youths, Ottawa

*Child Protection Report* (1986)—The Independent News Service for Professionals Working with Children and Youth, vol. X11, no. 15, July, p. 1. Washington, D.C.

Conte, J.R. (1986), *A look at child sexual abuse*, National Committee for Prevention of Child Abuse, Chicago

Crisp, L. (1991), 'The last taboo—nursery crimes', *Bulletin*, August 20, pp. 78–86

Curtis, M. and Noble, J. (1987), *Volunteer Management: A Resource Manual*, Volunteer Centre of South Australia, Adelaide

*Daily Mail*, Hull, 2 October, 1989

Davies, G. (April, 1992), Protecting the Child Witness in the Courtroom, Child Abuse Review, vol. no. 1, pp. 33–41

Devoss, J.A. and Newlon, B.J. (1986), Support groups for parents of sexually victimised children, *The School Counsellor*, vol. 34, pp. 51–8

De Young, M. (1982), *The Sexual Victimisation of Children*, McFarland, Jefferson (N.C)

Dube, R. and Hebert, M. (1988), 'Sexual abuse of children under 12 years of age: A review of 511 cases', *Child Abuse and Negect*, vol. 12, no. 3, p. 321

Finkelhor, D. (1979), *Sexually victimised children*, Free Press, New York

Finkelhor, D. (1984), *Child Sexual Abuse: New Theory and Research*, Free Press, New York

Finkelhor, D. (1986), A *source book of child sexual abuse*, Sage Publications, New York

Fishman, P. (1975), 'Interaction—The work women do', Paper presented at the American Sociological Association Meeting, San Francisco

Goldman, R. and Goldman, J. (1989), *Show me yours*, Melbourne, Penguin

Gordon, T. (1975), *Parent effectiveness training*, Plume, New York

Groth, A.N. (1977), 'The adolescent sex offender and his prey', *International Journal of offender therapy and comparative criminology*, vol. 21, pp. 249–54

Hassell, J. (1987), *What's wrong with bottoms?*, Century Hutchinson, Auckland, London, Sydney and Bergvlei (S. Africa)

Hetherington, P. (ed.) (1991), *Incest and the Community: Australian Perspectives*, Optima Press, Centre for West Australian History, University of Western Australia

Hollows, A. and Armstrong, H. (eds) (1989), *Working with sexually abused boys: An introduction for practitioners*, National Children's Bureau, London

Hunter, M. (1990), *Abused boys: the neglected victim of sexual abuse*', Fawcett Columbine, New York

Johnson, C.T. (1989), 'Child perpetrators—Children who molest other children: Preliminary findings', in *Child Abuse and Neglect*, vol. 12, pp. 219–29

Justice, B. and Justice, R. (1979), *The Broken Taboo*, Human Sciences Press, New York p. 104

Katz, L.G. and McClellan, D.E. (1991), 'The teacher's role in the social development of young children', ERIC Clearing House, Washington, DC

Kavaler, F. and Swire, M.R. (1983), *Foster-child health care*, Lexington Books, Lexington Mass

Kennedy, M. (1990), The deaf child who is sexually abused. Is there a need for a dual specialist'?, Nuffield Speech and Hearing Centre, London

Kreps, A. (1987), 'Breaking the silence on a taboo subject', *The Listener*, 23 July

Krug, R. (1989), 'Adult male reports of child sexual abuse by mothers: Case descriptions, motivations and long-term consequences', *Child Abuse and Neglect*, vol. 13, no. 1, p. 111

Longo, R.E. and Groth, A.N. (1983), 'Juvenile sexual offences in the histories of adult rapists and child molesters', *International Journal of Offender Therapy and Comparative Criminology*, vol. 27, pp. 150–5

MacFarlane, K. and Waterman, J. (1986), *Sexual abuse of young children*, Guilford Press, New York

McEwen, J. (1988), 'Child evidence: more proposals for reform', *Criminal Law Review*, quoted by Flin, R. and Boon, J., in Blagg *et al.* (1989) Child Sexual Abuse, Longman, London

Monaco, N.M. and Gaier, E.L. (1988), 'Differential patterns of disclosures of child abuse among boys and girls: Implications for practitioners', *Early Childhood Development and Care*, vol. 30, pp. 97–103

Mount, J. and Fetterman, R. (1989), 'An abuse prevention programme for deaf and hard of hearing children', Paper presented at the *CAID Convention*, June, San Diego, California

Rabiner, D. and Coie, J. (May 1989), 'Effects of expectancy on rejected children's acceptance by unfamiliar peers', *Developmental Psychology*, vol. 25, no. 3, pp. 450–7

Reich, J. (1984), *The treatment of child molesters: A manual*, State Psychiatric Institute, New York, referred to in Johnson, C.T. (1989)

Roberts, J. (1986), 'Fostering the sexually abused child', *Adoption and Fostering*, vol. 10, no. 1, pp. 8–11

Rosenthal, P. A., Rosenthal, S., (1989) 'Suicidal behaviour of preschool children', *AM. J. Psych.* 141, 520–525

Russell, D.E.H. (1983), 'The incidence and prevalence of intrafamilial and extrafamilial sexual abuse of female children', *Child Abuse and Neglect*, vol. 7, pp. 133–46

Ryan, G., Lane, S., Davis, J. and Isaac, C. (1987), 'Juvenile Sex Offenders: Development and Correction', *Journal of Child Abuse and Neglect*, vol. 11, no. 3, pp. 385–95

Salter, A. (1991), 'Accuracy of Expert Testimony in Child Sexual Abuse Cases: A case study of Ralph Underwager and Hollida Wakefield, New England Commissioners of Child Welfare Agencies, USA, summarised in *UPDATE*, vol. 4, no. 3, March

Schindler-Rainmen, E. and Lippitt, R. (1975), *The Volunteer Community* (2nd ed), International Authors, BV USA Pfeiffer & Co.

Schor, E.L. (1981), 'Health care supervision of foster-children', *Child Welfare*, vol. 60, no. 5, pp. 313–19

Schor, E.L. (1982), 'The foster-care system and health status of foster-children', *Pediatrics*, vol. 69, no. 5, pp. 521–8

Schor, E.L. (1983), 'Foster-care children: Reply', *Pediatrics*, vol. 71, no. 1, pp. 138–9

Sheard, J. (1986), *The Politics of Volunteering*, Advice and Development for Volunteering and Neighbourhood Care, London

Smith, H. and Israel, E. (1987), 'Sibling Incest', *Child Abuse and Neglect*, vol. 11, pp. 101–8

Spender, D. (1979), 'Don't talk, listen!', *Times Educational Supplement* N.3305. Nov. 3, p. 19

Spender, D. (1980), 'Talking in Class', in Spender, D. and Sarah, E. (eds), *Learning to lose—Sexism and Education*, The Women's Press, London

Swire, M.R. and Kavaler, F. (1977), 'The health status of foster children', *Child Welfare*, vol. 56, no. 10, pp. 635–54

*The News*, Adelaide, 22 October, 1991

*The Times*, London, 29 March, 1983

Tong, L., Oates, K. and McDowell, M. (1987), 'Personality development following sexual abuse', *Child Abuse and Neglect*, vol. 11, no. 3, pp. 371–84

*UPDATE*, vol. 4, no. 3, March 1991

Wallerstein, J.S. and Kelly, J.B. (1980), *Surviving the breakup: how children and parents cope with divorce*, 2nd ed. (1990), NY. Grant McIntyre Basic Books, London

Winton, M.A. (1990), 'An evaluation of a support group for parents who have a sexually abused child', *Child Abuse and Neglect*, vol. 14, pp. 397–401

Wood, H. (1990), 'Exposing Ritual Abuse', *Social Work Today*, 15 November, pp. 18–19

Yaffe, M. and Nelson, E.C. (eds) (1982), *The influence of pornography on behaviour*, Academic Press, London

Zimmerman, D. and West, C. (1975), 'Sex roles, interruptions and silences in conversation', in Thorne, B. and Henley, N. (eds), *Language and sex: Difference and dominance*, Newbury House, Rowley, Mass